THE NEW EGALITARIANISM

Kennikat Press
National University Publications
Political Science Series

THE
NEW
EGALITARIANISM

QUESTIONS AND CHALLENGES

edited by

DAVID LEWIS SCHAEFER

National University Publications
KENNIKAT PRESS // 1979
Port Washington, N. Y. // London

Manufactured in the United States of America

Published by
Kennikat Press Corp.
Port Washington, N.Y. / London

Library of Congress Cataloging in Publication Data
Main entry under title:

The New Egalitarianism.

(National university publications)
Bibliography: p.
1. Civil rights–United States–Addresses, essays, lectures. 2. Affirmative action programs–United States–Addresses, essays, lectures. 3. Political science–United States–Addresses, essays, lectures. 4. Equality–Addresses, essays, lectures. 5. Social justice–Addresses, essays, lectures. I. Schaefer, David Lewis, 1943–
JC599.U5N46   323.4'0973   78-27063
ISBN 0-8046-9220-3

*This book is dedicated
to the memory of
HERBERT J. STORING,
Professor of Political Science
the University of Chicago
1956–1977*

ACKNOWLEDGMENTS

The editor is grateful for permission to reprint the following materials (some of which have been slightly revised or condensed for inclusion in the present volume):

"On Meritocracy and Equality," by Daniel Bell, reprinted by permission from *The Public Interest*, no. 29 (fall, 1972), pp. 29–68.

"Liberal Democracy As A Mixed Regime," by Harvey C. Mansfield, Jr., reprinted by permission from *The Alternative: An American Spectator*, vol. 8, no. 9 (June–July, 1975), pp. 8–12.

"Of Populism and Texas," by Irving Kristol, reprinted by permission from *The Public Interest*, no. 28 (summer, 1972), pp. 3–11.

"The Socialist Ideal," by Bertrand de Jouvenel, reprinted by permission from *The Ethics of Redistribution* (Cambridge University Press, 1951).

"Intellectuals Have Consequences," by Colin Welch, reprinted by permission of Doubleday & Co., Inc., from the book *The Future That Doesn't Work*, edited by R. Emmett Tyrrell, Jr. Copyright © 1975, 1976, 1977 by The Alternative Educational Foundation, Inc.

"Western Guilt and Third World Poverty," by P. T. Bauer, reprinted by permission from *Commentary*, vol. 61, no. 1 (January, 1976), pp. 31–38; copyright © 1976 by the American Jewish Committee.

"The Last Train to Nihil," by Midge Decter, reprinted by permission of Coward, McCann, & Geoghegan, Inc., from *The New Chastity*. Copyright © 1972 by Midge Decter.

"American Women and Democratic Morals: *The Bostonians*," by Catherine H. Zuckert, reprinted by permission from *Feminist Studies*, vol. 3, no. 3/4 (spring–summer, 1976), pp. 30–50.

"Affirmative Action and the Principle of Equality," by Robert F. Sasseen, reprinted by permission from *Studies in Philosophy and Education*, vol. 9, no. 3 (spring, 1976), pp. 275–295.

"Is Busing Necessary?", by Nathan Glazer, reprinted by permission from *Commentary*, vol. 53, no. 3 (March, 1972), pp. 39–52; copyright © 1972 by the American Jewish Committee.

"About Equality," by Irving Kristol, reprinted by permission from *Commentary*, vol. 54, no. 5 (November, 1972), pp. 41–47; copyright © 1972 by the American Jewish Committee.

The editor also wishes to thank Holy Cross College for awarding him a Summer Research Grant and a Research Support Grant to assist the preparation of this volume; and Mrs. Jane Iannini for typing the manuscript.

CONTENTS

THE NEW EGALITARIANISM

David L. Schaefer

INTRODUCTION

This volume is inspired by the belief that an important shift has taken place in recent years in the liberal, egalitarian ethos that dominates policy making and political thinking in the American polity, and that this shift deserves a greater degree of critical scrutiny and reflection on the part of the general public than it has thus far received. Whereas justice traditionally has been understood in the United States to require an equality of rights or liberties—that is, an equality in the *treatment* of individuals by government—it is now widely argued that such "formal" equality is insufficient to achieve genuine justice. Rather, it is held to be incumbent on the government to take positive action to equalize the *results* that men achieve, in terms of income, status, and political influence. Theoretical justification for this shift in the goals of policy has been provided by such influential books as John Rawls's *A Theory of Justice*, Herbert Gans's *More Equality*, Christopher Jencks's *Inequality*, and the writings of some advocates of "women's liberation." Its practical effects can be seen in the "affirmative action" policies enforced by the Department of Health, Education, and Welfare; in the judicial requirement of school busing to overcome racial segregation even where such segregation results from housing patterns rather than from intentionally discriminatory policies; and in the frequent demand for a redistribution of income both within the United States and between this country and the "Third World."

Despite the widespread advocacy of the "new" egalitarianism[1] among academics, this movement has not gone unquestioned or unchallenged within the scholarly community. Nor has the questioning been limited to thinkers who could plausibly be branded "conservatives." In a

3

rhetorical coup reminiscent of that by which the advocates of the Constitution secured for themselves the title of "Federalists" in 1787, however, the new egalitarians have succeeded in calling themselves "liberals" and dismissing their opponents as "neoconservatives." This rhetoric has produced some startling changes in political terminology.[2] Whereas it was "liberal" fifteen years ago to advocate the equal treatment of persons without regard to race, that stance is now labeled "conservative"; a true "liberal" favors racial (and sexual) quotas in hiring, university admissions, and other areas. Although the "liberal" of past decades favored economic growth as a means to elevating the standard of living of the common man, economic expansion is now condemned for its alleged effect of depressing the standard of living of less developed nations. Whereas the most profound theorists of modern democracy, such as Rousseau and Tocqueville, had taught that the maintenance of political freedom critically depends on the inculcation of morality in the citizenry, and that this inculcation in turn is primarily the work of the family, present-day "libertarians" adopt a relativistic stance towards morality, and seek to insure that public policy will not favor heterosexuality over homosexuality, or married life over random sex. Some theoreticians of the women's liberation movement, among others, challenge the legitimacy of the family itself in their quest for a radical equality between the sexes.

Because I believe that the new egalitarianism embodies highly problematic consequences for America's well being, I have tried to collect in this book a number of essays that raise serious questions about various aspects of this movement. Neither my intention nor my principle of selection, however, has been polemical. Not all of the authors represented in this volume clearly hold the new egalitarianism as a whole, or in all of its particular manifestations, to be a bad thing. Some of the essays, in fact, have been chosen partly because they elucidate problems inherent in traditional liberalism that help to explain the rise and the appeal of the new egalitarianism. The other essays likewise differ considerably in both tone and substance. My aim throughout this anthology has been to find essays that will stimulate the reader to think, rather than necessarily to persuade him to adopt or reject a particular political position. And, along with several of the contributors, I believe that an adequate understanding of this issue is ultimately dependent on the consideration of the various teachings of such philosophers as Locke, Rousseau, Tocqueville, and Aristotle about the nature of justice and the good life.

Daniel Bell's essay "On Meritocracy and Equality" has been placed first among the readings in this anthology because it offers a broad survey of the purposes and problems of the contemporary egalitarian movement. "What is at stake today," Bell observes, "is the redefinition of equality." The intention of earlier American reformist movements in this century was to promote an equality of *opportunity* among individuals, both by combating arbitrary discrimination against individuals based on such factors as race, and by providing educational and other financial assistance to overcome the handicaps to advancement suffered by economically or culturally disadvantaged children. Such programs, even if not specifically mandated by the founding principles of the American regime, could be seen as fundamentally consistent with the Jeffersonian ideal of a "meritocracy," in which an individual's political, social, and economic position would be determined by his own talent and effort rather than his family background.

The disenchantment of contemporary intellectuals with the goal of equal opportunity, as Bell indicates, began with their rediscovery of a fact already well known to such philosophers as Locke and Tocqueville: that the equalization of opportunity does not eliminate, even if under some circumstances it may reduce, the inequalities in the rewards that men achieve as the result of differing amounts of natural ability, effort, or luck. Enamored with the goal of an actual equality of persons rather than the equalization of rights and opportunities, such American social scientists as James Coleman and Christopher Jencks have consequently redefined "equality of opportunity" itself to mean "equality of outcomes." The new test of a society's justness is to be, not the extent to which it enables individuals to secure rewards commensurate with their talent and effort, but the degree to which it equalizes their wealth, status, and political power.

As Bell's argument suggests, part of the cost of this movement towards a new concept of equality has been a threat to the other principle to which Americans have traditionally been at least equally dedicated: that of liberty. The attempt to overcome differences in the rewards obtained by different racial or ethnic groups entails the labelling of individuals, even against their will, as belonging to particular groups, and the elevation of group rights over individual ones. The difficulty of deciding the criteria by which groups should be distinguished from one another, and rewards determined, inevitably places a considerable degree of arbitrary authority in the hands of administrators charged with enforcing such policies as that of affirmative action. And a further consequence, in Bell's words, "is a thoroughgoing politicizing of society in which not only the market is subordinated to political decision but all institutions have to bend to the demands of a political center and politicize themselves." Thus, one may reasonably fear that the barriers erected by the American founders in order to prevent the subordination of the individual's life to the whims of government may be eroded.

Bell concludes his analysis with a plea on behalf of "a just meritocracy" as opposed to the imposition of "a rigid, dogmatic egalitarianism in matters where it conflicts with other social objectives and even becomes self-defeating." But as Bell indicates, the goal he propounds is unlikely to satisfy those contemporary egalitarians whose assault on traditional liberalism seems to be motivated less by justice than by *ressentiment.*

Bell attributes the contemporary controversy among different forms of egalitarianism in part to the ambiguity of the term "equality" itself. But the fact that contemporary writers find equality to be an ambiguous term does not mean that the goal it denotes, as understood by its original advocates, suffers from such ambiguity. An adequate evaluation of the contemporary arguments concerning equality in America requires that one first attempt to understand the sense in which the political and philosophic architects of American liberal democracy were egalitarians, and the reasoning underlying their position. It is in order to assist such understanding that the next two essays in this anthology are included.

In his article "Equality in America: The Declaration, Tocqueville, and Today," Richard W. Crosby attempts to elucidate the sense in which the authors of the Declaration of Independence intended their assertion that "all men are created equal" to be understood, and at the same time to explain the roots of the contemporary attempt to replace their standard of political equality and equality of opportunity with the demand for "equality of results." Through an examination of the political teachings of Hobbes and Locke, from which the principles of the Declaration were derived, Crosby endeavors to demonstrate that the American founders viewed the principle of natural equality primarily as a *means* to the preservation of liberty, rather than as an end in itself. He goes on to elucidate, with reference to the reflections of Alexis de Tocqueville, why a society based on the premise of men's natural equality nonetheless tends to inspire dissatisfaction with the consequences of liberty, and hence to create the possibility that liberty will ultimately be sacrificed for the sake of an equalization of men's economic and social, as well as political, position. If Crosby's argument is correct, the contemporary disenchantment with "meritocracy" as described by Bell is to be attributed less to the increased importance of "credentials" as a prerequisite to advancement in twentieth century society—although this is doubtless a factor—than to the underlying problems of isolation or "alienation" that Tocqueville found to be promoted by liberal individualism.

Harvey C. Mansfield, Jr.'s witty but difficult essay "Liberal Democracy as a Mixed Regime" is concerned, as Crosby's study is, with elucidating the intentions of the philosophic founders of modern liberal democracy. Mansfield, however, concentrates on explaining the sense in which liberal democracy was intended to reconcile equality with inequality in such a way as to benefit the citizenry as a whole. The intent underlying the egalitarian teaching of the modern "liberal" political philosophers, Mansfield argues, was never to deny the reality of inequalities in wisdom, talent, and virtue among men, but rather to harness and channel the superiorities some men enjoy in these qualities for the sake of the public good. Thus, the problem of combining the advancement of human excellence with popular consent, which classical political philosophy had tended to resolve more in theory than in practice, was for the first time to be given a practicable solution. The liberal solution has worked remarkably well, Mansfield argues, inasmuch as it has facilitated both the cultivation of the arts and sciences by some men and the development of a historically unrivaled material prosperity enjoyed—albeit unequally—by all. The continued maintenance of this solution is now threatened, however, as Mansfield indicates, by the failure of contemporary "liberals" to appreciate how they as well as the "democrats" benefit from it. Like Crosby, Mansfield points out that the main objections to the "injustice" of liberal society have been propounded, not by the "democrats" who supposedly suffer from it, but by the "liberals" who are its greatest beneficiaries. This phenomenon compels one to wonder about the real source of the ire of the new egalitarians against liberal democracy—a problem that will be given further examination in Irving Kristol's essay at the conclusion of this volume.

The policies advocated by the new egalitarians, as indicated in Bell's article, cover a wide range. But the core of their argument seems to concern the existence of allegedly unjust disparities of wealth and income, and the consequent need to redress these disparities through policies of "redistribution." Corresponding to the importance of this issue in its various aspects, the largest single section of the present anthology is devoted to examining the economic program of the new egalitarians. The essays included in this section challenge "redistributionist" policies on both moral and practical grounds.

Irving Kristol's "Of Populism and Taxes" deals with the issue of income equalization in the form in which that issue has most commonly been raised by American intellectuals and politicians in recent years: the demand for tax "reform." This demand generally embodies the charge that loopholes in the tax structure unfairly enable the rich and privileged to evade paying their fair share of the costs of government, thus depressing the income of the large majority who are unable to take advantage of such dodges. There are doubtless a number of particular inequities in the tax system—as should probably be expected in such a complex instrument of policy. While indicating that certain reforms are in order, however, Kristol argues that the basic premise of the most ardent reformers—the claim that improving the tax system will substantially elevate the standard of living of the majority—is simply untrue. Some of the so-called loopholes, such as the investment tax credit, the depreciation allowance, and the capital gains taxation rate, in fact serve to promote economic growth and hence ultimately to help supply tax revenues. Other special tax allowances, including those offered to the elderly, and the deduction of taxes on home mortgage interest, are unlikely to be abolished because they are primarily enjoyed, not by the rich, but by a broad segment of the electorate.

The argument of the new egalitarians against income inequality goes well beyond the demand for the elimination of tax loopholes, however. Radical egalitarians attack the legitimacy of the inequalities of wealth that characterize the United States and other societies, and assert the need for government action designed to bring about, if not an absolute equality of income, at least a considerable movement in that direction. This economic egalitarianism embodies an ethical view that is forthrightly challenged by Bertrand de Jouvenel in his examination of "The Socialist Ideal," excerpted here from his book *The Ethics of Redistribution.*

De Jouvenel's book, first published in England in 1951 at a time when the major foundations of the British "welfare state" had recently been laid, deals sympathetically with the moral impulse out of which socialism originally arose: the desire to replace a society of individual selfishness, competition, and conflict with "a new order of brotherly love." This impulse has been vitiated, however, De Jouvenel argues, by the "inner contradiction" of contemporary socialism: its simultaneous condemnation of materialism, and commitment to increasing the stock of material goods enjoyed by the generality of men. This contradiction has led in turn to the replacement of the original goal of social unity with the seemingly more modest one of "more equal consumption." But the advocates of this new goal, De Jouvenel contends, have failed to think through adequately either its feasibility or the true character of the kind of society that would result if it were instituted.

As Kristol has more recently done, De Jouvenel notes the lack of harmony between the "floor" that egalitarian intellectuals would like to establish on incomes and their desired "ceiling": because of the fewness of the truly rich as well as the amount of taxes they already pay, the confiscation of the "surplus" they presently enjoy and its redistribution among the poor would fall far short of providing the desired floor. A serious policy of income equalization would therefore require the vastly increased taxation of the middle class and the institution of a much lower maximum income than most people in Western societies—including the intellectuals themselves—seem likely to accept.

De Jouvenel is not arguing against governmental assistance to relieve the condition of the truly poor, who are unable to pay for the basic necessities of life. He distinguishes, however, between the policies necessary to help this "rearguard" and the redistributionist policies advocated by contemporary egalitarianism to raise the *median* income. The latter are motivated less by sympathy for suffering than by a "sense of scandal" at the superfluities enjoyed by the rich—a sense embodying "the subjective judgments of the policy-making class—in our time the lower-middle class." The bourgeois intellectual is less offended by poverty than he is by wealth. But his emphasis on the quantitative equalization of income abstracts from the *qualitative* characteristics of social life that may depend on the existence of an inequality of wealth.

The fundamental error of the redistributionists, De Jouvenel suggests, is their treatment of all income as "consumption," without regard to the kinds of activities that income may *produce*. The increase in the common man's enjoyment of material goods that is desired by the egalitarians can be achieved only at the expense of supporting the "unnecessary" goods that are produced and enjoyed by "people of uncommon tastes." These goods of course include many trivial frivolities; but they also include philosophy, art, serious literature and music—in short all of the "cultural" excellences that most distinguish man from the beasts. The accumulation of wealth may also be the prerequisite for educating and preparing men uniquely equipped to undertake the tasks of democratic statesmanship and public service: consider the Churchills and the Adamses, Washington and Jefferson, the Kennedys and Rockefellers. The dedication of society to promoting men's equal enjoyment of their private pleasures, without regard to the qualitative differences among those pleasures, as proposed by such egalitarians as John Rawls, would bring about something like what in Plato's *Republic* is called "the city of pigs."

Of course not all of the radical egalitarians want to carry their principle this far. Many propose that in the just society, the private support of cultural activities should be replaced by governmental sponsorship of them. But this proposal, as De Jouvenel indicates, is radically inconsistent with the egalitarian principle: if wealth is to be redistributed so as to equalize all people's "utilities," then the preferences of the majority as expressed in the market, ought to determine what activities are provided. If Beethoven suffers by comparison with the Beatles, so much the worse for Beethoven. In a truly egalitarian society, neither the charity of the wealthy nor the sponsorship of the government would give any special support to "high" culture.

Even if one allows the egalitarian principle to be inconsistently modified so as to authorize special support for the arts and sciences, a further consequence follows from the elimination of unequal wealth, as De Jouvenel indicates: the transfer of the power to determine what cultural activities will be supported, from private to public hands. Leaving aside the threat that such a centralization of power may pose (as Tocqueville feared) to individual liberty, the egalitarian argument then rests on an undemonstrated assumption that present-day governments are better equipped than private individuals to decide what constitutes an activity worthy of support. (The superiority of public television programming to that provided by the commercial networks in the United States might be taken as evidence in favor of governmental *participation* in financing such activities. But much of the sponsorship of the "public" stations has in fact come from private corporations and foundations. Moreover, it is precisely the high cultural level of public television programs that has caused some egalitarian intellectuals to attack them as "elitist.")

Cogent as they may be, De Jouvenel's arguments evidently proved insufficiently persuasive to bring about any reversal of the egalitarian course pursued by the makers of British social policy since World War II. In recent years the British government, spurred on by left-wing intellectuals and trade union leaders, has endeavored to advance substantially further towards the goal of minimizing inequalities of wealth. This movement has occurred simultaneously with the worsening of the country's severe economic problems; yet paradoxically, "social democracy" as practiced in England continues to represent for many American intellectuals a model that ought to be emulated in the United States. That British policy is far from constituting such a model was the theme of a book of essays by British and American observers published in 1977 and entitled *The Future That Doesn't Work: Social Democracy's Failures in Britain*. Colin Welch's essay "Intellectuals Have Consequences" is reprinted here from that volume.

Welch's argument is a trenchant critique of the thought of the English intellectuals who inspired the movement towards "social democracy," and the consequences of that thought. Welch portrays the egalitarian intellectuals as inspired by an inordinate pride rather than the sympathy for the down-trodden that they commonly profess: a pride that leads them to demand that nature, including the laws of economics, be remade to fit their "moral" ideals, without ever seriously examining either the feasibility or the worth of those ideals. Themselves privileged to pursue the "life of the mind" thanks to the previously unrivaled wealth and freedom of expression achieved by Western societies under capitalism, the intellectuals take both wealth and freedom for granted. Paying no attention to the actual economic means by which economic growth has been achieved, the egalitarians wish to concentrate on bringing about a "just" distribution of its fruits. But in so doing, Welch suggests, they are killing the proverbial goose that laid the golden egg. The growth of socialism and a burdensome system of taxation undermine the incentives to individual labor and achievement that are the prerequisites of social wealth.

Welch echoes Tocqueville's warning that the love of equality, if it becomes men's dominant passion, can easily threaten liberty. He cites the contempt felt by Fabian intellectuals like the Webbs for freedom and democracy. Of particular importance is Welch's critique of the commonly heard argument that freedom is a meaningless slogan without the general dispersion of the power to enjoy it. Society in general benefits from the products of great writers and artists, he notes, even though most of us lack the talent to be great writers or artists ourselves. The same can also be said of the accomplishments of great statesmen, scientists, and entrepreneurs. By contemptuously dismissing legal, "formal" freedom as valueless in itself, the egalitarian intellectuals encourage others to forget its importance, and thus prepare the minds of the common people to throw away their freedom if a tyrant should offer them bread and circuses instead. Yet should this consequence come about, it would be the intellectuals themselves (as Mansfield has also warned) who would be the most obvious losers.

In recent years the argument of those who advocate economic "redistribution" has added a new twist. In addition to demanding the reallocation of wealth within each Western nation, they now call for economic redistribution between the West and the "developing" nations of the Third World. Such a policy is said to be justified not only by the dire need of the less developed nations for substantial Western aid, but also by the alleged responsibility of the West for the impoverishment of its erstwhile colonies. Both the claim of Western "guilt" and the assumption that Western aid is the critical factor on which economic progress in the less developed world depends, are challenged by another English writer, P.T. Bauer, in his article "Western Guilt and Third World Poverty."

Step by step Bauer adduces facts that refute each of the allegations purportedly justifying the charge that Western "exploitation" has caused Third World poverty. It was the Third World's contact with the West that brought to it the very idea of material progress, he points out. Not only did the standard of living in large parts of the Third World rise enormously beginning with the advent of Western contact, those nations that were colonized often progressed much more rapidly than those that were not. The claim that Western economic gains from colonialism must have been earned at the expense of the colonized represents a misunderstanding of economic laws: incomes other than subsidies, Bauer points out, "are earned by the recipients for resources and services supplied, and are not acquired by depriving others of what they had." Nor can present-day "manipulation" of the terms of trade by the West be legitimately cited as a cause of Third World poverty: the external purchasing power of the less developed nations has increased greatly in recent decades according to Bauer, while those Third World nations that have little or no foreign trade are often among the poorest. Bauer also refutes the frequent argument that the West is impoverishing the Third World through its "excessive" consumption of natural resources. The ratio of per capita production to per capita consumption in the United States exceeds that in India; thus the net effect of American economic activities is to increase the stock of material goods available to all. In fact, it may be precisely the opportunity for increased consumption that, by serving as an incentive to labor, stimulates American workers to produce as much as they do.

In a curious way, Bauer argues, the West has indeed contributed to Third World poverty, but this is a quite different way from the one alleged by the redistributionists. In the first place, since changes induced by Western contact have substantially increased life expectancy in the less developed nations, more poor people are now alive than would otherwise have been the case. But a few would regret this change, or criticize the West for promoting it. Secondly, by encouraging governmental control over economic life in the Third World nations— partly through foreign aid given to these governments—the West has hampered economic growth in the Third World.

In its current policies toward the less developed countries, Bauer concludes, the West has been guided by an unthinking desire to assuage an unfounded sense of guilt, rather than by a realistic appraisal of the needs of the people of the Third World. The egalitarian ideology that holds the West's wealth to be a prima facie sign of guilt has in fact encouraged the West to confer respectability on the policies of shortsighted and oppressive Third World governments, afraid to criticize such governments lest the West again be found guilty of "imperialism."

One additional effect of the ideology of Western "guilt" as described by Bauer is to encourage a way of thinking that reduces the varied peoples of the Third World to an undifferentiated, homogeneous mass that must be forcefully transformed in order to achieve the Western intellectual's vision of "justice." This way of thinking, which treats the "disadvantaged" as objects to be manipulated by beneficent intellectuals who "know" what is good for others, is characteristic of a considerable amount of contemporary egalitarian thought. It is noteworthy, for instance, that John Rawls derives the principles of his widely admired "theory of justice" from a hypothetical "original position" in which human beings are deprived of the qualities, opinions, and passions that differentiate them from one another.[3] A similar attitude of hostility to the characteristics that distinguish human beings, and hence make them potentially or actually unequal to one another, is unmasked by Midge Decter in the thought of some leading advocates of women's liberation. Decter's argument therefore suggests an underlying link between the seemingly disparate goals of the economic egalitarians and certain elements of the so-called women's movement that makes it legitimate to view the latter as another form of the new egalitarianism.

In "The Last Train to Nihil," the concluding section of her book *The New Chastity*, Decter argues that the unifying thread of the women's liberation movement is a hostility, not merely to inequality, but to differentiation between the sexes. In the movement's denunciations of the family and of "sex stereotyping," Decter finds a rejection of the fundamental human condition and the desire to remake nature itself. The liberationists' lament that they are "victims," at a time when the opportunities available to women are greater than at any previous time in history, expresses a flight from responsibility for one's own life and a desire to be *deemed* equal to others regardless of whether one has achieved anything to merit their respect. (Here again the similarity to Rawls's doctrine is striking: consider his demand that human beings be granted not only an equality of rights, but "equality in the social bases of esteem," regardless of their accomplishments; and his endeavor to overcome "the arbitrariness found in nature.")[4] The attack on nature undermines any standard by which one could speak of an objective justice or injustice. Hence the liberationists' desire for a world where "there would be no men and no women" points, not to justice, but to nihilism.

If Decter is correct in arguing, however, that the situation of women in contemporary America is one of unparalleled liberty and opportunity, what causes can explain the popularity of the women's liberation movement? This question is addressed by Catherine Zuckert in her essay "American Women and Democratic Morals," a study of Henry James's *The Bostonians*. James, Zuckert contends, saw the condition of American women as an exemplification of "the possibilities and hidden defects of modern democratic life." While sympathetic to the *aims* of the "feminist movement," James "did not, apparently, believe that American women would solve their problems through political action." His novel dealing with that movement, both provides "a different view of 'the woman question' " from the prevailing one, and illustrates how that question embodies more fundamental difficulties inherent in democratic politics.

James's character Verena, Zuckert finds, embodies both the freedom enjoyed by American women and the unsatisfying character of that freedom. American women's freedom reflects the principle of the regime, as expressed in the Declaration of Independence: equal liberty for all, without any authoritative determination of the purpose for which that liberty should be exercised. The consequence, for Verena and others, is a lack of "identity" or purpose, and "a singular hollowness of character."

It is in the pursuit of purpose and achievement that some of the more able and interesting American women—like the leaders among other movements for "social justice"—dedicate their energies to promoting "reform," in this case, the attainment of legal equality between the sexes. But such movements cannot really satisfy the longings that give rise to them, precisely because their content derives from the very principles that have produced Verena's character and situation. Something in these women's way of life dissatisfies them, but they misconstrue the cause of that dissatisfaction because they share their fellow citizens' commitment to the principle of an ever-increasing equality.

The egalitarian principle as understood in America distorts the characters of both men and women according to James (and as feared by Tocqueville) because it isolates them from one another, reduces them to economic objects, and denies legitimate satisfaction to such passions as ambition and love. Because the Declaration's teaching of man's equality of rights tends naturally to collapse into the view that all human beings are simply equal, women such as Olive, whose longings are aristocratic, have "a bad conscience" about such longings. In order to satisfy their desire for superiority, such individuals must sublimate it into a commitment to egalitarian political movements, thus demonstrating their inequality to others in the very act of demanding equality. (The same could be said of the leaders of many other kinds of contemporary "reform" movements.) Similarly, because the abstract principle of human equality undermines the natural bonds of sentiment that connect particular human beings with one another, its acceptance turns the relation between the sexes into a battle for domination and possession, subordinating genuine love to utility. While the advocates of egalitarianism justify it by reference to the "brotherhood of man," such abstract principles have in fact much less power to interest human beings in each other's well being than the more particular ties that the egalitarian ideology undermines.

Precisely because he appreciated the opportunity that democratic freedom, rightly understood, provides for the development of human faculties, James was far from wishing, Zuckert indicates, for the restoration of an aristocratic political or social order. But being concerned, like Tocqueville, to prevent democratic freedom from degenerating into purposeless individualism, James tried to indicate how women's influence could serve as a check on that tendency. In order to exercise that influence, women need to come to terms with their own nature, rather than subordinating that nature to an abstract principle. James would presumably agree with Decter that the women's movement of our own time, with its ambition to obliterate the distinction between the sexes, represents both an unsalutary and a radically unnatural phenomenon. By making "having a career" the test of a woman's "liberation," the liberationists show themselves to be *insufficiently* "radical" in the literal sense: they unthinkingly accept the dominant, egalitarian principle of their times and the economic test of a person's worth, rather than questioning these principles.

In each of the substantive manifestations of contemporary egalitarianism, we have noted a tendency to pursue an abstract principle in relative disregard of particular facts and consequences. The same spirit is manifested in two of the fashionable "remedies" for alleged unjust inequalities: "reverse" discrimination and school busing. These remedies are examined critically in this volume by Robert Sasseen and Nathan Glazer, respectively.

Sasseen demonstrates that, whatever verbal subterfuges are employed to conceal the fact, the so-called affirmative action policy imposed on employers and educational institutions by the federal government in recent years amounts to a program of racial and sexual discrimination. By using the criterion of "underutilization" as a test of discrimination, the national bureaucracy in effect compels employers to hire, and universities to admit, specified percentages of women and favored minorities. Sasseen goes on to contrast the affirmative action principle with the understanding of equality on which the United States was founded. The "equal opportunity" protected by the Constitution is an equality of political rights and equality before the law, not a guarantee of equal economic and social status, which are to be attained by the individual's own efforts. To turn the government into an engine for imposing an equality of condition on men would undermine the individual freedom for the sake of which the American regime was established. In addition, the affirmative action system reintroduces racial distinction into a system which ought to be color blind, and thus implicitly sanctions other forms of private discrimination. As Sasseen warns, the notion that all inequality is a product of discrimination rests on no firmer a foundation than the equally false principle of fixed racial inequalities; to violate the principle of equality before the law in one direction is to invite others to reject it on other grounds.

Glazer's article "Is Busing Necessary?" raises a number of searching questions about the justness as well as the feasibility of court-ordered busing as a remedy for de facto racial segregation in public schools. Although this article was originally published in 1972, the issues it deals with remain unresolved, and Glazer's questions continue to be relevant to our situation.

The fundamental problem that concerns Glazer is how the national effort to repair the "monstrous wrong" of legally imposed racial segregation has been transformed into a policy of school busing that offends "the sense of right of great majorities" of people. The advocates of busing claim that this policy is required in order to give effect to the Supreme Court's original mandate to end school segregation in *Brown v. Board of Education*, and label opponents of this policy as racists and segregationists. Glazer endeavors to demonstrate on the other hand that there is a legitimate "third position" that opposes racial discrimination without demanding the imposition of busing.

Glazer begins by tracing the manner in which the courts have moved from outlawing legally mandated segregation in the South to attacking de facto segregation, resulting from patterns of residence, in cities throughout the country. In opposition to the claim that the new policy simply follows from the old one, Glazer draws an important distinction between judicial decisions that *expand* individual freedom, as the original rulings outlawing legal segregation did, and those that restrict it, as the busing decisions do. Something seems to be wrong with legal arguments that, while purporting to advance the cause of freedom, speak again and again of needing to prevent whites from "escaping" or "fleeing" the experience of integration. It does little to enhance one's confidence in the busing principle that few of the judges and lawyers who advocate it send their own children to integrated public schools. And it bespeaks an extreme contempt for ordinary men's opinions when the enforcers of busing simply dismiss parents' objections to it in cities like Boston as motivated by racism.

There are, Glazer argues, quite legitimate reasons for communities to believe that neighborhood schools are advantageous to them. For judges to set themselves up as supreme arbiters of educational policy in matters so open to argument hardly seems compatible with either the principle or the practice of democracy. What is more, there is little evidence that the legal compulsion of racial mixing in schools really achieves the goals it is supposed to serve, in terms either of black achievement or of community understanding.

School busing resembles each of the other egalitarian policies discussed in this volume—the equalization of wealth, status, and political influence; the abolition of distinctions between the sexes; and reverse discrimination—in purporting to serve the interest of the common man, yet being advanced much more by men who think themselves uncommon—the intellectuals—than by its supposed beneficiaries. Considering the deficiencies that the authors in this volume show to be intrinsic to the egalitarians' arguments, this attachment of contemporary intellectuals to a more or less radical egalitarianism evidently is in need of a further explanation than the objective circumstances of our society supply. Such an explanation is suggested by Irving Kristol in the final selection in this volume, his essay "About Equality."

As Harvey Mansfield, Jr., has noted, the liberal regime under which we Americans live is one that offers enormous benefits to the intellectual: above all, it provides him a historically unparalleled freedom to express his opinions, however unpopular or heretical they may be. Paradoxically, however (Kristol argues), the liberal regime is almost inevitably repulsive rather than attractive to the intellectual who lives under it. The problem is that the radical freedom of expression we now enjoy could be achieved only by making the mass of men indifferent to the importance of ideas. The liberal solution to the problem of government, originated by John Locke and other philosophers of the sixteenth through eighteenth centuries, is to liberate men's acquisitive instincts from moral and political control, and consequently to encourage the mass of men to concentrate on pursuing material goods in order to make their lives more comfortable, rather than becoming involved in the religious and political controversies that formerly troubled the world and caused persecutions, tyrannies, and civil wars. This solution has worked beautifully in the United States, in that it has produced a unique degree of prosperity, political stability, and individual freedom. But the way that people live in this society—their materialism, and their lack of a transcendent purpose such as religion and patriotism formerly provided—necessarily dissatisfies the intellectual, who concerns himself with "higher" things than money and sees himself as a leader of men.

American prosperity and freedom, and the value we place on "enlightenment"—that is, on the *practical* utility of ideas—have led to the development of an intellectual class of enormous numbers. These intellectuals passionately desire to distinguish themselves from other men. Yet imbued with the egalitarian principles of their regime, and conscious of their own often humble roots, intellectuals in modern democracy find the only legitimate distinction to lie (as Henry James indicates) in being *more* egalitarian than their "equals."

The desirability of sacrificing the freedom, domestic peace, and prosperity that Americans enjoy for the sake of achieving a "higher" purpose may well be doubted. But in any case, neither the peaceful egalitarians whose proposals are examined in this volume, nor would-be revolutionaries like Herbert Marcuse, actually offer men the vision of a society where life would be more meaningful and purposeful than at present. Rather, the "radicals'" vision of a good society seems to resemble Friedrich Nietzsche's portrait of the society of the "last man," a world of "no shepherd and one herd," one of universal conformity where life is reduced to "play."[5]

If we find such visions uninviting, we may feel reassured in the present crisis, as Kristol is, by contemplating the "natural recuperative powers" of "bourgeois" society. But given Kristol's own diagnosis of the problem, a merely passive sanguineness will not suffice. The crisis seems to require, in the first place, a thorough critical analysis of the charges leveled against the American regime by its egalitarian critics, and a thoughtful evaluation of their proposed "reforms," such as I believe the contributors to this volume (both in the present essays and in other works cited in "Suggestions for Further Reading") have helped to supply. A deeper problem, however, seems to lie in the character of the training and guidance that contemporary institutions of higher learning provide to the intelligentsia. If, as both Mansfield and Kristol suggest, the most influential intellectual critics of the American regime misperceive both the nature of that regime and the real causes of their own hostility to it, one must wonder how far what nowadays passes for "social science" lives up to its title. Despite their pretense of promoting "radical" criticism of American society, it increasingly appears that most departments of social science act primarily to propagate and reinforce a regnant ideology the grounds of which are seldom questioned, and which is antithetical to the preservation of a free regime.

The problem is exemplified, in part, by the failure of America's colleges and universities to provide their students with an adequate appreciation of the nature and the principles governing the operation of free institutions. One should recall that two such patriarchs of American liberty as Jefferson and Madison presupposed the need to *inculcate* "the true principles of liberty" in students of the law through the study of such works as *The Federalist* and the writings of John Locke.[6] What they had in mind, certainly, was not the dogmatic imposition of a particular ideology, but rather the thoughtful study of the American regime's fundamental principles without an awareness of which the regime could not perpetuate itself. A survey of contemporary higher education, however, would reveal a very different set of principles being inculcated, and a less open-minded mode of instruction, than Jefferson and Madison had in mind. Several leading college textbooks on American politics teach as undoubted fact the doctrine that—contrary to the claims of Jefferson, Lincoln, and the *Federalist*— the American regime is as "elitist" as any other, providing hardly (if any) more "meaningful" freedom than any other form of government. The belief that American institutions have any objective superiority to those of, say, Maoist China is, to say the least, out of fashion today. The bias of most American economics departments against the principles of free enterprise is similarly well known. And other social scientists dismiss as "repressive" prejudices the moral restraints upon which the preservation of freedom has traditionally been thought to depend.

Above and beyond the particular deficiencies of the teaching of social science, the contemporary academy suffers from a more serious flaw: its failure to provide most students with any serious understanding or appreciation of the greatest works of the human mind. In pursuit of studies that provide "relevance" and instill "commitment," the line between education on the one hand and journalism or entertainment on the other is rapidly being blurred if not erased. Thus, the writings of Plato, Rousseau, Dante and Shakespeare are given short shrift, replaced in the college curriculum by an ever-changing collection of contemporary scribblings. Such studies not only fail to induce the student to question in a genuinely radical way the dogmas of his time;

more importantly, they fail to make him aware of the possibility of a life of the mind that could satisfy his deepest longings. According to Plato and Aristotle, the political passion such as we find among our intelligentsia today is a misdirected form of the *eros* that points to philosophizing.[7] If the preservation of a regime dedicated to protecting the equal rights of man depends on the attitudes of the intelligentsia, then that preservation ultimately requires the restoration of the ideal of a truly liberal education.[8] The aim of such education cannot be, of course, the propagation of a race of philosophers; but it may reasonably aspire to instruct men both of the nature of human greatness and of the limits of political possibility. Thus, it may instill in them both a commitment to the pursuit of excellence and an appropriate measure of humility; an appreciation of the equal right of mankind to "life, liberty, and the pursuit of happiness," without the admixture of envy and misguided ambition that discolors the contemporary egalitarian movement.

1

The "New" Egalitarianism

Daniel Bell

ON MERITOCRACY AND EQUALITY

In 1958, the English sociologist Michael Young wrote a fable, *The Rise of the Meritocracy*. It purports to be a "manuscript," written in the year 2033, which breaks off inconclusively for reasons the "narrator" failed to comprehend. The theme is the transformation of English society, by the turn of the twenty-first century, owing to the victory of the principle of achievement over that of ascription (i.e., the gaining of place by assignment or inheritance). For centuries, the elite positions in the society had been held by the children of the nobility on the hereditary principle of succession. But in the nature of modern society, "the rate of social progress depend[ed] on the degree to which power is matched with intelligence." Britain could no longer afford a ruling class without the necessary technical skills. Through the successive school-reform acts, the principle of merit slowly became established. Each man had his place in the society on the basis of "I.Q. and Effort." By 1990 or thereabouts, all adults with an I.Q. over 125 belonged to the meritocracy.

But with that transformation came an unexpected reaction. Previously, talent had been distributed throughout the society, and each class or social group had its own natural leaders. Now all men of talent were raised into a common elite, and those below had no excuses for their failures; they bore the stigma of rejection, they were known inferiors.

By the year 2034 the Populists had revolted. Though the majority of the rebels were members of the lower classes, their leaders were high-status women, often the wives of leading scientists. Relegated during the early married years to the household because of the need to nurture high-I.Q. children, the activist women had demanded equality between the sexes—a movement that was then generalized into the demand for equality for all, and a classless society. Life was not to be ruled by "a mathematical measure," but each person would develop his own diverse capacities for leading his own life.[1] The Populists won. After little more than half a century, the Meritocracy had come to an end.

Is this, too, the fate of the post-industrial society? The post-industrial society, in its logic, is a meritocracy. Differential status and differential income are based on technical skills and higher education, and few high places are open to those without such qualifications. To that extent, the post-industrial society differs from society at the turn of the twentieth century. The initial change, of course, came in the professions. Seventy years or so ago, one could still "read" law in a lawyer's office and take the bar examination without a college degree. Today, in medicine, law, accounting, and a dozen other professions, one needs a college degree and accrediting, through examination, by legally sanctioned committees of the profession before one can practice one's art. For many years, until after World War II, business was the chief route open to an ambitious and aggressive person who wanted to strike out for himself. And the rags-to-riches ascent (or, more accurately, clerk-to-capitalist, if one follows the career of a Rockefeller, Harriman, or Carnegie) required drive and ruthlessness rather than education and skills. One can still start various kinds of small businesses (usually, now, by franchise from a larger corporation), but the expansion of such enterprises takes vastly different skills than in the past. Within the corporation, as managerial positions have become professionalized, individuals are rarely promoted from below but are chosen from the outside, with a college degree as the passport. Only in politics, where position may be achieved through the ability to recruit a following or through patronage, is the mobility ladder relatively open to those without formal credentials.

Technical skill, in the post-industrial society, is what economists call "human capital." An "investment" in four years of college, according to initial estimates of Gary Becker, yields, over the average working life of the male graduate, an annual return of about 13 percent. Graduation from an elite college (or elite law or business school) gives one a further advantage over graduates from "mass" or state schools. Thus the university, which once merely reflected the status system of the society, has now become the arbiter of class position. As the gatekeeper, it has gained a quasi-monopoly in determining the future stratification of the society.

Any institution which gains a quasi-monopoly power over the fate of individuals is likely, in a free society, to be subject to quick attack. Thus the Populist revolt which Michael Young foresaw several decades hence has already begun, at the very onset of the post-industrial society. One sees this today in the derogation of the I.Q. and the denunciation of theories espousing a genetic basis of intelligence; in the demand for "open admissions" to universities; in the pressure for increased numbers of blacks, women, and specific minority groups such as Puerto Ricans and Chicanos on the faculties of universities, by quotas if necessary; and in the attack on "credentials" and even schooling itself as the determinant of a man's position in society. A post-industrial society reshapes the class structure of society by creating new technical elites. The populist reaction, which has begun in the 1970s, raises the demand for greater "equality" as a defense against being excluded from that society. Thus the issue of meritocracy versus equality.

The credentials society. Initially, equality of opportunity was the main preoccupation. The explicit fear created by a post-industrial society is that failure to get on the educational escalator means exclusion from the privileged places in society. A meritocratic society is a "credentials society" in which certification of achievement—through the college degree, the professional examination, the license—becomes a condition of higher employment. Education thus becomes a defensive necessity, as Lester Thurow has observed (in *The Public Interest*, No. 28, Summer 1972):

As the supply of educated labor increases, individuals find that they must improve their educational level simply to defend their current income positions. If they don't, others will and they will find their current jobs no longer open to them. Education becomes a good investment not because it would raise people's incomes above what they would have been if no one had increased his education, but rather because it raises their income above what it will be if others acquire an education and they do not. *In effect, education becomes a defensive expenditure necessary to protect one's "market share."* The larger the class of educated labor and the more rapidly it grows, the more such defensive expenditures become imperative.

The logical outcome of these fears is a demand on the part of disadvantaged groups for "open admissions" to universities. The underlying rationale of this demand has been the argument that social class origin of the parent was the primary factor skewing selection in the occupational system, and that open admissions to colleges would enable minority groups to compete more fairly in the society. To that extent, open admissions is no more than the historic American principle that everyone should have a chance to better himself, no matter where he starts. It is also the optimistic American belief that giving any student more education will do him good. This was the logic behind the land-grant college acts; it was the long-standing practice of the public universities, outside the East, even before World War II.[2]

But for some the extension of this demand has become an attack on the meritocratic principle itself. As one proponent of open admissions, Jerome Karabel writes:

As long as open admissions remains limited to a few institutions, it poses no threat to the meritocracy. Recruitment into the elite will be based not on *whether* one went to college, but on *where* one went to college. Universal open admissions, however, would destroy the close articulation between the meritocracy and the system of higher education; further, by the very act of abolishing hierarchy in admissions, it would cast doubt on hierarchy in the larger society.

That argument, however, if pushed to its logical conclusion, would mean that admission to all higher schools in the country, from Parsons College to Harvard, should be by lot. And the further conclusion, since elite schools would still be defined by the faculty, would be to make teaching assignments in the national university system a matter of lot as well.

Opening admissions is a means of widening equality of opportunity by broadening access to the university for potential students. But there is also the question of place in the university structure itself—in the faculty, staff, and administration. In their comprehensive study of the American occupational structure, Peter Blau and Otis Dudley Duncan have shown that almost all the different minority groups have been able to achieve commensurate status, power, and economic rewards—with the exception of women and blacks. Clearly, if there is discrimination—on the basis of sex, or color, or religion, or any criterion extraneous to professional qualification—there is no genuine equality of opportunity. The second effort to widen equality has been the effort to expand the number of places for minorities in the system.

In the 1960s, the government declared it a matter of public policy that "affirmative action" had to be taken to rectify the discrimination against minorities. The policy of affirmative action was first proclaimed by President Johnson in an Executive Order in 1965. It stated that on all federal projects, or in any employment situation that used federal money, employers had to prove they had sought out qualified applicants from disadvantaged groups; had to provide special training where necessary, if qualified applicants could not be found immediately; and had to hire preferentially from among minority-group members when their qualifications were roughly equal to those of other applicants. This program, combined with others such as Head Start and compensatory education programs, was designed to redress a historic cultural disadvantage and, quite deliberately, to give minority-group members, especially blacks, an edge in the competition for place.

In the first years of the affirmative action program, efforts were directed primarily within the skilled trades—especially the building trades, where there had been a deliberate policy of racial exclusion. In the early 1970s, the Nixon Administration, acting through the Department of Health, Education, and Welfare (HEW), extended the program to universities, and each school with federal contracts was asked to provide data on the number of minority persons in each position, academic and non-academic, and to set specific goals for increasing the number of minority-group persons in each classification. Edward Shils summarized the order as follows:

Universities were informed that for each category of employee in the university it would be necessary to specify rates of remuneration and number in each category by "racial breakdown, i.e., Negro, Oriental, American Indian, Spanish-surnamed Americans...." This has to be accompanied by an " 'Affirmative Action Program' which specifically and succinctly identif[ies] problem areas by division, department location and job classification, and includes more specific recommendations and plans for overcoming them." The "Affirmative Action Program" must "include specific goals and objectives by division, department and job classification, including target completion dates on both long and short ranges as the particular case may indicate. Analytical provision should be made for evaluating recruitment methods and sources; the total number of candidates interviewed, job offers made, the numbers hired with the number of minority group persons interviewed, made job offers, and hired...."

From discrimination to representation. The initial intention of the Executive Order was to eliminate *discrimination.* But discrimination is difficult to prove, especially when the qualifications required for a job are highly specific. And the government's test became: Are the members of the minority groups to be found in employment, at every level, in numbers equal to their proportion in the population? Or, if women earned 30 percent of the Ph.D.s, are 30 percent of the faculty women? What this meant, in theory, was to set "target" figures for women and blacks. In practice, this has meant quotas, or priorities in hiring, for persons from these groups.

What is extraordinary about this change is that, without public debate, an entirely new principle of rights has been introduced into the polity. In the nature of the practice, *the principle has changed from discrimination to "representation."* Women, blacks, and Chicanos now are to be employed, as a matter of right, in proportion to their number, and the principle of professional qualification or individual achievement is subordinated to the new ascriptive principle of corporate identity.[3]

The implications of this new principle are far-reaching. One can "logically" insist on quotas where the skill is homogeneous, where one person can readily substitute for another. But by focusing on group identity rather than the person, by making the mechanical equation of number of women Ph.D.s to number of positions they should hold, the government assumes that "educated labor" is "homogeneous"—that individual talent or achievement is less important than the possession of the credential. This may be true in many occupations, but not in university teaching and research, where individual merit is the singular test. Putting someone in a tenure position, which is capitalized at three quarters of a million dollars, is very different from hiring a black rather than a white plumber; simply having the degree is not necessarily the qualification for the high position.

Furthermore, quotas and preferential hiring mean that standards are bent or broken. The inescapable assumption of the ascriptive criterion as regards tenured university positions is that minority persons are less qualified and could not compete with others, even if given a sufficient margin. What effect does this have on the self-esteem of a person hired on "second-class" grounds? And what effect does it have on the quality of a university, its teaching and research and morale, if its faculties are filled on the basis of quotas?

And quite apart from their effects, the quotas themselves are no simple matter. If "representation" is to be the criterion of position, then what is the logic of extending the principle only to women, Blacks, Mexicans, Puerto Ricans, American Indians, Filipinos, Chinese, and Japanese (the categories in the HEW guideline)? Why not to Irish, Italians, Poles, and other ethnic groups? And if representation is the criterion, what is the base of representation? At one California state college, as John Bunzel reports, the Mexican Americans asked that 20 percent of the total work force be Chicanos, because the surrounding community is 20 percent Mexican-American. The black students rejected this argument and said that the proper base should be the state of California, which would provide a different mix of blacks and Chicanos. Would the University of Mississippi be expected to hire 37 percent black faculty because that is the proportion of blacks in the population of Mississippi? And would the number of Jews in most faculties in the country be reduced because the Jews are clearly overrepresented in proportion to their number?

And if ethnic and minority tests, why not religion or political beliefs as the criteria of balanced representation? [Former] Governor Reagan of California...said that conservatives are highly underrepresented in the faculties of the state universities, a fact evident when the political coloration of those faculties is compared with voting results in California; should conservatives therefore be given preference in hiring? And should particular communities be asked to support the teaching of certain subjects (or the presence of certain books in school libraries) which are repugnant to the beliefs of that community—a question first raised in the Virginia House of Burgesses and a principle restated by the Tennessee legislature in the 1920s in barring the teaching of evolution in a Fundamentalist state?

The historic irony in the demand for representation on the basis of an ascriptive principle is its complete reversal of radical and humanist values. *The liberal and radical attack on discrimination was based on its denial of a justly earned place to a person on the basis of an unjust group attribute.* That person was judged—and excluded—because he was a member of a particular group. But now it is being demanded that one must have a place primarily because one possesses a particular group attribute. The person himself has disappeared. Only attributes remain. The further irony in all this is that according to the radical critique of contemporary society, an individual is treated not as a person but as a multiple of roles that divide and fragment him and reduce him to a single dominant attribute of the major role or function he plays in society. Yet in the reversal of principle we now find that a person is to be given preference by virtue of a role, his group membership, and the person is once again "reduced" to a single overriding attribute as the prerequisite for a place in the society. That is the logic of the demand for quotas.

II

The issues of schooling, of income, of status have all become matters of social policy because equality has been one of the central values of the American polity. But there has never been a clear-cut meaning to equality, and the earliest form of the idea in the seventeenth century was quite different from the popular form it assumed by the third decade of the nineteenth century. Those who founded the colonies—in New

England, at least, beginning with the Pilgrims of the Mayflower Compact—had an image of themselves as a "community of virtuous men who understood themselves to be under sacred restraints." There was an equality, but in the Puritan sense of an equality of the elect. Among the Founding Fathers the idea of virtue and of election by ability (if no longer by grace) predominated. A curious blend of Roman republican imagery and Lockean thinking—since both emphasized agrarian virtues and labor—informed their language. The central theme was independence, and the conditions whereby a man could be independent. But in the very use of Lockean language there was an implicit commitment to a hierarchy—the hierarchy of intellect. Since thought was prized, it was assumed that some men "thought" better than others, were more able, more intelligent—and so formed the natural aristocracy.

The initial departure from this was symbolized by the "Jacksonian persuasion." Thought was replaced by sentiment and feeling, each man's sentiments were held to be as good as any other's. This is what gives point to the striking observations of Tocqueville. The opening lines of *Democracy in America* are:

No novelty in the United States struck me more vividly during my stay than the equality of conditions. It was easy to see the immense influence of this basic fact on the whole course of society. It gives a particular turn to public opinion and a particular twist to the laws, new maxims to those who govern and particular habits to the governed.

Reflecting on the power of this new principle, Tocqueville concluded:

Therefore the gradual progress of equality is something fated. The main features of this progress are the following: it is universal and permanent, it is daily passing beyond human control, and every event and every man helps it along. Is it wise to suppose that a movement which has been so long in train could be halted by one generation? Does anyone imagine that democracy, which has destroyed the feudal system and vanquished kings, will fall back before the middle classes and the rich? Will it stop now, when it has grown so strong and its adversaries so weak?

In nineteenth-century America, however, the notion of equality was never sharply defined. In its voiced assertions it came down to the sentiment that each man was as good as another and no man was better than anyone else. What it meant, in effect, was that no one should take on the air of an aristocrat and lord it over other men. To this extent, it was a negative reaction to the highly mannered society of Europe, and travelers to this country at the time understood it in those terms. On its positive side, equality meant the chance to get ahead, regardless of one's origins; that no formal barriers or prescribed positions stood in one's way. It was this combination of attributes—the lack of deference and the emphasis on personal achievement—which gave nineteenth-century America its revolutionary appeal, so much so that when the German '48ers came here, including such members of Marx's Socialist Workers Club as Kriege and Willich, they abandoned socialism and became republicans.

The redefinition of equality. What is at stake today is the redefinition of equality. A principle which was the weapon for changing a vast social system, the principle of equality of opportunity, is now seen as leading to a new hierarchy, and the current demand is that the "just precedence" of society, in Locke's phrase, requires the reduction of all inequality, or the creation of *equality of result*—in income, status, and power—for all men in society. This issue is the central value problem of the post-industrial society.

The principle of equality of opportunity derives from a fundamental tenet of classic liberalism: that the individual—and not the family, the community, or the state—is the basic unit of society, and that the purpose of societal arrangements is to allow the individual the freedom to fulfill his own purposes—by his labor to gain property, by exchange to satisfy his wants, by upward mobility to achieve a place commensurate with his talents. It was assumed that individuals will differ—in their natural endowments, in their energy, drive, and motivation, in their conception of what is desirable—and that the institutions of society should establish procedures for regulating fairly the competition and exchanges necessary to fulfill these diverse desires and competences.

As a principle, equality of opportunity denies the precedence of birth, of nepotism, of patronage or any other criterion which allocates place, other than fair competition open equally to talent and ambition. It asserts, in the terms of Talcott Parsons, universalism over particularism, achievement over ascription. It is an ideal derived directly from the Enlightenment as codified by Kant, the principle of individual merit generalized as a categorical imperative.

The social structure of modern society—in its bourgeois form as the universalism of money, in its romantic form as the thrust of ambition, in its intellectual form as the priority of knowledge—is based on this principle. Estate society, in the eighteenth century and earlier, had given honorific precedence to land, the Army, and the Church, and only the birthright of inheritance could provide access to these institutions. Even where there was nominal mobility—the institutions of the Red and the Black—commissions in the Army (as in England up to the middle of the nineteenth century) were only by purchase, and benefices in the Church were available through family connection. Modernity meant the uprooting of this stratified order by the principle of openness, change, and social mobility. The capitalist and the entrepreneur replaced the landed gentry, the government administrator took power over the Army, and the intellectual succeeded the priest. And, in principle, these new positions were open to all men of talent. Thus there occurred a complete social revolution: a change in the social base of status and power, and a new mode of access to place and privilege in the society.

The post-industrial society adds a new criterion to the definitions of base and access: Technical skill becomes a condition of operative power, and higher education the means of obtaining technical skill. As a result, there is a shift in the distribution of power as, in key institutions, technical competence becomes the overriding consideration. In industry, family capitalism is replaced by managerial capitalism; in government, patronage is replaced by civil service and bureaucratization; in the universities, the exclusiveness of the old social elites, particularly WASP domination of the Ivy League colleges, breaks up with the inclusion of ethnic groups, particularly the Jews. Increasingly, the newer professional occupations, particularly engineering and economics, become central to the decisions of the society. The post-industrial society, in this dimension of its status and power, is the logical extension of the meritocracy; it is the codification of a new social order based, in principle, on the priority of educated talent.

In social fact, the meritocracy is thus the displacement of one principle of stratification by another, of ascription by achievement. In the past this new principle was considered just. Men were to be judged and rewarded on the basis not of birth or primordial ties but of individual merit. Today that principle is held to be the new source of inequality and of social, if not psychological, injustice.

The case against meritocracy. The socioligical and philosophical objections to the meritocracy are of a contradictory and overlapping nature:

1. If one assumes that a meritocracy is purely a selection by intelligence, and that intelligence is based on inherited genetic differences, then privilege is obtained on the basis of an arbitrary genetic lottery, which is the antithesis of social justice.

2. There can never be a pure meritocracy because high-status parents

will invariably seek to pass on their positions, either through the use of influence or simply by the cultural advantages their children inevitably possess. Thus after one generation a meritocracy simply becomes an enclaved class.

3. There is considerable social mobility in the United States, but it is less related to schooling or ability or even family background than to intangible and random factors such as luck and competence in the particular job one falls into. Christopher Jencks and his associates, in a review of the effect of family and schooling on mobility, conclude:

Poverty is not primarily hereditary. While children born into poverty have a higher than average chance of ending up poor, there is still an enormous amount of economic mobility from one generation to the next. There is nearly as much economic inequality among brothers raised in the same homes as in the general population....

...there is almost as much economic inequality among those who score high on standardized tests as in the general population. Equalizing everyone's reading scores would not appreciably reduce the number of economic "failures."...

Our work suggests, then, that many popular explanations of economic inequality are largely wrong. We cannot blame economic inequality primarily on genetic differences in men's capacity for abstract reasoning, since there is nearly as much economic inequality among men with equal test scores as among men in general. We cannot blame economic inequality primarily on the fact that parents pass along their disadvantages to their children, since there is nearly as much inequality among men whose parents hold the same economic status as among men in general. We cannot blame economic inequality on differences between schools, since differences between schools seem to have very little effect on any measurable attribute of those who attend them. Economic success seems to depend on varieties of luck and on-the-job competence that are only moderately related to family background, schooling, or scores on standardized tests.

Thus, a situation of inequality exists which is justified on the basis of achievement or meritocracy but does not actually derive from them, so that the rewards of mobility, or, at least, the degrees of inequality in reward, are not justified.

4. A meritocracy instills a competitive feeling into society which is damaging to those who succeed and even more so to those who fail. Jerome Karabel writes:

A meritocracy is more competitive than an overtly-based class society, and this unrelenting competition exacts a toll both from the losers, whose self-esteem is damaged, and from the winners, who may be more self-righteous about their elite status than is a more traditional ruling group. Apart from increased efficiency, it is doubtful whether a frenetically competitive inegalitarian society is much of an improvement over an ascriptive society which, at least, does not compel its poor people to internalize their failure.

5. The principle of equality of opportunity, even if fully realized on the basis of talent, simply recreates inequality anew in each generation, and thus becomes a conservative force in society. In its most vulgar form, this is the argument that equality of opportunity has been the means by which some (e.g., the Jews) have sought to get "theirs" in society and to deny latecomers (e.g., blacks) a fair share of the spoils. This is the argument employed in New York City, for example, where it is charged that in the school system Jews "used" the merit system to dispossess the Catholics, who had risen through patronage, but that the merit system now is a means of keeping out blacks from high places in the system. In its pristine form, this argument says social justice should mean equality not at the start of a race, but at the finish, equality not of opportunity but of result.

The Coleman Report. This change in social temper—the distrust of meritocracy—occurred principally in the last decade. The Kennedy and Johnson Administrations, as a double consequence of the civil rights revolution and the emphasis on higher education as a gateway to better place in the society, had made equality the central theme of social policy. The focus, however, was almost completely on widening equality of opportunity, principally through the schools: on compensatory education, Head Start programs, manpower training to improve skills, school integration, busing ghetto children to suburban schools, open admissions, and the like. It was clear that black and poor children were culturally disadvantaged, and these handicaps had to be eliminated. The image that President Johnson used, in proclaiming the policy of affirmative action, was that of a shackled runner:

Imagine a hundred yard dash in which one of the two runners has his legs shackled together. He has progressed 10 yards, while the unshackled runner has gone 50 yards. At that point the judges decide that the race is unfair. How do they rectify the situation? Do they merely remove the shackles and allow the race to proceed? Then they could say that "equal opportunity" now prevailed. But one of the runners would still be forty yards ahead of the other. Would it not be the better part of justice to allow the previously shackled runner to make up the forty yard gap; or to start the race all over again? That would be affirmative action towards equality.

The change in attitude, however, began with the realization that schooling had little effect in raising the achievement or reducing the disparate standing of black children relative to white. In 1966, Professor James Coleman of Johns Hopkins University, carrying out a mandate of the Civil Rights Act of 1964, concluded a massive survey of 4,000 schools and 600,000 students. The Office of Education, which sponsored the research, and Coleman himself had expected to find gross inequality of educational resources between black and white schools and to use these findings as an argument for large-scale federal spending to redress the balance. But the report, *Equality of Educational Opportunity*, found that there was little difference between black and white schools in such things as physical facilities, formal curricula, and other measurable criteria; it also found that a significant gap in achievement scores between black and white children was already present in the first grade, and that despite the rough comparability of black and white schools, the gap between the two groups had widened by the end of elementary school. The only consistent variable explaining the differences in scores *within* each racial or ethnic group was the educational and economic attainment of the parents. As Coleman wrote:

First, within each racial group, the strong relation of family economic and educational background to achievement does not diminish over the period of the school, and may even increase over the elementary years. Second, *most of the variation in student achievement lies within the same school, very little of it is between schools*. The implication of these last two results is clear: family background differences account for much more variation in achievement than do school differences.

But there was no consistent variable to explain the difference *between* racial groups, not even family background—which is why some persons have fallen back on genetic explanations.

The Coleman findings dismayed the educational bureaucracy, and at first, received little attention. Issued in July 1966, the document was not reported in the *New York Times* or the newsweeklies. But as the explosive finds gradually became known, the Coleman Report became the center of the most extensive discussion of social policy in the history of American sociological debate, and the source of vehement public recrimination on such questions as compulsory integration, school busing, and the like.[4]

Much of the controversy over the Coleman Report dealt with integration: Some interpreted it, as did Coleman himself, in part, as a mandate to mix lower-class black schoolchildren with middle-class whites to provide stronger peer-group pressures for achievement; black-power advocates saw it as justification for black control of black schools in order to strengthen the black child's control over his own destiny; and still others felt that additional money spent on schools would be a waste, since schools were ineffective in reducing the achievement gaps between the races or between social classes.

But in the long run, the more important aspect of the report was less its findings than its major thesis, which was the redefinition of equality of opportunity. Coleman had been explicitly charged to determine the extent of inequality in the educational *resources* available to black and white children, the assumption being that social policy had to equalize the "inputs" into the educational process. But what Coleman took as his criterion was achievement, or results. In effect, he redefined equality of opportunity *from equal access to equally well-endowed schools (inputs) to equal performance on standardized achievement tests (equality of outcomes).* As he put it in the title of his *Public Interest* essay, the focus had to shift from "equal schools to equal students."

What Coleman was saying was that the public schools—or the process of education itself—were not the social equalizers American society imagined them to be. Children achieved more or less in relation to family background and social class, and these were the variables that would have to be changed. Equality would not be attained until an average public school in Harlem produced as many high achievers as one in Scarsdale.

Equality of result. The argument has been pushed one step further by Christopher Jencks. If the focus was on the "equal student," then the problem was not even the distinction between Harlem and Scarsdale. In reanalyzing the Coleman data, Jencks found that students who performed best on achievement tests "were often enrolled in the same schools as the students who performed worst," and this, he declared, was potentially the most revolutionary revelation in the Report: "In the short run it remains true that our most pressing political problem is the achievement gap between Harlem and Scarsdale. But in the long run it seems that our primary problem is not the disparity between Harlem and Scarsdale but the disparity between the top and bottom of the class in both Harlem and Scarsdale."

One can carry this still another step to the disparity among children of the same family. And Jencks in fact has done so: "There is nearly as much economic inequality among brothers raised in the same homes as in the general population. This means that inequality is recreated anew in each generation, even among people who start life in essentially identical circumstances." For Jencks, inequality is not inherited. There is no single consistent variable which explains who gets ahead and why.

It is as much luck as anything else.

The logic of this argument is developed by Jencks in his book, *Inequality*. Not only can one not equalize opportunity, but even if one could, equalizing opportunity does not appreciably reduce the inequality in results. He concludes quite bluntly:

Instead of trying to reduce people's capacity to gain a competitive advantage on one another, we will have to change the rules of the game so as to reduce the rewards of competitive success and the costs of failure. Instead of trying to make everybody equally lucky or equally good at his job, we will have to devise "insurance" systems which break the link between vocational success and living standards.[5]

The aim of social policy, thus, has to be equality of result—by sharing and redistributive policies—rather than equality of opportunity.

If equality of result is to be the main object of social policy—and it is the heart of the populist reaction against meritocracy—it will demand an entirely new political agenda for the social systems of advanced industrial countries. But no such political demand can ultimately succeed without being rooted in some powerful ethical system, and for this reason the concept of equality of result has become the Archimedean point of a major new effort to provide a philosophical foundation—a conception of justice as fairness—for a communal society.

In the nature of human consciousness, a scheme of moral equity is the necessary basis for any social order; for legitimacy to exist, power must be justified. In the end, it is moral ideas—the conception of what is desirable—that shape history through human aspirations. Western liberal society was "designed" by Locke, Adam Smith, and Bentham on the premise of individual freedom and the satisfaction of private utilities; these were the axioms whose consequences were to be realized through the market and later through the democratic political system. But that doctrine is crumbling, and the political system is now being geared to the realization not of individual ends but of group and communal ends. Socialism has had political appeal for a century now not so much because of its moral depiction of what the future society would be like, as because of material disparities within disadvantaged classes, the hatred of bourgeois society by many intellectuals, and the eschatological vision of a "cunning" of History. But the normative ethic was only implicit; it was never spelled out or justified. The claim for equality of result is a socialist ethic (as equality of opportunity is the liberal ethic), and as a moral basis for society it can finally succeed in obtaining men's allegiance not by material reward but by philosophical justification. An effort in politics has to be confirmed in philosophy. And an attempt to provide that confirmation is now under way.

III

The starting point for the renewed discussion of inequality—as for so much of modern politics—is Rousseau. In his *Discourse on the Origin and Foundations of Inequality Among Men* (the "Second Discourse"), Rousseau sought to show that civil society ineluctably generates inequality. For Rousseau, the state of nature was a psychological construct that showed what men would be like without society. In nature and in society, there are two kinds of dependence. As he wrote in *Emile*, there is "dependence on things, which is the work of nature; and dependence on men, which is the work of society. Dependence on things, being non-moral, does no injury to liberty and begets no vices; dependence on men, being out of order, gives rise to every kind of vice, and through this master and slave become mutually depraved." The movement from nature to society is a change in the character of dependence.

For Rousseau, there are also two kinds of inequality: One is natural or physical (such as age, health, strength); the other, moral or political inequality, is based on convention and established by the consent of men. Inevitably, however, as society developed, the first led to the second:

Each one began to look at the others and to want to be looked at himself, and public esteem had a value. The one who sang or danced the best, the handsomest, the strongest, the most adroit or the most eloquent became the most highly considered; and this was the first step toward inequality and, at the same time, toward vice.

Since mind, beauty, strength, skill, merit, and talent established the rank and fate of men, it was necessary to have these qualities, or to dissemble:

...for one's advantage, it was necessary to appear to be other than what one in fact was. To be and to seem to be became two altogether different things; and from this distinction came conspicuous ostentation, deceptive cunning, and all the vices that follow from them.... Finally, consuming ambition, the fervor to raise one's relative fortune less out of true need than in order to place oneself above others, inspires in all men a base inclination to harm each other, a secret jealousy all the more dangerous because, in order to strike its blow in greater safety, it often assumes the mask of benevolence....

Vanity thus was one source of inequality. The other was material differences rooted in property. Property in and of itself is good and productive. Labor gives a person the right to the soil, and continuous possession is transformed into property, thus establishing "the first rules of justice." Things in this state "could have remained equal if talents had been equal...but this proportion was soon broken; the stronger did more work; the clever turned his to better advantage; the more ingenious found ways to shorten his labor." And one man thus had more than another.

Thus does natural inequality imperceptibly manifest itself along with contrived inequality; and thus do the differences among men, developed by those circumstances, become more perceptible, more permanent in their effects, and begin to have a proportionate influence over the fate of individuals...Thus, as the most powerful or most miserable made of their force or their needs a sort of right to the goods of others, equivalent to them to the right of property, the destruction of equality was followed by the most frightful disorder....

Inequalities of various kinds become formalized, "but in general, wealth, nobility or rank, power and personal merit [are] the principal distinctions by which one is measured in society." Of these four types of inequality,

as personal qualities are the origin of all the others, wealth is the last to which they are reduced in the end because, being the most immediately useful to well-being and the easiest to communicate, it is easily used to buy all the rest: an observation which can permit a rather exact judgment of the extent to which each people is removed from its primitive institution, and the distance it has traveled toward the extreme limit of corruption.

Thus, "from the extreme inequality of conditions and fortunes...come scores of prejudices equally contrary to reason, happiness and virtue." This is what one finds "in discovering and following...the forgotten and lost routes that must have led man from the natural state to the civil state."

Since man cannot live in the state of nature, the problem is how to reduce the dependence of man upon man and yet make him a social person instead of a natural person. Rousseau's answer, of course, is the social contract, the tie by which men forswear both natural liberty and conventional liberty to gain moral liberty. One renounces one's self— one's vanity and the desire to dominate others—by becoming a member of the community; and the community itself is a single personality, a whole of which each citizen is a part.

These clauses [of the social contract], rightly understood, are reducible to one only, viz. the total alienation to the whole community of each associate with all his rights; for, in the first place, since each gives himself up entirely, the conditions are equal for all; and the conditions being equal for all, no one has any interest in making them burdensome to others.

The price of equality, then, is that "an individual can no longer claim anything"; he has no individual rights, "his person and his whole power" are dissolved into the general will. Equality is possible only in community through the eclipse of the self. Thus Rousseau pursued one logic of the meaning of equality.

Mill and the logic of representation. For Rousseau, who sees social nature as ruled by passion and vice, equality is not an end in itself but a means of achieving civic virtue and making virtuous men; in his hierarchy of purposes, he retains the classical view of the goals of society. For a second, more diffuse kind of political thought, the purpose of equality is social peace, and its guiding principle is utility.

Democracy is by nature contentious because men constantly covet what other men have. Not all societies invite invidious comparisons. The peasant did not compare his lot with the lord; he had his allotted place in the scheme of things and accepted it fatalistically. Democracy, with its normative commitment to equality, inevitably provides an evaluative yardstick for measuring discrepancies in status, wealth, and power. Where one is barred from modifying these discrepancies, the result is often—in Nietzsche's term—*ressentiment,* or envy, anger, and hatred toward those at the top. As Max Scheler has noted:

Ressentiment must therefore be strongest in a society like ours, where approximately equal rights (political and otherwise) or formal social equality, publicly recognized, go hand in hand with wide factual differences in power, property and education....Quite independently of the characters and experiences of individuals, a potent charge of *ressentiment* is here accumulated by the very structure of society.

Ressentiment is the chief psychological fuel of disruption and conflict, and the problem for the society is how to reduce it. Since inequality is not random but patterned—the discrepancies are grouped—all groups have to be included in the society and enabled to use the political system as a means of redressing other forms of inequality. Thus, the chief instrument of social peace is representation.

The rationale for this system was laid down by John Stuart Mill in his *Representative Government.* "The interest of the excluded is always in danger of being overlooked," he wrote. The group he had in mind, at the time, was the working class. Although the other classes no longer "deliberately" sought to sacrifice the interests of the working class to themselves, the very fact that the workers were excluded meant that questions were never regarded from their viewpoint. Mill went so far as to argue that representative government can only exist when there is proportional representation, and one chapter of his book, entitled "Representation of Minorities," explores the Hare system for this kind of election, "a scheme which has the almost unparalleled merit of carrying out a great principle of government in a manner approaching to ideal perfection as regards the special object in view . . . ." What is good about that principle of government is that "it secures a representation, in proportion to numbers, of every division of the electoral body: not two great parties alone, with perhaps a few large sectional minorities in particular places, but every minority in the whole nation, consisting of a sufficiently large number to be, on principles of equal justice, entitled to a representative."

The logic of minority representation is the quota. Any polity, to obey the dictates of equal justice, would have to insist that its representative body be made up of social units equal in proportion to the diverse composition of its membership. The Democratic Party, in its . . . rules for the 1972 convention, did exactly this in stipulating that all state parties had to take "affirmative steps" to make their delegations representative of their respective state populations in terms of minority groups, women, and young people (those from 18 to 30).

The problem of quotas. But this raises two serious problems. First, how does one define a legitimate "interest," or social unit, or minority corporate group? In the early years of the Republic, it was argued that the states were the legitimate units of representation, and the Constitution, before it was amended, gave state legislatures the duty of electing each state's two senators. In the 1930s and after, the legitimate units seemed to be the "functional groups"—business, farmers, and workers. In the 1960s and 1970s, the units came to be biologically defined (sex, color, age) and culturally defined (ethnic, religious) groups. Yet if one sits in a representative body on the basis of age, sex, ethnic group, religion, or occupation, is that single corporate identity to be the overriding attribute which guarantees one's place? It is an elementary sociological fact that a person has not a single identity but a multiple number of roles. Does a black woman under 30 have three votes rather than one? Or must she choose a single attribute to be "quotaed" for?

Second, if political bodies are composed entirely of corporate groups, what happens to numerical majority rule? Do the few larger corporate bodies outvote the smaller ones? The blacks, for example, one of the most disadvantaged groups in American society, make up about 11 percent of the population. In a few cities they are a majority, but these cities do not have sufficient financial resources for rehabilitation or improvement. The sociologist Herbert Gans has argued that no numerical majority will ever tax itself, or redistribute its wealth, to aid a minority, so that in a majoritarian society the lot of blacks will never be greatly improved. In consequence, he argues that if equality is to be achieved, minority groups should be given special veto rights in the society. This is, in effect, the principle of the "concurrent majority" which John C. Calhoun sought before the Civil War to protect the Southern states from being outvoted by the North.[6] It is also the logic behind the idea of "community control" over social resources such as schools, housing, and the like. But is there then any wider social or public interest? If corporate or community groups are to control the decisions which affect their lives, by what right can one deny a Southern community the right to practice segregation? And if a local group vetoes the passage of a highway through its neighborhood, does it not thus impose a higher tax cost on its neighbors by insisting on this relocation?

The purpose of inclusive representation of all minorities is to reduce conflict, yet the history of almost all societies shows that when polities polarize along a single overriding dimension—be it class, religion, language, tribe, or ethnic group—there is bound to be violent conflict; and when there are numerous "cross-cutting" identities—in Holland, where there are both class and religious political parties, Catholic and Protestant workers divide so that neither religion nor class wholly captures a single allegiance—there is a greater degree of checks and veto power in the society. In short, can the principle of quota representation in the polity, defined along communal or particularistic lines, escape either the polarization or the fragmentation of the polity, and the fate of ataxia for the society?

Rawls and fairness. If Rousseau sought equality of result for the sake of virtue, and Mill equal representation proportionate to one's interest for the purpose of social stability, John Rawls wants to establish the priority of equality for reasons of justice. As he elegantly declares, "justice is the first virtue of social institutions, as truth is of systems of thought."[7]

What is justice? It cannot be the greatest good for the greatest number, for the price of this may be injustice for the lesser number. It has to be a distributive principle for judging competing claims—i.e., the appropriate division of social advantages. For Rawls, this is justice as fairness, and the foundation of fairness rests, initially, on two principles:

First: each person is to have an equal right to the most extensive basic liberty compatible with a similar liberty for others.

Second: social and economic inequalities are to be arranged so that they are both (a) reasonably expected to be to everyone's advantage, and (b) attached to positions and offices open to all.

The first principle deals with equal liberties of citizenship—freedom of speech, vote, and assembly; eligibility for office; and so on. The second deals with social and economic inequalities—the distribution of income and wealth, differences in the degree of authority, and the like. It is with the second principle that we are concerned. The controlling terms in the propositions are the ambiguous phrases "to everyone's advantage," and "equally open to all." What do they mean?

Rawls's argument is complex, yet lucid. "Equally open" can mean either equal in the sense that careers are open to the talented, or equal in the sense of "equality of fair opportunity." The first simply means that those who have the ability and the drive are entitled to the place they have earned; this is the conventional liberal position. But Rawls notes that it does not take account of the distortions arising out of social contingencies. "In all sectors of society," Rawls writes, "there should be roughly equal prospects of culture and achievement for everyone similarly motivated and endowed....Chances to acquire cultural knowledge and skills should not depend upon one's class position, and so the school system, whether public or private, should be designed to even out class barriers."

The liberal principle accepts the elimination of social differences in order to assure an equal start, but it justifies *unequal result* on the basis of natural abilities and talents. For Rawls, however, "natural" advantages are as arbitrary or random as social ones.

There is no more reason to permit the distribution of income and wealth to be settled by the distribution of natural assets than by historical and social fortune.... The extent to which natural capacities develop and reach fruition is affected by all kinds of social conditions and class attitudes. Even the willingness to make an effort, to try, and so to be deserving in the ordinary sense is itself dependent upon happy family and social circumstances. It is impossible in practice to secure equal chances of achievement and culture for those similarly endowed, and therefore we may want to adopt a principle which recognizes this fact and also mitigates the arbitrary effects of the natural lottery.

Therefore, Rawls concludes, one cannot equalize opportunity, one can only bend it towards another purpose—the equality of result.

No one deserves his greater natural capacity nor merits a more favorable starting place in society. But it does not follow that one should eliminate these distinctions. There is another way to deal with them. The basic structure can be arranged so that these contingencies work for the good of the least fortunate. Thus we are led to the difference principle if we wish to set up the social system so that no one gains or loses from his arbitrary place in the distribution of natural assets or his initial position in society without giving or receiving compensating advantages in return.[8]

The question thus turns from "equally open to all," to the distribution of chances for place—the distribution of primary social goods or values—to the meaning of "everyone's advantage." This phrase, for Rawls, can be defined in terms of either the "principle of efficiency," or the "difference principle."

The efficiency principle is congruent with what welfare economists call "Pareto optimality." The allocation of goods or utilities is efficient when one reaches the point where it is impossible to change an existing distribution pattern so as to make some persons (even one) better off without at the same time making some other persons (at least one) worse off. For Rawls the difficulty with the principle of efficiency is that, as a matter of fairness, it cannot specify *who* is better off or who is not worse off. A utilitarian principle, "Pareto optimality" is interested only in a net social balance and is indifferent to actual individuals.

The "difference principle." The "difference principle" states that if some persons are to be better off, the less advantaged are also to be better off, and in some circumstances even more so. If one gains, so must the others. "The intuitive idea is that the social order is not to establish and secure the more attractive prospects of those ,better off unless doing so is to the advantage of those less fortunate."[9]

This leads Rawls to his more general conception of social justice, or the social ideal:

All social primary goods—liberty and opportunity, income and wealth, and the bases of self-respect—are to be distributed equally unless an unequal distribution of any or all of these goods is to the advantage of the least favored.

For this reason, too, Rawls rejects the idea of a meritocracy. Although the meritocratic idea *is* democratic, it violates the conception of fairness:

The meritocratic social order follows the principle of careers open to talents and uses equality of opportunity as a way of releasing men's energies in the pursuit of economic prosperity and political domination. There exists a marked disparity between the upper and lower classes in both means of life and the rights and privileges of organizational authority. The culture of the poorer strata is impoverished while that of the governing and technocratic elite is securely based on the service of national ends of power and wealth. Equality of opportunity means an equal chance to leave the less fortunate behind in the personal quest for influence and social position. Thus a meritocratic society is a danger for the other interpretations of the principles of justice but not the democratic conception. For, as we have just seen, the difference principle transforms the aims of society in fundamental respects.

The difference principle has two implications for social policy. One is the principle of redress for individuals:

This is the principle that undeserved inequalities call for redress; and since the inequalities of birth and natural endowment are undeserved, these inequalities are to be somehow compensated for. Thus, the principle holds that in order to treat all persons equally, to provide genuine equality of opportunity, society must give more attention to those with fewer native assets and to those born into the less favorable social position. The idea is to redress the bias of contingencies in the direction of equality. In pursuit of this principle greater resources might be spent on the education of the less rather than the more intelligent, at least over a certain time of life, say the earlier years of school.

The second is the more general principle that talent is to be regarded as a social asset, and its fruits should be available to all, especially the less fortunate.

[The difference principle] transforms the aims of the basic structure so that the total scheme of institutions no longer emphasizes social efficiency and technocratic values. We see then that the difference principle represents, in effect, an agreement to regard the distribution of natural talents as a common asset and to share in the benefits of this distribution whatever it turns out to be. Those who have been favored by nature, whoever they are, may gain from their good fortune only on terms that improve the situation of those who have lost out.

We have here a fundamental rationale for a major shift in values; instead of the principle "from each according to his ability, to each according to his ability," we have the principle "from each according to his ability, to each according to his need." And the justification for need is fairness to those who are disadvantaged for reasons beyond their control.

The end of liberalism. With Rawls, we have the most comprehensive effort in modern philosophy to justify a socialist ethic. In this redefinition of equality as equity, we can observe the development of a political philosophy which will go far to shape the last part of the twentieth century, as the doctrines of Locke and Smith molded the nineteenth. The liberal theory of society was framed by the twin axes of individualism and rationality. The unencumbered individual would seek to realize his own satisfactions on the basis of his work—he was to be rewarded for effort, pluck, and risk—and the exchange of products with others was calculated by each so as to maximize his own satisfactions. Society was to make no judgments between men—only to set the procedural rules—and the most efficient distribution of resources was the one that produced the greatest net balance of satisfactions.

Today we have come to the end of classic liberalism. It is not individual satisfaction which is the measure of social good, but redress for the disadvantaged as a prior claim on the social conscience and on social policy.[10] Rawls's effort in *A Theory of Justice* is to establish the principle of fairness, but he pays little attention, other than using the generic term "disadvantaged," to *who* is to be helped.[11] Yet in contemporary society, inevitably, the disadvantaged are identifiable largely in group terms, and the principle of equity is linked with the principle of quota representation.

The claim for group rights stands in formal contradiction to the principle of individualism, with its emphasis on achievement and universalism. But in reality it is no more than the extension to hitherto excluded social units of the group principle which has undergirded American politics from the start. The group process—which was the vaunted discovery of the "realists" of American political science—consisted largely of economic bargaining between functional or pressure groups operating outside the formal structure of the political system. What we now find are ethnic and ascriptive groups claiming formal representation both in the formal political structure and in all other institutions of the society.

These claims are legitimated, further, by the fact that America has been a pluralist society, or has come to accept the principle of pluralism rather than the homogeneity of Americanism. But pluralism, in its classic conceptions, made a claim for the cultural identity of ethnic and religious groups and for the institutional autonomy of cultural institutions (e.g., universities) from politics. Pluralism was based on the separation of realms. But what we have today is a thoroughgoing politicizing of society in which not only the market is subordinated to political decision but all institutions have to bend to the demands of a political center and politicize themselves. Here, too, there has been another change. In functional group politics, membership was not fixed, and one could find cross-cutting allegiances or shifting coalitions. Today the groups that claim representation—in the political parties, in the universities, in the hospitals, and in the community—are formed by primordial or biological ties; and one cannot erase the ascriptive nature of sex or color.

And yet, once one accepts the principle of redress and representation in the group terms that were initially formulated, it is difficult for the polity to deny those later claims. That is the logic of democracy which has always been present in the ambiguous legacy of the principle of equality.

IV

Any principle inevitably has its ambiguities, for no moral situation is ever clear-cut, particularly in the case of equal opportunity versus equal result, where the conflict is between right versus right, rather than right versus wrong. What, then, are the difficulties and the contradictions in the principle of fairness, and are they of sufficient weight to render it nugatory?

First, what is the meaning of disadvantage? What is the measure of fairness? Is it objective or subjective? Often a sense of unfairness depends upon expectation and the degree of deprivation. But by whose standard? One measure, Rawls writes,

is a definition solely in terms of relative income and wealth with no reference to social position. Thus, all persons with less than half the median income and wealth may be taken as the least advantaged segment. This definition depends only upon the lower half of the distribution and has the merit of focusing attention on the social distance between those who have the least and the average citizen.

But for most persons the question of unfairness or deprivation is not some fixed or absolute standard but a comparison with relevant others. We know from many sociological studies that large disparities of income and status are accepted as fair if individuals feel that it is the will of God, or justly earned, while small differences, if arbitrary, will often seem unfair. Orderlies in a hospital compare their income with that of a nurse but not that of a doctor. Thus relative deprivation and reference group (to use the sociological jargon) at each point stipulate the degree of disparity. But are we to accept the subjective evaluations of individuals as the moral norm, or an objective standard, and on what basis? The point is not clear.

If disadvantage is difficult to define, there is a different kind of problem in the identification of "the least fortunate group." Rawls writes:

Here it seems impossible to avoid a certain arbitrariness. One possibility is to choose a particular social position, say that of the unskilled worker, and then to count as the least advantaged all those with the average income and wealth of this group or less. The expectation of the lowest representative man is defined as the average taken over this whole class.[12]

Problems of borderlines and shadings apart—and in practical terms these are great—the identification of social position in this fashion raises a serious psychological question. One of the important considerations of moral philosophy has been to avoid the labelling, or public stigmatization, of the disadvantaged. This is one of the reasons why reformers have always fought a "means test" as the criterion for public aid and tried to provide help as a right. It is one of the reasons (administrative matters aside) why proposals for the redistribution of income have suggested that a stipulated sum be given to all persons, and that money above a certain level be recouped by taxation. Yet Rawls writes: "...we are entitled at some point to plead practical considerations in formulating the difference principle. Sooner or later the capacity of philosophical or other arguments to make finer discriminations is bound to run out." But it is exactly at those points where principle has to be translated into rule and case that the problems of public policy and administration begin.

The question of labelling and redress leads back to a more general contradiction, the relation of equality to a principle of universalism. One of the historical gains of equality was the establishment of a principle of universalism, so that a rule—as in the rule of law—applied equally to all, and thus avoided administrative determination between persons. For example, in the Constitution, this meant the outlawing of bills of attainder, which are aimed at one person; a law has to be written with a sufficient degree of generality to cover all persons within a category. In criminal law, we apply *equal punishment* to those who have violated the same law, regardless of the ability to bear punishment, and two men convicted of speeding are fined $25 each though one is a millionaire and the other a pauper. The law does not inquire into their status differences; there is equal liability. And the court is enjoined from so prying in order to avoid the enlargement of judicial power which would enable the judge to make determinations between persons; his function is solely to find out whether they are guilty or not. Yet where wealth and income are concerned, we have in some areas gone far in the opposite direction.

Under the income-tax law, which was adopted in this century, not only do individuals not pay an equal amount (e.g., $500 each), they do not even pay equal proportions (e.g., 10 percent each, which would lead to different absolute amounts on varying incomes). In principle, they pay progressively higher proportions as incomes rise. Here ability—the ability to pay—becomes the measure. It may well be that in the area of wealth and income one wants to establish the principle "from each according to his ability, to each in accordance with another's needs"; the principle of justice here applies because *marginal* amounts must be compared. (If two persons pay the same amount, in one case it comes to half his income, in the other case only a tenth, and the same principle is at work in proportionate taxes.) But, in the larger context, the wholesale adoption of the principle of fairness in all areas of life shifts the entire society from a principle of equal liability and universalism to one of unequal burden and administrative determination.

The ground of fairness is a generalized social norm founded on a social contract. It is based, Rawls says, on the theory of rational choice whereby individuals declare their own preferences, subject to the principle of redress and the principle of difference; and this rational choice would push the societal balance toward the social norm. Now, utility theory can order the preferences of an individual and define the rational conduct of the individual; and, in utility theory, society is rightly arranged when we have a net balance of individual gains or losses on the basis of the person's own preferences in free exchange. But here we run up against a difficulty. If rationality is the basis of the social norm, can we have a social-welfare function that amalgamates the discordant preferences of individuals into a combined choice which recapitulates the rationality of the individual choice? If one accepts the theoretical argument of the Arrow impossibility theorem—which shows that a rational combined choice is not possible—we cannot (observing the conditions of democracy and majority choice) have a social-welfare function.[13] What the social norm is to be then becomes a political question, subject to either consensus or to conflict—extortion by the most threatening, or collective bargaining in which people eventually accept some idea of trade-off. But if the decision is political, there are then no clear theoretical determinations, set by principles of rational choice of what the social norm should be—unless, in the Rousseauan sense, the body politic is a "single" personality. We may want a social norm for reasons of fairness, but in the structure of rational choice procedures we cannot define one.

If the definition of a social norm, then, is essentially a political one, the principle of helping the least fortunate as the *prior* social obligation may mean—in a sociological as well as statistical sense—a regression toward the mean. If it is assumed that we have reached a post-scarcity stage of full abundance, this may be a desirable social policy. But if this is not so—and it is questionable whether it can ever be so—and if one defines society, as Rawls does, "as a cooperative venture for mutual advantage," why not allow greater incentives for those who can expand the total social output and use this larger "social pie" for the mutual (yet differential) advantage of all?

It is quite striking that the one society in modern history which consciously began with a principle of almost complete equality (including almost no wage differentials)—the Soviet Union—gradually abandoned that policy, not because it was restoring capitalism but because it found that differential wages and privileges served as incentives and were also a more rational "rationing" of time. (If a manager's time is worth more than that of an unskilled worker, since he has to make decisions, should he be expected to wait in line for a crowded tram or be given a car of his own to get to work?) Even those societies which have had relatively small differentials in income and incentives in the post-World War II years, such as Israel and Yugoslavia, have gradually widened these differences in order to stimulate productivity. And one of the chief pieces of advice which sympathetic economists have given to Fidel Castro to restore his stumbling economy (which has been largely organized on the basis of moral exhortation and the donation of extra labor time) is to make greater use of material incentives and wage differentials. In the United States, the major period when social programs could be most easily financed was from 1960 to 1965, when the increase in the rate of economic growth, not the redistribution of income, provided a fiscal surplus for such programs.

The difficult and thorny question, in the end, is not just priority— who should be helped first—but the degree of disparity among persons. How much difference should there be in income between the head of a corporation and a common laborer, between a professor at the top of the scale and an instructor? The differences in pay in a business firm are on the order of 20:1, in a hospital of 10:1, and in a university of 5:1. What is the rationale for these differences? What is fair? Traditionally, the market was the arbiter of differential reward, based on scarcity or on demand. But as economic decisions become politicized, and as the market is replaced by social decisions, what is the principle of fair reward and fair differences? Clearly this will be one of the most vexing questions in a post-industrial society.

A striking fact of Western society over the past 200 years has been the steady decrease in income disparity among persons—not by distribution policies and judgments about fairness, but by technology, which has cheapened the cost of products and made more things available to more people. The irony, of course, is that as disparities have decreased, as democracy has become more tangible, the expectations of equality have increased even faster, and people make more invidious comparisons ("people may suffer less but their sensibility is exacerbated"), a phenomenon now commonly known as the "Tocqueville effect." The revolution of rising expectations is also the revolution of rising *ressentiment*.

The real social problem, however, may be not the abstract question of "fairness" but the social character of *ressentiment*, and the conditions which give rise to it. The fascinating sociological puzzle is why in the democratic society, as inequality decreases, *ressentiment* increases. That, too, is part of the ambiguous legacy of democracy.

A just meritocracy. The difficulty with much of this discussion is that inequality has been considered as a unitary circumstance, and one single principle the measure of its redress, whereas in sociological fact there are different kinds of inequality. The problem is not *either/or* but what *kinds* of social and moral differences. There are, we know, different kinds of inequality—differences in income and wealth, status, power, opportunity (occupational or social), education, services, and the like. There is not one scale but many, and the inequalities in one scale do not correlate perfectly with inequality in every other.[14]

We can, for example, insist on a basic social equality in that each person is to be given respect and not to be humiliated on the basis of color, or sexual proclivities, or other personal attributes. This is the basis of the civil rights legislation outlawing modes of public humiliation such as Jim Crow laws, and setting forth the principle of complete equal access to all public places. This principle also makes sexual conduct a purely private matter between consenting adults.

We can reduce invidious distinctions in work, whereby some persons are paid by the piece or the hour and others receive a salary by the month or year, or a system whereby some persons receive a fluctuating wage on the basis of hours or weeks worked and others have a steady, calculable income. We can assert that each person is entitled to a basic set of services and income which provides him with adequate medical care, housing, and the like. These are matters of security and dignity which must necessarily be the prior concerns of a civilized society.

But one need not impose a rigid, dogmatic egalitarianism in matters where it conflicts with other social objectives and even becomes self-defeating. Thus, on the question of wage or salary differentials, there may be good market reasons for insisting that the wages of a physician and dentist be greater than those of a nurse or dental technician, for if each cost the patient roughly the same (if one could for the same price have the services of a better qualified person), no one would want to use a nurse or dental technician, even in small matters. The price system, in this case, is a mechanism for the efficient rationing of time. If as a result of differential wages the income spread between the occupations became exceedingly high, one could then use the tax laws to reduce the differences.

But the point is that these questions of inequality have little to do with the issue of meritocracy, if we define the meritocracy as those who have an *earned* status or have achieved positions of rational authority by competence. Contemporary populism, in its desire for wholesale egalitarianism, insists in the end on complete levelling. It is not for *fairness,* but against *elitism;* its impulse is not justice but *ressentiment.* What the populists resent is not power (which they seek for the undifferentiated mass) but authority—the authority represented in the superior competence of individuals. In the populist sociology, for example, the authority of doctors should be subject to the decisions of a community council, and that of professors to the entire collegiate body (which in the extreme versions includes the janitors).

But there cannot be complete democratization in the entire range of human activities. It makes no sense, in the arts, to insist on a democracy of judgment. Which painting, which piece of music, which novel or poem is better than another cannot be subject to popular vote—unless one assumes, as was to some extent evident in the "sensibility of the 1960s," that all art is reducible to experience and each person's experience is as meaningful to him as anyone else's. In science and scholarship achievement is measured and ranked on the basis of accomplishment—be it discovery, synthesis, acuity of criticism, comprehensive paradigms, statements of new relationships, and the like. And these are forms of intellectual authority.

Sociologists have made a distinction between power and authority. Power is the ability to command which is backed up, either implicitly or explicitly, by force. That is why power is the defining principle of politics. Authority is a competence based upon skill, learning, talent, artistry, or some similar attribute. Inevitably it leads to distinctions between those who are superior and those who are not. A meritocracy is made up of those who have earned their authority. An unjust meritocracy is one which makes these distinctions invidious and demeans those below.

Rawls has said that the most fundamental good of all is self-respect. But the English sociologist W. G. Runciman has made a useful distinction between respect and praise. While all men are entitled to respect, they are not all entitled to praise.[15] The meritocracy, in the best meaning of that word, is made up of those worthy of praise. They are the men who are best in their field, as judged by their peers.

And just as some individuals are worthy of praise, so are certain institutions—e.g., those engaged in the cultivation of achievement, the institutions of science and scholarship, culture and learning. The university is dedicated to the authority of scholarship and learning and to the transmission of knowledge from those who are competent to those who are capable. There is no reason why a university cannot be a meritocracy, without impairing the esteem of other institutions. There is every reason why a university has to be a meritocracy if the resources of the society—for research, for scholarship, for learning—are to be spent for "mutual advantage," and if a degree of culture is to prevail.

And there is no reason why the principle of meritocracy should not pertain in business and government as well. One wants entrepreneurs and innovators who can expand the amount of productive wealth for society. One wants men in political office who can govern well. The quality of life in any society is determined, in considerable measure, by the quality of leadership. A society that does not have its best men at the head of its leading institutions is a sociological and moral absurdity.

Nor is this in contradiction with the fairness principle. One can acknowledge, as I would, the priority of the disadvantaged (with all its difficulty of definition) as an axiom of social policy, without diminishing the opportunity for the best to rise to the top through work and effort. The principles of merit, achievement, and universalism are, it seems to me, the necessary foundations for a productive—and cultivated—society. What is important is that the society, to the fullest extent possible, be a genuinely open one.

The question of justice arises when those at the top can convert their authority positions into large, discrepant material and social advantages over others. The sociological problem, then, is how far this convertibility is possible. In every society, there are three fundamental realms of hierarchy—wealth, power, and status. In bourgeois society, wealth could buy power and deference. In aristocratic society, status could command power and wealth (through marriage). In military and estate societies, power could command wealth and status. Today it is uncertain whether the exact relations between the three any longer hold: Income and wealth (even when combined with corporate power) rarely command prestige (who knows the names or can recognize the faces of the heads of Standard Oil, American Telephone, or General Motors?); political office does not make a man wealthy; high status (and professors rank among the highest in prestige rankings) does not provide wealth or power. Nor does the existence of a meritocracy preclude the use of other routes—particularly politics—to high position and power in the society.

But even within the realms the differences are being tempered; and the politics of contemporary society makes this even more likely in the future. Wealth allows a few to enjoy what many cannot have; but this difference can—and will—be mitigated by a social minimum. Power (not authority) allows some men to exercise domination over others; but in the polity at large, and in most institutions, such unilateral power is increasingly checked. The most difficult of all disparities is the one of status, for what is at stake is the desire to be different and to *enjoy* the disparity. With his usual acuteness, Rousseau observed: "[It is] the universal desire for reputation, honors and preferences, which devours us all, trains and compares talents and strengths...stimulates and multiplies passions; and making all men competitors, rivals or rather enemies how many reverses, successes and catastrophes of all kinds it causes..."

Yet, if vanity—or ego—can never be erased, one can still observe the equality of respect due to all and the differential degree of praise owed to some. As Runciman puts it, "a society in which all inequalities of prestige or esteem were inequalities of praise would to this extent be just." It is in this sense that we can acknowledge differences between individuals. It is to that extent that a well-tempered meritocracy can be a society not of equals, but of the just.

Richard W. Crosby

EQUALITY IN AMERICA:
THE DECLARATION, TOCQUEVILLE, AND TODAY*

INTRODUCTION

The United States has been called many things, some descriptive, some prescriptive, some friendly, some not. It is significant that the most frequent characterizations are political, as if the political were in some way the heart or soul of what the United States *is: viz.* some kind of democracy. But there seems to be some discomfort with simply saying we are a democracy, because that word does not accurately describe the regime and because it is insufficient as a prescription for what the regime should be. Therefore, we hear the United States most often referred to as a liberal democracy (or less often as a constitutional democracy or a democratic republic). "Liberal democracy" is both descriptive and prescriptive: we are and should be a regime in which the people rule while protecting liberty. An alternative description/ prescription, "egalitarian democracy," has had no such currency, perhaps because it is less euphonious or is thought to be redundant (democracy is egalitarian). But the ear can become accustomed to cacophony in political discourse, and redundancy in the service of the good is no vice. What seems to be reflected in the unpopularity of "egalitarian democracy" is precisely a doubt that such a regime would be good. Should equality be *the* goal of the regime (and how liberal could such a regime be)?

Some contemporary critics of the United States assert that the problem with the regime is that it is insufficiently egalitarian, insufficiently democratic. The country should shift its aim from "equality of opportunity to equality of results."[1] The radicalism of such a shift is

53

cloaked by the language used. The new egalitarians in their appeal for "equality of results" tap the reservoir of public approbation for some kind of equality. Approval of movement from the familiar ("equality of opportunity") to the unfamiliar ("equality of results") is greased and eased by a rhetorical sleight of hand. But this legerdemain is possible because the United States *is* "dedicated to the proposition that all men are created equal." After all, the fundamental premise of the Declaration of Independence, the founding document of the regime, is the self-evident truth of man's natural equality. In tapping this egalitarian strain, are not the new egalitarians being faithful to the central tenet of the American creed?

This essay seeks to demonstrate the following:

1. The universal teaching of the Declaration of Independence has no necessary egalitarian implications for civil society and actually requires that inequality be the essential characteristic of civil society.

2. The United States did in fact incorporate what are called egalitarian elements (political equality and equality of opportunity), but these were understood by the Founders as approximations of natural *liberty* which were consistent with the libertarian purpose of the regime and were not expected to issue in an equality of results.

3. It is possible, even likely, as was demonstrated by the French political theorist Alexis de Tocqueville, for a society characterized by political equality and equality of opportunity to rededicate itself to the purpose of securing equality of results but with a concomitant and necessary loss of liberty.

I. THE DECLARATION OF INDEPENDENCE: ALL MEN ARE CREATED EQUAL

The Declaration's statement that all men are created equal is a description of the prepolitical condition of man, before "governments are instituted among men." The fact of man's natural equality is, however, decisive for the institution of government. From it is derived the purpose of government (to secure rights equally possessed by men), and the only legitimate mode for the establishment of government: the consent of the people. Without that consent any government's powers are not just: the government lacks legitimacy.

What is meant by man's natural equality and why does it issue in these requirements for government? In its abbreviated presentation of the natural rights teaching, the Declaration does not elaborate the meaning of natural equality. For that elaboration, it is necessary to turn to the original authors of the natural rights doctrine.

Thomas Hobbes was, I believe, the first political philosopher to argue the crucial political significance of man's natural equality. I also believe that it is his understanding of this primary political fact, transmitted with some modification by John Locke, that constitutes the meaning and political significance of the Declaration's statement: all men are created equal.

According to Hobbes, inequality is characteristic of man's civil state after the establishment of government. But before this, men were equal in that each could do the "greatest things" to one another, namely, kill each other.[2] Because of man's natural equality, there is no natural title for one man to rule another. This is the decisive fact about both man and the state of nature. It is this natural equality which renders the state of nature a state of war and impels man to seek relief from the horrors of a condition of natural equality.

Men in civil society observe that this state abounds in inequality—of wealth, wit, beauty—but they are mistaken when, on the basis of such inequality, some men claim to rule other men.[3] For these inequalities which may develop in civil society are dependent upon the existence of government for their efflorescence. Something more fundamental must serve as the basis of government itself, and that something is man's natural equality in the ability to kill.[4] But neither the inequalities of civil society nor the natural equality of man seem to provide a title to rule. How then, given that man is not naturally a social creature, given that nature dissociates men,[5] is rule to be legitimately established?

Men are, according to Hobbes, equal in another fundamental sense. They are equally desirous of the "greatest thing," the preservation of their lives, and each man has "the liberty...to use his own power, as he will himself, for the preservation of his own nature—that is to say, of his own life—and consequently of doing anything which, in his own judgment and reason, he shall conceive to be the aptest means thereunto."[6] Men equal in ability to kill, acting in accord with this right of nature come into conflict. "The state of equality is the state of war."[7] The impossibility of securing the "greatest thing," life, in this condition of natural equality pushes men toward civil society. The last and crucial expression of natural equality is in consenting to be governed. But this is an expression of equality of natural right, of that *liberty* which each man equally possesses "to use his power...for the preservation of...his own life." Out of fear, men exercise their natural right and consent to be governed, i.e., they consent to renounce natural equality, the equality of ability to kill (which becomes a virtual monopoly of the government), and the equal right to do anything which conduces to self-preservation.

Far from being a title to rule, consent is a renunciation of the claim to rule.

"Therefore inequality was introduced by a general consent; this inequality. . . is no longer to be accounted an unreasonable thing."[8] By consenting to be governed, which means the establishment of inequality, men seek to secure the crucial object of the right of nature (life), which object was rendered insecure in the natural state of equality. Where there is government, the various and unequal talents of men which were latent and suppressed in the state of nature can manifest themselves in action: in "industry. . ., culture of the earth. . ., navigation. . ., commodious building. . ., arts, letters. . . ."[9] In short, civilization has a chance to flourish.

Of course, it is not Hobbes but John Locke who is rightly said to be the source of the Declaration's doctrine. But it has been shown that although

the first impression of Locke's state of nature seems very unlike Hobbes's state of nature, [there are] three significant similarities. . . . The state of nature is the home—and the only home—of the state of war: the state of nature is "an ill condition" "not to be endured." Secondly, the source, content, and end of the law of nature can be stated, briefly and not inaccurately, in the word *self-preservation*. And finally, Locke's teaching is not unlike Hobbes's in the assertion that "civil government is the proper remedy for the inconveniences of the state of nature."[10]

Locke is also not unlike Hobbes in his understanding of the significance of equality within the state of nature. The state of nature is "a state of perfect freedom" and "a state also of equality." And that, as for Hobbes, is the problem. It is a state of equality because no man has the natural power and therefore claim to rule another.[11]

In seeking his preservation "in that state of perfect equality, where naturally there is no superiority or jurisdiction of one, over another, what any may do. . .everyone must needs have a right to do."[12] Thus within this natural state of equality, "inconveniences" arise. "For all being kings as much as he, every man his equal, and the greater part no strict observers of equity and justice, the enjoyment of the property [life, liberty, and estate] he has in this state is very unsafe and insecure. This makes him willing to quit a condition, which however free, is full of fears and continual dangers. . . ."[13]

And for Locke as for Hobbes, natural equality is manifest in the act of consent to establish civil society, but not necessarily beyond. "But though men when they enter into society, give up the equality, liberty, and executive power they had in the state of nature. . ., yet it being only with the intention in every one the better to preserve himself, his liberty and property."[14]

This Hobbesean-Lockean understanding of equality is, I believe, also the Declaration's. "All men are created equal" is the description of man in the state of nature. Because of an equality of passion (from which rights arise) and ability, neither of which provide a title or possibility of rule and both of which create "an ill condition" "not to be endured," government is established among men, that government gaining its legitimacy from the consent of those to be governed. The Declaration requires no particular *form* of government: the right to consent is not a title to rule. The form (democracy, aristocracy, limited monarchy) can be whatever (to the people) "shall seem most likely to effect their safety and happiness." (The essence of the Declaration's indictment of George III is that he is an unfit prince, which entails the possibility of a fit prince, i.e., one who secured these rights.) Because the state of natural equality is barely endurable, government of almost any kind is a great boon, so "that mankind are more disposed to suffer, while evils are sufferable, than to right themselves by abolishing the forms to which they are accustomed." If anything, there is a bias in the Declaration for any form of government other than the worst form, absolute monarchy.[15]

Although the form of government is not specified, the *purpose* of government is: to secure these rights, life, liberty and the pursuit of happiness.

For Hobbes natural liberty is an enemy of the most important natural right, life. Therefore, upon entering civil society, it must be given up. Locke and the Declaration assert that the protection of life and liberty, the liberty to pursue happiness however the individual defines that happiness, are compatible. It is because Locke and the founders thought that the pursuit of property would constitute an essential part of the pursuit of happiness for most men that they could afford this crucial revision of Hobbes. The pursuit of property could be civilized, so that this liberty could be allowed without bringing back the anarchic conditions of the state of nature. Which is to say a regime might be constructed which could be libertarian because it was not simply egalitarian.

II. POLITICAL EQUALITY AND
EQUALITY OF OPPORTUNITY

"The democratic teaching of the Declaration begins with natural equality but does so in order to conserve conventional inequality, for example, inequality of wealth and inequality of political authority, which is what is meant by government."[16]

Natural equality is antithetical to government. It must be curbed, civilized, politicized before it can be safely incorporated into civil society; it must be transformed into political equality. The regime which attempts this delicate enterprise is democracy. Although democracy is not the form of government required by the Declaration of Independence, in some form it may be that regime which to the people, especially the American people in 1776, "seems most likely to effect their safety and happiness." But the argument for democracy, as for any form of government, is that it best serves the specified end of government: the security of rights. It is a means toward an end and is therefore subordinate to the end.[17]

To secure rights is the preeminent goal of government. But if this goal can be accomplished by a government based on the popular principle (political equality), by that very fact a part of man's natural rights will have been secured within civil society. The popular principle can be seen as a deduction from the fact of natural equality (and therein lie both its attractiveness and its potentially antisocietal tendencies). Since it is selfish rights that government is to protect, each individual "self" *may* be the best judge of what measures and laws are indeed in his interest. Civil society with government based on the popular principle may make possible what was impossible in the state of nature, for men to be judges in their own case. Popular government is then that paradoxical experiment which tries to reintroduce on the level of civil society a similacrum of that natural equality which was the cause of man's flight from the state of nature. (Equality of opportunity is the parallel attempt in the nonpolitical realm.) "Majority rule...derogates least from the natural equality from which civil society took its origin."[18]

The founders in establishing the regime were aware of the paradox of popular government and tried to resolve it. Although the authors of *The Federalist* could say: "The streams of national power ought to flow immediately from that pure original fountain of all legitimate authority [the consent of the people],"[19] power still has flowed *from*, i.e. it is no longer entirely located there. And it was to "flow from" in such a way that actual political authority was unequally distributed, de facto because de jure. Political equality was to be diluted, not primarily because the size of the country necessitated representation, but because the representative principle would better serve the legitimate ends of government.[20]

Representation, even in its most direct form in the House of Representatives but even more in the indirect modes of electing the Senate and President, not to mention the Supreme Court, was "to refine and enlarge the public views, by passing them through the medium of a chosen body of citizens, whose wisdom may best discern the true interest of their country, and whose patriotism and love of justice, will be least likely to sacrifice it to temporary or partial considerations."[21] This sort of representation may occur because, on the one hand, the people will choose their betters as their natural representatives (the argument of *Federalist* #35), and on the other because the offices in the *national* government will be sufficiently grand to attract men of ambition.

Political equality remains only at the level of the franchise (and not completely even there) and in the openness of most offices to anyone who wishes to run. But the offices themselves are of varying importance and power. Inequality is introduced, however, not to harbor privilege but to fulfill the purpose of government, and to correspond to the inequalities of talent that civil society has allowed to flower.

The constitutional order seeks not only to preserve some semblance of natural equality in the political realm, it also tries to provide more than a semblance of natural equality in the nonpolitical realm. Because of the importance of the social realm, the function of government is emphatically limited. For Hobbes, it is limited to protecting life, but because life is so endangered by other men and other nations, absolutism is justified. By expanding the number of rights which government is to protect and channelling the liberty to pursue happiness in a certain way, government can be truly limited (in the sense of not impinging on individuals). A milder government is possible only if some extragovernmental means can be found for men satisfying their wants. Locke found such a means in the pursuit of property. The political shrinks in importance (becomes in fact limited) in so far as it becomes less necessary for men to be kept off each other's backs. Our concept of limited government expects men to be doing more important things (pursuing their happiness) while government merely provides hospitable conditions for that pursuit (which is to say that most men's political interests and activities will be as limited and secondary as is the purpose of government). But the question is: how *can* men be left free to pursue happiness without re-creating the state of nature within civil society? Just as political equality seems to reproduce the unacceptable situation of men judging in their own cases, so allowing man something like natural liberty to pursue happiness would seem to invite those inconveniences that made the state of nature unendurable.

Federalist #10 provides the outline of an ingenious solution to both these problems. To simplify, the problem is that a devotion to liberty in the social sphere and to the popular principle in the political seems to create the possibility of a chaos like that in the state of nature. Solution: *really* free men; tear down all the old, conventional barriers to gain (provide equal opportunity) so that they will embark on a multiplicity of peaceful money-making ventures, such a variety that they will be unable to coalesce into a single-willed majority. In so doing men are free but harmless, and the wealth of nations or of a nation will be created.

A *"civilized, modern* nation [such as that envisioned by *Federalist* #10] is one in which there is an enormous degree of liberty and in which nature is . . . given the greatest scope."[22] But *Federalist* #10 sees this as at once a problem and the solution to the problem. In particular, it is the emancipation of "the different and unequal faculties of acquiring property" (which it becomes the "first object of government" to protect) that *could* be the problem but becomes the solution, within the framework of law (the Constitution) and the large, commercial republic.

Liberty channelled in a certain way is safe. Conflict over the goods that make life comfortable and pleasant can be minimized by commerce, especially if the size of the nation and the development of technology make possible an ever-increasing abundance, and such conflict need never embroil the political sphere. The large, commercial republic that is freer and more prosperous than any nation of whatever size at whatever time in history is an extraconstitutional solution. Or, put more accurately, it reflects the modern idea that the purpose of government is to provide the conditions which allow men to go about their more important, private business. The Constitution is a necessary condition for the large, commercial republic, and the crucial importance of representation is that it makes great size possible.

In the political realm, it is possible to adhere to the popular principle because it can be civilized (both within the Constitution by creating a factual inequality of offices and extraconstitutionally by the fracturing effects of the large, commercial republic on a factious majority). Similarly, in the social and economic realm, liberty can be allowed and even encouraged because it is rendered benign and even beneficial in the pursuit of wealth. Such liberty creates abundance and thereby national power. As David Potter has said, "in America 'liberty' [means] 'freedom to grasp opportunity' and 'equality' also means 'freedom to grasp opportunity'; [they] have become almost synonymous."[23] The constitutional order envisioned by *Federalist* #10, as the necessary condition for this assimilation of the meanings of liberty and equality, counts on and itself furthers the destruction of the old, conventional barriers to opportunity. It may even be sufficient to lower those barriers and present to the eyes of men, as now attainable, the fruits of this abundant continent. Thus equalized and opened, opportunity may be sufficient to spur the pursuit, to make the many (in Locke's phrase) industrious and rational. On what grounds could one cavil with the fact intended by the founders, that "from the protection of different and unequal faculties of acquiring property, the possession of different degrees and kinds of property immediately results"?[24] What could divert some from the promises (and to a large extent, the reality) of liberty and abundance, and make them demand equality of results?

III. Tocqueville

Tocqueville provides one scenario, as they say today, for the transformation of the world of *Federalist* #10 into that sought by the new egalitarians.

To put Tocqueville's projection in terms used previously, Americans may find themselves too close to the state of nature for comfort. The reproduction within civil society of an untrammeled liberty approximating natural liberty and of that dissociation of men characteristic of the state of nature leaves men fearful and their primary desire for comfort unsatisfied. To escape this too natural civil state, they consent to a "soft" despotism which embodies the principle of equality of results. A new founding may occur which at least is faithful to the old principles in the sense that popular consent is required and forthcoming.

Tocqueville argues for this possibility as follows: In America, "hereditary wealth, the privileges of rank, and the prerogatives of birth have ceased to be . . . ."[25] Freed from those conventional restraints, men see it as their right and hope to attain the good things in life. But the democratic regime in America not only frees men, "it tends to isolate them from each other, to concentrate every man's attention upon himself."[26] The dissociation and selfishness of the state of nature are reproduced. But most important,

it lays open the soul to an inordinate love of material gratification. . . . Of all the passions which originate in or are fostered by equality, there is one which it renders peculiarly intense and which it also infuses into the heart of every man; I mean the love of well-being. The taste for well-being is the prominent and indelible feature of democratic times."[27]

This, of course, is what the American founders and their mentors intended. This pursuit of well-being results in inequality.

When men living in a democratic state of society are enlightened, they readily discover that they are not confined and fixed by any limits which force them to accept their present fortune. They all, therefore, conceive the idea of increasing it. If they are free, they all attempt it, but all do not succeed in the same manner. The legislature, it is true, no longer grants privileges, but nature grants them. As natural inequality is very great, fortunes become unequal as soon as every man exerts all his faculties to get rich.... The inequality of fortunes augments in proportion as...their liberty increases.[28]

Civil liberty allows the flowering of differences only latent in the state of nature and issues in inequality: "all do not succeed in the same manner." And there is the rub. Tocqueville mentions a sect in his time which proposed "to concentrate all property in the hands of a central power" and then distribute it to individuals "according to their merits." Tocqueville finds the system of *Federalist* #10 superior to this, but goes on to show that men may demand such a central power whose criterion for distribution is not merit but that natural, brute equality of all men.

John Stuart Mill observed that Tocqueville assumed the democratic revolution would continue "until all artificial inequalities shall have disappeared from among mankind; those inequalities only remaining which are the natural and inevitable effects of the protection of property."[29] Although Tocqueville sees this inevitable inequality as natural and just, he is aware that democratic men may reject it. That inequality which civil society allows to develop may become the irritant which, together with irritating approximations of natural liberty and natural dissociation, may lead democratic man to create a civil society without liberty, but with mass homogeneity, and equality of results—a society in which the only vestige of nature as a standard is in the demand that all men be in fact equal and consent to their bondage.

"When there is no longer any principle of authority..., men are speedily frightened at the aspect of this unbounded independence. The constant agitation of all surrounding things alarms and exhausts them. As everything is at sea in the sphere of the mind, they determine at least that the mechanism of society shall be firm and fixed; and, as they cannot resume their ancient belief, they assume a master."[30] But it is not only "in the sphere of the mind" that everything is at sea. In the economic arena, "the taste...for easy success and present enjoyment" (which "all men then have" in a "democratic period")[31] is not satisfied. Instead, the pursuit of their own welfare is accompanied by

the vague dread that constantly torments them lest they should not have chosen the shortest path which may lead to it.... [A native of the United States] clutches everything, he holds nothing fast, but soon loosens his grasp to pursue fresh gratifications.... His is a bootless chase of that complete felicity which forever escapes him.... [He is filled with] anxiety, fear, and regret...his mind [is] in ceaseless trepidation...."[32]

Men in a democracy will seek relief from this "joyless quest for joy." And since it is liberty which is the condition of his unhappy pursuit of happiness, liberty must be sacrificed, in the name of equality.

There is, in fact, a manly and lawful passion for equality that incites men to wish all to be powerful and honored. This passion tends to elevate the humble to the rank of the great; but there exists also in the human heart a depraved taste for equality, which impels the weak to attempt to lower the powerful to their own level and reduces men to prefer equality in slavery to inequality in freedom.[33]

Democracy predisposes men toward the second, depraved taste for equality.

The ambition of those who are below...is irritated in exact proportion to the great number of those who are above.... It cannot be denied that democratic institutions strongly tend to promote the feeling of envy in the human heart; not so much because they afford to everyone the means of rising to the same level with others as because those means perpetually disappoint the persons who employ them. Democratic institutions awaken and foster a passion for equality which they can never entirely satisfy. This complete equality eludes the grasp of the people...The lower orders are agitated by the chance of success, they are irritated by its uncertainty; and they pass from the enthusiasm of pursuit to the exhaustion of ill success, and lastly to the acrimony of disappointment. Whatever transcends their own limitations appears to be an obstacle to their desires, and there is no superiority, however legitimate it may be, which is not irksome in their sight.[34]

The solution which satisfies the longing for equality, especially equality of goods, relieves the tensions and restlessness of the pursuit of happiness, and abandons liberty, is "soft despotism."

I seek to trace the novel features under which despotism may appear in the world. The first thing that strikes the observation is an innumerable multitude of men, all equal and alike, incessantly endeavoring to procure the petty and paltry pleasures with which they glut their lives. Each of them, living apart, is as a stranger to the fate of all the rest. . . . He exists only in himself and for himself alone; and if his kindred still remains to him, he may be said at any rate to have lost his country.

Above this race of men stands an immense and tutelary power, which takes upon itself alone to secure their gratifications and to watch over their fate. That power is absolute, minute, regular, provident, and mild. It would be like the authority of a parent if, like that authority, its object was to prepare man for manhood; but it seeks, on the contrary, to keep them in perpetual childhood. . . . For their happiness such a government willingly labors; but it chooses to be the sole agent and the only arbiter of that happiness; it provides for their security, foresees and supplies their necessities, facilitates their pleasures, manages their principal concerns, directs their industry, regulates the descent of property, and subdivides their inheritances; what remains, but to spare them all the care of thinking and all the trouble of living?

Thus it everyday renders the exercise of free agency of man less useful and less frequent; it circumscribes the will within a narrower range and gradually robs a man of all the uses of himself. The principle of equality has prepared men for these things; it has predisposed men to endure them and often to look on them as benefits.

. . .the will of man is not shattered, but softened, bent, and guided; men are seldom forced by it to act, but they are constantly restrained from acting. Such a power does not destroy, but it prevents existence; it does not tyrannize, but it compresses, enervates, extinguishes, and stupefies a people, till each nation is reduced to nothing better than a flock of timid and industrious animals, of which the government is the shepherd.[35]

Perhaps paradoxically, this sacrifice of freedom is done freely. This government derives its powers from the consent of the governed. The only difference between it and the Declaration's prescription for just government is that it no longer has as part of its purpose the dangerous protection of liberty. But it may indeed be that form of government which to the people seems "most likely to effect their safety and happiness." It is a total escape from the state of nature, wherein man is free, dissociated, and insecure. By transforming the Declaration's description of prepolitical man, "all men are created equal," into a prescription for civil society, "make men in fact equal," it associates men into an enslaved herd. The state of nature, as the American regime tried to approximate it, becomes the ill condition not to be endured.

IV. CONCLUSION

Both the end and the means of its attainment are common to Tocqueville and the new egalitarians. The only difference is that the latter approve and Tocqueville disapproves. Equality of cognitive skills, occupational status, income, and job satisfaction are the explicit goals of contemporary egalitarianism. And it is to be government's job to bring these about. The problem is to gain consent. And here it has been suggested that the envy, though the word is not used, of the lower orders be tapped.[36] It is admitted that the many must undergo a process of "enlightenment" before they will demand of government equality of results. But it seems that it is precisely the many who are most resistant to such suggestions.[37] It is the few, academics or intellectuals, who seem infatuated with the idea of equality of results (always, of course, in the name of the many), which gives some plausibility to Irving Kristol's provocative suggestion that those seeking equality do so, not for reasons of justice, but because *they* wish to rule.[38]

I do not mean to deny that an argument for the justness of an equality of results can be made. I do mean to suggest that the egalitarianism of the Declaration of Independence and the kinds of equality introduced into civil society by the founders cannot be appealed to as a justification for the principle of equality of results. Further, I wonder whether equality of results can be achieved without sacrificing liberty, while acknowledging that popular consent might be forthcoming for such a sacrifice.

Harvey C. Mansfield, Jr.

LIBERAL DEMOCRACY AS A MIXED REGIME

In recent years the parts of the coalition of which the Democratic party is composed have been exposed to view. In the election of 1972, the coalition came unstuck as Democratic voters divided into enthusiasts for McGovern or against Nixon and supporters of Wallace and Nixon. In 1976, they were back together but still suspicious of each other. Whether the coalition will dissolve further or be drawn tighter I cannot say, but my interest is not so much in the future history of parties as in what these events reveal about the character of liberal democracy as a regime. They reveal that this regime is a mixture, usually made in a party coalition, of liberals and democrats.

The "liberals" are, of course, the McGovern enthusiasts in our example, those generally known as "liberals"—but not only they, as we shall see. Such liberals might be called "opinion leaders" or identified by class or group, but I will define them as men of ambition who have enough demonstrable talent to think themselves capable of being outstanding in some way. Their ambition is usually moderate and varied, but it is real; and it is very important to them not to do merely what others do, to think what others think, or to be what others are. The "democrats," the ordinary voters (including most McGovern voters in 1972), are otherwise. They want what passes for a competence, no less than what most people have but no more; and they want this with security, more for the sake of their dignity (their "standard" of living) than for any level of comfort, and more against injustice than against loss. They prefer a quiet, private life, and are satisfied with the praise and esteem of their friends. Last but not least, the democrats are many and the liberals are relatively few.

Now since our regime is often called a liberal democracy, and liberal democracy is a regime that takes pride in diversity, why should it be necessary to discover that liberal democracy is a mixture of liberals and democrats? The answer is that the liberals resist being defined as I have defined them. They want to think of themselves as democrats, as I have defined *them.* This resistance, I will try to show, lies at the root of the troubles of liberal democracy today, including those of liberal democrats in the 1972 election, because liberal democracy is so mixed as to conceal intentionally the ambitions of liberals. To see why and how this was done, we must consider the classical source of the mixed regime in Aristotle's political science, out of which, and against which, liberal democracy was conceived.

According to Aristotle, almost all modern, civilized regimes are democracies or oligarchies. They may be defined as the rule of the many and of the few; in fact, since it happens that the poor are many and the rich few (questionable in contemporary America), they are the rule of the poor and of the rich. The difference between the poor and the rich is highly visible to all, including the poor and the rich, and it is perhaps most impressive to ordinary men or "democrats" who judge life by the level of security and comfort. This difference is perhaps also the first observation of a traveller in a foreign land: "how do people live here?" means "how well do they live?", which means "how well-off are they?"

Yet Aristotle's classification of these regimes by the number who rule is significant of their similarity: both the poor and the rich (as such), and hence their regimes, are concerned above all with wealth; and a regime of the "have-nots" does not differ in *quality* from a regime of the "haves." We know that any share of wealth can be expressed as a quantity of money to make it comparable with other wealth; so when wealth is the end of politics, citizens are comparable and countable as quantity. Democracies constituted as rule of the poor—that is, most democracies of which we have experience—are in a sense indistinguishable from oligarchies. As the poor seek to become rich, they behave as the rich do: they expropriate the expropriators, and fall into faction and conflict. For wealth considered as pure quantity—as an end in itself rather than as a means to a certain quality of life—is an unstable principle. One never knows how much is enough either for comfort and security or for dignity of life. The security (not to mention comfort) of a mortal body seems to be an ideal (if we may call it that) impossible of realization, and quantified dignity measured in money is perfectly relative to the indignity of other men and therefore intensely competitive.

Indeed, what is the dignity of having more money as opposed to more of anything else? What can be the value of having more unless we know more *what*? This question applies against poor and rich alike, since we need to know what the rich do with their money and what the poor would do with theirs. It is not enough to answer for the poor that they would like to survive; their right to life implies a certain quality in human life. Mere quantity offers no basis for a human right to survive, for there are other species more numerous than ours with more mouths to feed and other species less numerous than ours which are more in danger of extinction. Both ants and eagles are more needy than the human poor. But even in our ecological concern, we are concerned for the survival of species, not for mere number but for the number of a certain species or kind or what. The certain quality of human life is not so easily defined as is that of other species. When we look at the human community we do not see the uniform qualities of ants and eagles; rather, we see first of all a difference between rich and poor which appears to lead nowhere—into a meaningless dispute over quantity, not toward a definition of quality. This indetermination of humanity—our inability to see easily what we are—obliges us to make claims as to what we are in some less visible respect to which all men do not obviously measure up. These are claims as to what we ought to be. Such claims are almost inevitably partisan because they begin from a quality each of us thinks he has and proceed to generalize or absolutize this quality as the human quality. Thus the establishment of human dignity involves us in the promotion of some humans over others, one individual over others, one party over others, one country over others. In our day atomic weapons have made human beings an endangered species, but in no way have they helped to define a human being. So the diverse claims by which men assert themselves to be human continue to cause political conflict in our day as in Aristotle's. It does not seem possible either to reduce political conflict without defining human dignity, or to define human dignity without risking political conflict. Contrary to B.F. Skinner, the problem of security and the problem of dignity arise together and cannot be solved separately.

Therefore, when Aristotle puts together a mixed regime of the rich and the poor, he seeks a standard by which to mix them, an understanding of the human good or virtue. The rich and the poor must be defined according to this standard in order that they be mixed, because as mere quantities of wealth or human bodies they can attempt to solve political disputes only by outcounting their opponents or preponderating over them. But since it is never clear what they are counting, the result of the count is always open to dispute and will be disputed. Because of their failure to appreciate quality, the rich and the poor cannot find out what they are in disputing each other, although it is true that when they face each other, certain qualities typical of the rich and poor are called forth. These qualities are tautness in the rich, as they find they are few and must defend themselves against the poor, and softness in the poor, as they seek to embrace everyone in order to deny privileges to the few. At this point one can speak of oligarchical and democratic qualities. More precisely, however, one must speak of the formal character of qualities, which are "oligarchic" insofar as they define themselves against others and "democratic" by the willingness of matter to receive them. We are reminded of the forms and the potentiality of matter in Aristotle's less political treatises, but we are also reminded of the liberals and democrats in liberal democracy: liberals exhibit outstanding qualities and democrats receive them with enthusiasm, tolerance, or disgust. Evidently the quality of the mixed regime is not established until the oligarchical and the democratic contributions are brought together, and we still do not know what they contribute to. Someone is needed to help the partisans move toward the quality that is the standard of their mix, someone who has knowledge of human virtue. The dialectic of party conflict does not move toward resolution on its own. Without a helping hand parties win and lose in defense or pursuit of wealth.

The difficulty is that the standard of human dignity and political sovereignty is not visible. Aristotle says that ". . . it is not so easy to see beauty of soul as beauty of body" (*Politics* 1254b 39). We may take this for a considerable understatement, but we cannot overlook the fact that he says beauty of soul can be seen. This is Aristotle's task in constructing the mixed regime: to find a standard which makes invisible virtue visible so that men can see beauty of soul. Invisible virtue is the intellectual virtue that most men, including most rulers, cannot recognize or appreciate. Such virtue cannot be the basis of political agreement in the situation, which of course continues today because it is the unchangeable human condition, where the vast majority of mankind is quite satisfied with its share of wisdom, each with his own. Against this majority intellectual virtue cannot even defend itself, much less instruct others. Or perhaps it could defend itself by instructing others. To do so, the man of intellectual virtue or the man who seeks it, the philosópher, would have to become a political scientist for his own sake as well as for the benefit of the community. He would have to make his virtue political and to make politics receptive to his virtue. He would aid the democratic and oligarchical parties to define themselves in accordance with a standard that improves and mixes their qualities while elevating them above the concern for mere wealth. The political scientist aids the parties, and neither neglects them nor rules them. He must not neglect them because they cannot fashion their own mixed regime unaided, and he does not rule them because he cannot.

If the mixed regime is made to a standard of human virtue, then it cannot merely mix democracy and oligarchy as they are found. This would be a mixed regime in which both poor and rich rule, sharing the offices but not ceasing to be or to consider themselves poor and rich. Although together, poor and rich would remain intact in a sort of democracy. Not the many but all would rule, as accords with the claim of democracy to be the rule of all, that is, both few and many. But this regime would surely degenerate into an unmixed partisan regime at the first opportunity for poor or rich to impose itself on the other, and it would not have any basis but common concern for wealth. Another mixed regime would mix poor and rich by splitting the difference between them, as when a small quantity of wealth above the lowest poverty defines a citizen. As the first mixed regime is a sort of democracy this is a sort of oligarchy with a property qualification, but low enough to include many democrats. It is based not on what is common to both extremes but on what is between them; it presupposes or calls for the existence of a middle class between the poor and the rich. This mixed regime is then an improvement on the first because it begins to overcome the most visible difference in a society: the middle class is visibly neither poor nor rich. Yet the middle class as such is not essentially superior to the poor and the rich; it would be like the poor if necessary and like the rich if possible. Lacking a quality of its own, it has difficulty in defending itself from the claims of the extremes, and when one extreme asserts itself the middle class regime, too, easily degenerates into a partisan regime.

A third mixed regime to transcend the poor and the rich is needed. To construct such a regime the political scientist must satisfy two contrary requirements in what will maintain the regime. For attracting the partisans to the regime, it is necessary that both democracy and oligarchy be visible to them so that they can find something to like; but for maintaining the regime, no part of it should desire any other regime. The problem is that attracting the partisans does not diminish but rather increases their desire for democracy or oligarchy unmixed. How can they be weaned away from the very taste by which they are attracted?

Aristotle's solution is in the ordering of the regime. The political scientist takes the democratic mode of lot and the oligarchical or aristocratic mode of choice and combines them in the various offices to make an order. The democratic and oligarchic modes are there to appeal to the partisans, but they have been formalized in accordance with the qualities of democracy and oligarchy so that they contribute to a whole. The democratic quality of "open to all" and the oligarchical quality of "reserved for the few" are preserved and in view, but arranged in a visible order reflecting the intention of the legislator. The visible order implies the existence of an invisible order in the soul of the legislator, since bodies in any order may be taken to imply soul. The American government, for example, is not a mere haphazard combination of diverse parts but a certain order of institutions from which we could infer an intention of the founders even if we did not have ample evidence that one (or more than one) exists. When Aristotle discusses the distribution of the three parts of regimes in Book 4 of the *Politics*, he separates them as activities of the soul or of the rational soul: deliberating, judging, and the ruling that connects them. Each part of the regime is then shown to have many possible orderings with different degrees of democracy and oligarchy so that the whole regime in its intricacy can vary to show the legislator's intention visibly and with easy discrimination. Democracy and oligarchy are mixed and transcended by transforming them into qualities of the soul, while the soul of the legislator is made visible in the order of democratic and oligarchical institutions. The partisans would be led from their initial allegiance to the modes by which they were attracted to an appreciation of the ordering of the whole, and thus to participation in the legislator's bipartisan intention.

The partisans may well resist this invitation. It is no part of Aristotle's political science to underestimate the resistance men offer to proposals made for their own good. On the contrary, it could be said that he develops the standard for the mixed regime from this very resistance. Men resist having their own good imposed on them out of a sense that no other can have the concern for preserving one's body as will equal the interest of its resident. One's body even resents instructions from one's own soul, as we know. This spirited resistance of the body against the tyranny of the soul, even or especially against beneficial tyranny, is itself an activity or part of the soul. It serves to defend the body but it also transcends mere preservation of the body when, for example, a man dies in his own self-defense. In politics, such spirit can be understood as the basis for the democratic claim of freedom. The many democrats are poor, but since poverty is a mere lack, they cannot advance a claim to rule because they are poor. Poverty is nothing to be proud of. The democrats claim rule because they represent the claim of the body against the soul yet made within the soul.

When the democrats advance the claim of freedom, they assert that all free bodies are equal and transform individual selfishness into good-natured democratic openness. But when freedom is exercised in choice, oligarchical exclusion comes into use; for after the choice what is chosen must be defended against what is rejected and indiscriminate democratic openness cannot be sustained. At the same time oligarchical choice can be directed to the legislation of better qualities than the defense of wealth (for wealth when defended can be considered a quality). The freedom of man is specified in qualities visible in the habits of a people living under a legislated regime, and just as the order of a regime implies the intention of a legislator, the visible habits of a people imply the existence of a certain moral virtue in their souls. Moral virtue can be inferred, and also produced, from the very resistance men offer to their own good, because that resistance presupposes a special dignity in the matter or quantity of human beings. Moral virtue is not exactly a virtue of the soul; it is the habit of using the body as if the body had soul. Therefore, it is most easily inferred, and beauty of the soul is most visible, in the noblest deeds. For making virtue visible, Aristotle relies on the splendor of moral virtue. Political peace and stability in the mixed regime are built on what can be seen in or inferred from the deeds of the noblest political men. They must be trained to appreciate the worth of politics, and the city has to be persuaded to accept them and to be inspired by them as was Sparta by its sacrifices for (or to) Brasidas (*Nicomachean Ethics*, 1134b 24). This mixed regime when fully developed is nothing less than aristocracy, and rare if not impossible. Every lesser mixed regime depends on its possibility and reflects some of its shine. Yet beyond the visible mixed regime is the invisible mixed regime. Democracy and oligarchy can be mixed only in the soul of the best man which is out of public view but concerned for the public good; compared to this soul, all visible arrangements are more or less mediocre and merely attempt where he succeeds. Invisible virtue is made visible in Aristotle's mixed regime, but the standard of the mix remains the best soul.

The modern mixed regime of liberal democracy is very different from this one, indeed conceived against this one. Its basis is democracy, not aristocracy, yet strangely it begins from democracy and proceeds to aristocracy, like Aristotle. The modern mix is based on the equality of man, for all are said to be equal in an original state of nature. No man is naturally the ruler of any other; and in society all live as they please with rights that secure their liberty. Having followed Aristotle's reasoning, we might wonder how it is possible to maintain the dignity of the human over the non-human if some men are not considered natural rulers over others. But this was precisely the intention of the founders or proto-founders of liberal democracy, John Locke and his friends. They desired passionately to defend the dignity of man which they saw endangered by the enslavement of men to priests and priestly education. To counter this menace, their defense of human dignity took the form of a denial of the superiority of soul, because it was soul and its invisible virtue which gave the priests their handle with which to manipulate men. They accepted the equality of man because it was a necessary consequence of the primacy of body, and they left human dignity at human liberty out of the same necessity.

Another consequence is that the democratic and oligarchical parties are transformed into democrats and liberals as described above. Since man's freedom must be kept from implying the superiority of soul, the democrats who were asserters of freedom according to Aristotle must be restrained from making the characteristic claim by which they transcend mere quantity. Their resistance is now understood as malleable matter, and the democrats become the unassertive, "apathetic" many. They are now the beneficiaries rather than the asserters of freedom; in exchange for their standard of dignity they are promised and given a rise in their standard of living. Democracy, now known as "pure democracy," yields to liberal democracy in which the party conflict is no longer between democrats and oligarchs but within the oligarchs or liberals. For the liberals, the ambitious men, are now the sole asserters of freedom. Freedom for them means just what it means to the people, which is living as you please; but since it pleases them to excel in some way, the consequence of liberty for all is unequal honors and wealth for the few. The principle of equality results in equal liberty, justifying inequality for the few who are able to take better advantage of equal liberty. Yet although these profiteers of equal opportunity have a good thing for themselves, their self-assertion is for the benefit of the democrats rather than against them. They use soul or reason in defense of body, not to flaunt their superior qualities; so in effect they assert not only their own dignity but human dignity in general. And because they are allowed to use soul in defense of body, they are not expected to use body as if it were soul, in the way of moral virtue. Their qualities are impressed on the inert class, the "opinion followers," in some degree, but the difference in ambition remains. The democrats approve or tolerate ambition; the liberals have it. This difference is not overcome in the mix of honors and benefits characteristic of liberal democracy.

There are two principal rights in a liberal democracy and two kinds of liberals to exploit them. The first is the right of acquiring private property. It is justified for the common good, but—or and—the few best acquisitors profit most. The opportunities of free enterprise awaken the desires of talented men, but also engage their competitiveness. Their ambition for political honors is turned at least partly to what is called "success" in economic matters. To be "successful" is to compete not only to make money, but for the sake of competing—to win, to overcome "a challenge." Those in our day who drop out of competitive acquisition do not call it a hog trough but call it a "rat race," and this despite the fact according to them that the Establishment is run by pigs. In Locke's more stately language, the "quarrelsome and contentious" are diverted from politics to the making of money, where yet much of their political ambition can be satisfied. This is good for them and others; for the result as we have seen is to "increase the common stock of mankind."

Liberalism recognizes the need of some men to aspire to more than they need, and channels this need for excess into the common benefit. Let the contentious engage in the bloodless killing of commerce. Their success may at worst bankrupt their rivals, and it helps the people, the democrats. The rich are allowed to remain rich, rather encouraged to become ever richer, if they turn to a private life in a privatized society. Their ostentation is more or less confined to certain "exclusive" neighborhoods and country clubs; it is not directly political and not obvious in the halls of power. The rich do not rule as rich, although they surely exert influence. The poor in the meantime live a more comfortable life, and do not have to feel envious of a class that visibly rules because it is rich.

The other right is the right of free speech, which we also find in Locke's political philosophy. This right is justified as for the common good in the doctrine that the government has no business caring for souls. We are thus informed that the common good is to be found in caring for the body, but it is also implied that the common good so defined needs to be continually defended against attempts to define it as something more. Such attempts, as we have seen in Aristotle's political science, arise naturally from the partisan assertions and counter-assertions of the democrats and oligarchs to be found in every regime. Accordingly, the right of free speech at the beginning was asserted from a polemical stance against religion and soul-caring. Although it took the form of a universal openness to speech whatever its content or source, free speech was brought forth with intent to oppose and exclude the speech characteristic of priests and their scholarly clerks. In both respects, the right of free speech was a typical partisan assertion. Its early asserters in the seventeenth century opposed, but could not drive out offensive soul-speech because of the endemic human susceptibility to it, and so even today, when fire-breathing votaries of religion are sometimes indistinguishable from flaming liberals, there is need of a group that will defend the doctrine supporting free speech.

It is evident that the doctrine that the government has no business caring for souls protects both the democratic principle of living as you please and the liberal-democratic right of acquiring private property. Living as you please is surer with the body that is surely yours, even if temporarily (and as to mortality, perhaps science will find a cure for it), than with a soul that may be someone else's or no one's or yours on condition of good behavior. And the right of acquiring private property must be protected against limitations whose source is concern for the soul of a greedy man, though not against limitations whose purpose and effect are to "increase the common stock of mankind" and to ensure that the bodies of the poor are fed, preserved, and made fit and comfortable. Liberalism is necessarily laisser-faire with regard to the soul but not with regard to the body, and old-fashioned laisser-faire liberals opposed the "social legislation" of interventionist liberals on behalf of the bodies of the poor mainly because it feared the effect on their souls: with coddled bodies the poor would forget to live as they please and begin asking the government to care for their souls. This fear has been countered with the thought that unless their bodies are made comfortable, the poor will ask the government to care for their souls.

Yet when all this has been said to prove that the right of free speech is for the common good, one must still ask the question we are accustomed to ask about the right of free enterprise: who profits most? The answer, obviously, is those who speak the best. Just as under free enterprise the best money-makers profit the most, so under free speech the best speakers earn the highest reputation if not the most money— though frequently they get both. These speakers run the gamut from poets, philosophers, and scientists to the big thinkers and polished *artistes* at the bottom of the media; in sum, we know them as intellectuals. Intellectuals have much more freedom in liberal democracy than in the ancient democracies, and as is the case with the businessmen, we may suppose that this is allowed with respect for the ambition and pugnacity which they might otherwise waste in hostility for the vulgar and anti-democratic scheming. There is something of honorable ambition in the name "intellectual" as compared to "philosopher"—lover of wisdom—which is not altogether effaced in the Marxian formula "worker of the brain." Patrick Henry's ringing cry "Give me liberty or give me death!" has been restated with routine bravado in the slogan "publish or perish" but without softening the firm impression that the intellectual of our day is still full of fight and eager for the highest prizes of scholarly controversy.

This, then, is another group with a stake in the privatized life of liberal society whose privileges are justified as for the common benefit, or at least as having "redeeming social value." Again, although this group exerts influence, its ostentation is not directly political. In America today it thrives in the universities and in the media, two institutions which may be said to converge in the domain of public television. It is not oppressive mastery to be confronted with the opportunity of watching public television.

These two groups, businessmen and intellectuals, are the "liberals" of liberal democracy. They make use of another group of liberals, the politicians. For liberal democracy does not mix without the work of skilled politicians who must build alliances and persuade both other liberals and democrats to see and to act in accordance with their interests. The unpolitical or less political liberals make use of politicians to ally with the people, that is, with the democrats or with different groups of democrats. At present businessmen are concentrated in the Republican party, while intellectuals flock to the Democratic party. In obedience to the fundamental democracy of the modern mixed regime, these two groups of unequals seek to advance their claims under the banner of equality. Each of them is very complacent about its own inequality, but constantly accusing the other of being anti-democratic.

Businessmen live with easy conscience in fine houses, drive expensive cars and hold important offices of management while complaining of high-sounding ignorance from pretending upstarts ("effete, intellectual snobs") who have never met a payroll and/or do not know what it is to work. Intellectuals, for their part, take for granted their ability to publish their undying thoughts in indelible ink, to be quoted in the media and to receive the adulation of the young; but they despise know-nothing businessmen who have never taught a class and/or do not know what it is to study. They say that America suffers terribly from *economic* inequality and some of them are socialists; but they propose to nationalize only the means of producing economic articles, never the means of artistic or intellectual expression, and they have an ultimate, existential concern for the well-being of the copyright law. Thus, both kinds of liberals are induced by their political alliances, which are determined by the fundamental mixing principle of liberal democracy, to deny that they are in any way remarkable. To show or perhaps to feel their loyalty in the alliance, they blame others for elitism but do not admit it of themselves.

Early liberal philosophers and statesmen such as Locke and the authors of *The Federalist* carefully worked out the new mixed regime. They specified the rights and duties of liberals in regard to democrats while making it clear that the unequal qualities of men are in the service of the more fundamental equality of man. They have made the benefits of this regime visible to the democrats, who remain generally loyal to it; but it may be doubted whether they succeeded in making the benefits visible to the liberals. Now we have theories of pluralist liberalism which almost suppose that liberal society is an automatic system of interest groups that nearly does away with the political problem of mixing liberals and democrats. In these theories it is as if the liberals were just collectivities of democrats having therefore no duties to the democrats. Liberals do not govern society because society does not need to be governed; there is no *noblesse,* so no requirement that *noblesse oblige.*

Such theories have been criticized in recent years by the radicals. The radicals ask why it is that in liberal democracy, liberals happen to come out on top? It must be that they govern from behind the scenes in an Establishment, a network of indirect and informal government which cleverly ensures their dominance. The Establishment must be exposed and "all power to the people." But the "people" in the radicals' slogan contains their own ambitious selves eager for honor and power. The radicals are "liberals" too, and they fall to their own critique of liberalism. If they are now in eclipse, it is partly because no Establishment in liberal society has appeared with such boring frequency as that of the radical movement.

The problem in liberal democracy is in the liberals, not the democrats. The liberals have forgotten they are liberals, and now believe they are democrats. It is not that they are virtuous men wishing to maintain a prudent obscurity before the unremarkable many; the liberals have been more democratic in their demands than the democrats, and thus have become invisible to themselves. Out of embarrassment the younger and even some of the older liberals dress and behave in such a way that no one could accuse them, on superficial acquaintance, of being gentlemen. They do not see how they profit more from equal rights, and so they take their own inequality for granted. They do not see that they as liberals must contribute to the whole, but instead they use their unequal status to destroy tolerance for unequal status. They speak as if the whole were not a mix but merely democratic, and as if it could be created by the verbal exertions of partisan extremism. Tocqueville expressed his fear that American democracy would suffer from "individualism," by which he meant the danger that former aristocrats in a democracy would sulk and live privately in apathy. Today the two wings of our liberal aristocrats reveal an active hostility to each other and at the least an inadequate comprehension of liberal democracy as a mixed regime. It may be that they lost sight of themselves at the time when the intellectuals came under the influence of romanticism and Marxism and, to put it mildly, lost their sense of community with businessmen, then dubbed the bourgeoisie. Whatever the cause, the groups that Locke joined were put asunder. Now they have taken refuge with the many, and have justified their own privileges by attacking others'.

In liberal democracy, the mixing principle does not make virtue visible. Liberal democracy therefore has a dual advantage over the ancient mixed regime of a more democratic appearance and a more oligarchical reality. The result should please both parties, but the trouble is that liberal oligarchs have been taken in by the appearance more than the democrats. They are allowing or urging liberal democracy to be transformed into an extreme democracy to which men who wish to excel cannot contribute and in which they cannot live without increasing frustration, self-delusion and hypocrisy. I do not propose a return to Aristotle's moral splendor, or to the exemplary arrogance of the British aristocracy, but to the wisdom of that liberal democrat Thomas Jefferson, who frankly spoke of democracy's need for natural aristocrats—though to be sure in a private letter. The success of the mixed regime of liberal democracy depends on a recognition that it *is* a mixed regime, and that although liberals can *contribute* to democracy, they cannot *become* democrats and should not try.

2
Economic Equality

Irving Kristol

OF POPULISM AND TAXES

What is populism and why is everyone suddenly saying such nice things about it? The answer to that last question, at least, is easy enough: When a populist spirit is abroad in the land, most Americans are always eager to say nice things about it. After all, populism as a political movement is indisputably based on popular passions and popular resentments, and very few commentators today are willing to adopt a critical posture toward it, lest they stand accused of the awful ideological error of "elitism." During the 1950s, the late Richard Hofstadter (among others) could explore the connections in American history between political populism and political paranoia—the belief that the world is being misdirected by some kind of mischievous conspiracy against the "common man." The perception of such a connection permits one to understand some of the more interesting aspects of American populist movements: their tendency toward xenophobia and racism for one thing, their extraordinary ineptitude at significant institutional reform for another. But, in recent years, Hofstadter's work has been nibbled at by a flock of younger historians who are maddened by his very detachment from populist clichés. In America, intellectuals are now more consistently populist than the populace itself. Political populism is a natural temptation for a democratic people, but the populist idea seems to have become something like a secular religion for the democratic intellectual, who is convinced that "the people" represent a holy congregation and, therefore, that their indignation is the wrath of God. Indeed, when the American people sensibly resist the populist temptation—when they exhibit a preference for a politics of calm deliberation over a politics of passionate resentment—they are likely to be rebuked by their intellectuals for their disgusting "apathy."

What is populism? Oddly enough, I believe the classical Marxist definition is the most accurate: Populism in America is the radicalism of the petit-bourgeois sensibility—the radicalism of the traditional-minded and nostalgia-ridden "common man," a radicalism of the sullen, the bewildered, the resentful, the anxious, the frustrated. It is, Marxism goes on to say, a "false" class consciousness in that it is myth-ridden and essentially "escapist"; it is therefore a very dangerous form of radicalism because, in the end, it is more likely to be captured by unscrupulous right-wing demagogues than by proper socialist theoreticians. This interpretation of populism is doubtless schematic and even melodramatic, as Marxist interpretations tend to be. But I think it to be more valid than not, and I would remark that the ease with which so many of yesterday's quasi-Marxist radicals have transformed themselves into today's self-styled "populists" is a sad commentary on the condition of American political thinking in the 1970s.

Still, when all this has been said, considerably less than everything has been said. Populism may be a natural temptation in a democracy, but large numbers of citizens are not likely to succumb to this temptation unless circumstances move them to do so. Vox populi is not vox Dei, but when people feel the times are out of joint, then they are in fact out of joint—there is no higher court to appeal to. The rise of a populist temper is a sure sign that something has gone wrong, and that reforms are very much in order. A populist upsurge always points to very real problems that ought to be on our political agenda. But populism itself usually misperceives these problems, and the solutions it proposes are, more often than not, illusory.

WHAT KIND OF TAX REBELLION?

It seems generally agreed that a major cause of the present populist discontent is taxation. But, typically, the populist temper seizes hold of this matter and twists it into a familiar paranoid shape; the tax issue, it proclaims, arises out of the manipulation of our tax laws by "vested interests" so that the rich are getting away scot-free while the common man bears the whole tax burden. The answer, obviously, is to soak the rich.

Now there is, as it happens, something to be said for soaking the rich. But that is not really the problem, nor is it really any kind of a solution. The average American, no matter what he may sometimes say or what is said in his name, is not rebelling against tax inequities. *He is rebelling against taxes, period.* He is rebelling against increased property and sales taxes. He is rebelling against the hidden tax that inflation represents. He is rebelling against all those itemized deductions from his paycheck—against the fact that his "take-home pay" diverges more and more from his formal salary, so that his hard-won wage increases seem to exist only on paper and never find their way into his pocket.

Since most social critics are members of the upper-middle class, for whom the income tax looms so large, it is easy to exaggerate the importance of the income tax for the American working man. True, as his wages increase he moves "progressively" up into higher tax brackets. But the actual impact of this process is minimal, since we are talking about relatively small spurts in income. The average American worker is *not* paying a greater proportion of his salary to Internal Revenue than he was ten years ago; as a result of the Kennedy and Nixon tax reforms, he is more likely to be paying less. He is, however, witnessing a greater proportion of his salary being preempted by inflation—itself the consequence of increased government spending on such things as welfare, education, medicare, medicaid, etc. He also sees more of his salary being funneled off into social security, supplementary private pensions, early retirement schemes, medical insurance, etc. Between 1965 and 1971, his weekly earnings rose by 12 percent, but what we call his "real spendable earnings" did not increase at all. The American worker finds this frustrating. He resents this whole process, which bureaucratically insists on improving his longer-term prospects at the expense of his shorter-term ones—on improving his general welfare at the expense of his specific well-being. In short, he resents the present structure of the welfare state, and his "tax rebellion" is an expression of this resentment. This intense dissatisfaction of the working class and lower-middle class over the issue of "taxes" is not a uniquely American phenomenon. The same resentment is clearly visible in Britain, France, Germany, and Sweden—nations where the question of tax inequities is barely raised at all.

What is occurring is very interesting and very troubling: The middle-class psychology which has created the welfare state is on a collision course with a working-class psychology which, while not rejecting any of the benefits of the welfare state, nevertheless feels victimized by it. This may be short-sighted on the part of the working-class—but, then, it is in the nature of working-class people to be more short-sighted (to have a shorter "time horizon") than middle-class people; since their lives offer fewer gratifications, working-class people tend to want them more immediately. And there may well be more than short-sightedness involved. After all, it is the middle class that manages our welfare state, whereas our working class is managed by it—and it is a lot more fun to manage than be managed. Many workers who are angry at those deductions from their paycheck would take pride in making those deductions on a voluntary basis. They could then find personal satisfaction in providing for their own and their children's future. It is pleasing to fulfill such responsibilities in a "manly" way; it is apparently much less pleasing to have a bureaucratic process do this *to* you and *for* you.

How to get out of this impasse is not a subject we have given much thought to. Indeed, we have for the most part failed to realize just what kind of impasse we are in. Instead we tend to permit ourselves to be caught up in the populist current, and to believe that a populist reform—a more "progressive" tax system—will provide the answer to populist discontent. Just how illusory such a notion is may be inferred from the following report in the *New York Times* for May 19, 1972:

For many New Jersey political leaders it didn't seem to make any sense. Here was a Republican Governor urging a Legislature controlled by Republicans to approve the most progressive, urban-oriented, socially conscious tax-reform program ever proposed in the state's history. Appearing before a joint legislative session in the crowded Assembly chamber this afternoon, Gov. William T. Cahill recommended a $2-billion tax program that included a graduated state income tax and a state-wide property tax of $1 on every $100 of true value.

He promised that the new taxes would cut local property taxes in New Jersey by an average of 40 per cent and enable the state to assume the entire financial responsibility of operating the public schools....

Stripped to its essentials, it is a controversial program that would bear down hardest on the wealthy, predominantly Republican communities in the suburbs and offers sizable tax relief and new urban aid to the predominantly Democratic poor people in the cities and the working-class communities immediately surrounding them....

It would follow, then, that the Governor should be able to count heavily on the cities and the Democrats in his effort to reform what he calls "an unjust, regressive tax system which places the greatest burden on those least able to pay."

In reality, some of the most strident opposition to any reforms will come from blue-collar neighborhoods who stand to benefit the most from them.

For example, a number of legislators from the cities, such as Anthony Imperiale of Newark, contend—probably rightly—that virtually all their constituents are opposed to any kind of new taxes, regardless of any accompanying reduction in local taxes.

"I can't put my finger on it," Mr. Imperiale said today, but it was apparent that the same sense of political, economic and social alienation that is encouraging thousands of working-class Democrats in New Jersey to support Gov. George Wallace of Alabama would also be a major factor in determining their opposition to any reforms.

One can fairly predict that many middle-class reformers will find, to their surprise, that the populace is going to be quick to bite the hand that aims to feed it. The populace doesn't want to be fed; it wants more freedom to graze on its own.

TAXING THE RICH

I am not suggesting that there are no inequities in our tax system. On the contrary, there are many and their elimination or reformation is highly desirable. But one has to have a clear idea of what this will accomplish. It will *not* have any significant effect on the distribution of income in the United States, and it will *not* have any significant effect on the tax burden of the average American. It will *not* of itself finance the prospective growth of existing social programs (e.g., national health insurance, day-care centers, etc.). Its purpose will be primarily symbolic: to reassure the American people that the tax system is "fair." Such reassurance is clearly needed today, and therefore the importance of such symbolic reforms cannot be overestimated.

One such reform, in my opinion, would affect the present way in which corporate executives can acquire and exercise stock options. The problem here is that corporate executives still think of themselves as businessmen—i.e., entrepreneurs—who ought to get rich if they are successful. This is a dangerous misconception. Executives ought to get tempting salaries, and these salaries ought not to be taxed with exceptional severity[1]—but no corporate executive ought to feel entitled to get rich on the job. He is not a risk-taking entrepreneur, since his risks are no greater than that of any other employee of the corporation, and he is entitled to the kinds of benefits other employees get—nothing more. I would say he is not even entitled to a special bonus system—unless, in those years when the corporation does badly, he is willing to accept an equivalent negative bonus (i.e., pay cut).

Another useful reform would be to abolish the tax advantage which the purchase of tax-free municipal and state bonds now offers to those in the higher tax brackets. This advantage is not nearly so scandalous as various newspaper reports would have one believe. It is perfectly true that a wealthy citizen can avoid all taxes by putting his capital into tax-exempts. But it is also true that, since the yield on tax-exempts is only about two-thirds of the yield on taxable bonds, he is in effect paying a 33 percent tax for the privilege of not having to bother filing a return. This is a lot more than zero; on the other hand, it is substantially less than he would otherwise pay, if this option were not open to him. Various plans have been developed[2] for abolishing tax-exempt bonds while not damaging the ability of localities to borrow money. It is time that some such plan were put into effect.

There are still other possible reforms one could mention, but there is no need to list them here. The point I wish to emphasize—and it is not really controversial in itself—is the mainly symbolic character of such reforms. They will not raise much in the way of new revenue; they will not affect the ordinary person's tax burden; they will leave no trace on the distribution of income. They are desirable on grounds of equity and their impact will be almost totally psychological. Obviously, these are not the kinds of results that those who take populist rhetoric seriously have been led to expect. Such results, if they are to be obtained, will involve far more drastic reforms—and, for better or worse, each of these reforms would have serious costs, economic and political.

It would be easy, for instance, to raise quite a few billions by increasing the corporate income tax and decreasing the depreciation[3] allowances offered to corporations who invest in new capital equipment. But the effect of this would be to slow economic growth in the private sector, to decrease the number of jobs created therein, and ultimately to diminish the tax revenues generated by it. One can fairly predict that, after a few months of such a "sluggish economy," the political pressure for restoring depreciation allowances and cutting corporate taxes would be irresistible.

The abolition of the capital gains tax, and the taxation of all income at normal rates, would raise perhaps an extra $8 billion—*on paper.* In actuality, it would probably raise only a tiny fraction of that, since people with substantial capital gains would simply refuse to sell their stocks or properties, preferring to borrow against them if they should need cash. Why, they will ask, is it "fair" to treat capital gains as income when capital losses cannot be written off against income? This would seem to be one of those cases when a tax sets itself into direct opposition to elementary self-interest and to the taxpayer's own sense of justice— and when this happens, it is the tax which usually loses out. The same thing would doubtless be true for a cumulative lifetime inheritance tax, which, putting a tax bill of $200,000 on an estate of $500,000 and going up from there (e.g., a tax of over $500,000 on a million dollar estate), would yield $4 billion—on paper. In real life, the incentive for avoidance of such a tax, seen as "confiscatory," would be so great that the only ones to benefit would be the tax lawyers who would figure out ways to soften that tax-bite. Anyone who is skeptical of his ability to succeed in this should himself immediately consult a tax lawyer: He will discover that he has needed one all along.

There are some reforms that would unquestionably bring in the money—only no one is ever going to enact them. If you abolish tax benefits for those over 65, you would pick up some $9 billion a year. And if you abolished the tax-deductibility of interest payments on home mortgages, you would pick up over $20 billion a year. But who is going to pass such legislation? It is all very well to argue, as some academics do, that if we got rid of all of these tax preferences for various groups in the population, we could have, not only a simpler tax system, but a much lower general tax level for everyone. Were we in a position to design our tax system afresh, that would be an eminently sensible procedure. But we are in no such position, and it is quite futile to try to persuade large numbers of people to surrender substantial and tangible tax benefits in favor of a prospective tax reform that *might* leave them slightly better off. That is just not going to happen.

THE RICH—TOO FEW, AND TOO MANY

The trouble with the idea of lightening the average man's tax burden through soaking the rich is that there are both too few and too many rich—depending on how you define that category. The top one percent of our income distribution—families with over $50,000 a year income—number only 700,000, and they already pay out 46 percent of their income in taxes. The top 5 percent consists of 3.5 million families with income of $30,000 or over; these pay out about 33 percent of their income in taxes. There is unquestionably more tax revenue to be got here—but not easily: These people don't think of themselves as being "rich," the rest of the population doesn't think of them in this way, either, and the millions of people in this bracket will therefore fight hard and effectively against any kind of discriminatory increase in their taxes. The same is even truer for those 14 million families in the top 20 percent, who make over $18,000 in income. As for the tens of millions of people in the $10,000–$18,000 bracket—well, these are the very people who are already populist rebels against our prevailing tax rates! The idea of taxing them more harshly for the benefit of those with below-median incomes is not to be taken seriously.*

It is precisely because of the fact that income distribution in a modern industrial society takes the shape of a diamond, rather than a pyramid, that income *re*-distribution turns out to be so hellishly difficult. It can hardly be an accident that countries with such different economic and social policies as the United States, Britain, France, Germany, and

Sweden should have an almost identical pre-tax distribution of income, and still roughly comparable post-tax distribution. In all of these countries there are both too few "rich," and too many, for taxes to be a powerful instrument of economic equality.

Such a recognition of the limits of tax policy will depress those who believe that the distribution of income is a major problem for American society today. But is it, really? My own guess is that, left-wing intellectuals and academics apart, no one is terribly exercised by this issue. It is in the nature of democratic politics that practically any discontent expresses itself in terms of a demand for greater "equality," when what is actually being demanded is fairness or efficiency—or even special privilege! I have suggested that much of our working-class discontent is over the structure of the welfare state: I would add that this discontent is exacerbated by the ways in which the welfare state is spending its tax revenues—for ever-growing welfare rolls, for an educational system that seems to be falling apart, for a police force that cannot cope with increased criminality, for low-income housing that converts itself into instant slums, for medicaid to the poor which inflates medical costs for the non-poor, etc. It would not be an exaggeration to say that much of the present discontent with taxation is provoked by the fact that the welfare state, which these taxes support, is *too* committed to equality—to expenditures that benefit primarily the minority who are poor.

The populist demand for "equality," back in the 1890s, was in reality a protest against the emerging new shape of American society, in which the large corporation was to be a central institution. What the Populists basically wanted, and what in the end they got, was for government to take effective action to curb the economic power and political influence of the corporations. That end achieved, the populist spirit gradually melted away. Today, populist dissent, as I see it, is once again concerned with the emerging new shape of American society. It is a society in which bureaucracies—governmental, judicial, professional, educational, corporate—make the crucial decisions which affect the common man's life (e.g., busing his children away from their neighborhood school, appropriating part of his salary to support people he thinks unworthy of support, etc.). Most of these decisions involve specific costs to him, while promising only future benefits, some of which are vaguely "social." It is no wonder that his anxiety becomes touched with paranoia, and that he should smell foul conspiracy.

There is no conspiracy—but there is a problem. It is not a problem of income distribution or of inequities of taxation. The problem is the bureaucratization of American society—and the fact that this bureaucratization has failed to accomplish the only thing no bureaucracy dare fail at: the efficient delivery on its promises. Populist dissent today is directed *against* liberal politics—even when it votes for an "anti-establishment" liberal politician. Liberals may find this incredible: How can the people possibly be against liberal politics, when liberal politics so sincerely has the larger interests of the people at heart? So long as this question can be asked so ingenuously, we shall not have got very far in coping with the upsurge of populist dissent in the 1970s.

Bertrand de Jouvenel

THE SOCIALIST IDEAL

I propose to discuss a predominant preoccupation of our day: the redistribution of incomes.

The process of redistribution. In the course of a lifetime, current ideas as to what may be done in a society by political decision have altered radically. It is now generally regarded as within the proper province of the State, and indeed as one of its major functions, to shift wealth from its richer to its poorer members. "An exceedingly complex machinery has grown up piecemeal"[1] to provide money benefits, free services, goods and services below cost. . . . Its purpose is to redistribute incomes and especially, it is generally assumed, the incomes of the richer, which are drained by progressive taxation, and at the same time affected by rent control, limitation of dividends, and requisition of assets.

Our subject: the ethical aspect. A spirited controversy is now raging on what is termed "the disincentive effect of excessive redistribution." It is known from experience that in most cases, though by no means in all, men are spurred by material rewards proportional or even more than proportional to their effort, as for example in "time and a half." Making each increase of effort less rewarding than those which preceded it, whilst at the same time lowering, by the provision of benefits, the basic effort necessary to sustain existence, can be held to affect the pace of production and economic progress. Thus the policy of redistribution is subject to heavy fire. The attack, however, is made on grounds of expediency. Current criticism of redistribution is not based on its being undesirable but on its being, beyond a certain point, imprudent. Nor do

88

champions of redistribution deny that there are limits to what can be achieved, if it is proposed, as they wish, to maintain economic progress. This whole conflict of which so much is made today is a borderline quarrel, involving no fundamentals.

I propose to skirt this field of combat and shall assume here that redistribution, however far it may be carried, exerts no disincentive influence, and leaves the volume and growth of production entirely unaffected. This assumption is made in order to center attention upon other aspects of redistribution. To some the assumption may seem to do away with the need for discussion. If it were not going to affect production, they will say, redistribution would have to proceed to its extreme of total equality of incomes. This would be good and desirable. But would it? Why would it? And how far would it? This is my starting-point.

Dealing with redistribution purely on ethical grounds, our first concern must be to distinguish sharply between the social ideal of income equalization and others with which it is sentimentally, but not logically, associated. It is a common but ill-founded belief that ideals of social reform are somehow lineal descendants of one another. It is not so: redistributionism is not descended from socialism; nor can any but a purely verbal link be discovered between it and agrarian egalitarianism. It will greatly clarify the problem if we stress the contrasts between these ideals.

Land redistribution not equivalent to redistribution of income. What was demanded in the name of social justice over thousands of years was land redistribution. . . . There is a clear contrast between redistribution of land and redistribution of incomes. Agrarianism does not advocate the equalization of the produce, but of natural resources out of which the several units will autonomously provide themselves with the produce. This is justice, in the sense that inequality of rewards between units equally provided with natural resources will reflect inequality of toil. In other words, the role played by inequality of "capital" in bringing about unequal rewards is nullified. What is equalized is the supply of "capital."

Now the idea of eliminating the influence of capital from functions determining income is not an archaic one: it runs right through social thought at all times. When Marx said that value was made up of labor only, he was in fact resorting by wishful thinking to a state of affairs which seem inherently right. That the idea of rewards in proportion to the contribution made was a basic one with the classical economists is plain enough: they were concerned to show that this would be the outcome of a perfectly competitive system, and to them the initial distribution of property was always a disturbing factor.

Agrarian reformers are often claimed by the socialists as their forerunners. They are not; but the two groups do have one preoccupation in common: both want to eliminate the effect of an unequal distribution of property.

Socialism as the City of Brotherly Love. Agrarianism can be summed up under the heading of *fair rewards.* Socialism aims even higher than the establishment of "mere" justice. It seeks to establish a new order of brotherly love. The basic socialist feeling is not that things are out of proportion and thus unjust, that reward is not proportional to effort, but an emotional revolt against the antagonisms within society, against the ugliness of men's behavior to each other.

It is of course logically possible to minimize antagonism by minimizing the occasions on which men's paths cross. Thus, the agrarian solution lies in the economic sovereignty of each owner on his well delimited field, which is equal in size to that of his neighbor. But this is not possible in modern societies, where interests are intertwined as in a Gordian knot. To cut the knot means reversion to a ruder state. But there is another solution: it is a new spirit of joyful acceptance of this interdependence; it is that men, called to serve one another ever increasingly by economic progress and division of labor, should do so "in newness of spirit,"[2] not as the "old" man did who grudgingly measured his service against his reward, but as a "new" man who finds his delight in the welfare of his brethren.

The pattern is easily recognizable: it is the Pauline pattern of law and grace, as transformed by Rousseau. For Rousseau, social progress increases strife: it arouses man's desires and, as he comes to stand in too close propinquity to his fellows, his self-love is turned into wickedness because he finds that they do not serve him enough or that they hinder him too much. Rousseau's answer to this, an answer which he believed to be valid only if introduced as a preventive and never as a cure,[3] was the displacement of man's center of affections, love of the whole being substituted for self-love. This is the fundamental pattern of socialist thought. It is from Rousseau again that socialism derives its belief that social antagonism arises from "objective situations," the removal of which should remove strife. And socialism has singled out private property as the basic "situation" creating antagonisms: it creates firstly the essential antagonism between those with property and those without, and secondly the struggle among the propertied.

How to do away with antagonism: socialist goal, and socialist means.
The socialist solution then is the destruction of private property as such.
This is to erase the contrast between men's positions and thereby do
away with tension. The proletariat, made conscious of its solidarity in
its struggle to do away with property, will, when victorious, absorb into
itself the now proletarianized remainder. Social antagonisms would
thereby be extinguished and the force of repression formerly called for
by the existence of antagonisms in order to preserve civil peace in an
atmosphere of war, that is, the power of the State, will become
unnecessary. This power must then of itself wither away.

This promise that the State will wither away is fundamental to
socialist doctrine, because the disappearance of antagonisms is the
fundamental aim of socialism; but it has somewhat suffered from being
bandied about in political controversy. Some shrewd critics of socialism
have very properly taken the withering away of the State as the criterion
of socialist success, thereby causing annoyance to their opponents. In
the dust of combat the fact that the State is expected to wither away as
an instrument of repression and of police power has been somewhat lost
sight of, and in fairness it does not seem that enlarged functions of the
State, by themselves, prove a failure of socialism but only the
preservation and *a fortiori* the enlargement of police powers. It is,
however, only too evident that police powers are at their greatest where
the destruction of private property has been most completely achieved:
a plain fact which refutes socialist belief.

It is clear for all to see that the destruction of private property has not
done away with antagonisms or given rise to a spirit of solidarity
permitting men to dispense with police powers; and it is further
apparent that what spirit of solidarity there is seems to have as its
necessary ingredient the distrust and hatred of another society, or of
another section of society. The warlike intentions of foreign powers
seem to be a basic postulate of the collectivist State, and may even be
attributed by one collectivist State to another, or, if the process of
socialization has not been completed, to the aggressive disposition of
the capitalist classes, backed by foreign capitalists. Thus the solidarity
obtained is not, as intended, a solidarity of love, but, at least in part, a
solidarity in strife. Clearly, this is not consonant with the basic intention
of socialism: "the fruit of righteousness is sown in peace of them that
make peace."[4]

Yet the socialist ideal is not to be summarily dismissed. We do aspire
to something more than a society of good neighbors who do not
displace landmarks, who return stray sheep to their owner, and refrain
from coveting their neighbor's ass. And indeed a community based not

upon economic independence but upon a fraternal partaking of the common produce, and inspired by the deep-seated feeling that its members are of one family, should not be called utopian.

The inner contradiction of socialism. Such a community works. It has worked for centuries and we can see it at work under our very eyes, in every monastic community. But it is to be noticed that these are cities of brotherly love *because* they were originally cities built up by love of the Father. It is further to be noticed that material goods are shared without question *because* they are spurned. The members of the community are not anxious to increase their individual well-being at the expense of one another, but then they are not very anxious to increase it *at all*. Their appetites are not addressed to scarce material commodities, and thus competitive; they are addressed to God, who is infinite. In short, they are members of one another not because they form a social body but because they are part of a mystical body.

Socialism seeks to restore this unity without the faith which causes it. It seeks to restore sharing as amongst brothers without contempt for worldly goods, without recognition of their worthlessness. It does not accept the view that consumption is a trivial thing, to be kept down to the minimum. On the contrary it adheres to the fundamental belief of modern society that there must be ever more worldly goods to be enjoyed, the spoils of a conquest of nature which is held to be man's noblest venture. The socialist ideal is grafted on to the progressive society and adheres to this society's veneration of commodities, its encouragement of fleshly appetites and pride in technical imperialism.

The moral seduction of socialism lies in the fact that it repudiates the methodical exploitation of the personal interest motive, of the fleshly appetites, of egoism, which held pride of place in the economic society it has undertaken to supersede; yet that, in so far as it has endorsed this society's pursuit of ever-increasing consumption, it has become a heterogeneous system, torn by an inner contradiction.

If "more goods" are the goal to which society's efforts are to be addressed, why would "more goods" be a disreputable objective for the individual? Socialism suffers from ambiguity in its judgment of values: if the good of society lies in greater riches, why not the good of the individual? If society should press towards that good, why not the individual? If this appetite for riches is wrong in the individual, why not in society? Here, then, is at least a prima facie incoherence, indeed a blatant heterogeneity.

Further, so long as the general purpose of society is the conquest of nature and the enjoyment of its spoils, is it not logical that this purpose should determine the characteristics of that society? Is not society shaped by its predominant desire, by the end towards which it tends? Is it not possible that many unpleasant traits of society are functionally related to its basic purpose? And is not their unpleasantness inherent in the purpose, so that any different society one seeks to build up with the same purpose must display the same characteristics, possibly under a different guise?

The productivist society may be likened to the military society. That which is meant for war must in its structure show characteristics appropriate to war. An army, or a military society, embodies many traits which are indefensible, by the standards of a "good society." But military hierarchy and discipline cannot be done away with as long as victory remains the purpose—though of course they can be amended. In the same manner, there may be a relation between the structure of productivist society and its purpose. And there is much to be said for the view that socialism's higher aspirations were doomed when it accepted the general purpose of modern society—as Rousseau indeed foresaw.

The socialist belief, that is to say the noble ethical aim of a society rid of its antagonisms and transformed into a city of brotherly love, has gone into decline. The measures which were once believed to lead towards that goal are still pressed for and in no small degree achieved. But they are increasingly advocated as ends, or as means to something other than the "good society" previously pictured, the vision of which now floats free from its anchor to what was formerly believed to be its means of achievement. Socialism, properly so called, is disintegrating, in that the component parts of a formerly compact edifice of beliefs seem to be operating almost autonomously, and for something differing from the original socialist ideal. . . .

Redistribution and the scandal of poverty. What has now come to the fore, as against the ideal of fair rewards, and brotherly love, is the ideal of more equal consumption. It may be regarded as compounded of two convictions: *one*, that it is good and necessary to remove want and that the surplus of some should be sacrificed to the urgent needs of others; and *two*, that inequality of means between the several members of a society is bad in itself and should be more or less radically removed.

The two ideas are not logically related. The first rests squarely upon the Christian idea of brotherhood. Man is his brother's keeper, must act as the Good Samaritan, has a moral obligation to help the unfortunate, an obligation which rests most heavily, though not exclusively, upon the most fortunate.[5] There is, on the other hand, no prima facie evidence for the current contention that justice demands near equality of material conditions. Justice means proportion. The individualist is entitled to hold that justice demands individual rewards proportionate to individual endeavors; and the socialist is entitled to hold that it demands individual rewards proportionate to the services received by the community.[6] It seems therefore reasonable to deny simultaneously that our present society is just, and that justice is to be achieved by the equalization of incomes.

It is however a loose modern habit to call "just" whatever is thought emotionally desirable. Attention was legitimately called in the nineteenth century to the sorry condition of the laboring classes. It was felt to be wrong that their human needs were so ill-satisfied. The idea of proportion then came to be applied to the relation between needs and resources. Just as it seemed improper that some should have less than what was adjudged necessary, so it also seemed improper that others should have so much more.

The first feeling was almost the only one at work in the early stage of redistributionism. The second has gained almost the upper hand in the latter stage.[7]

Socialists, at the inception of the move towards redistribution, took rather a disdainful attitude; the initial measures were in their eyes mere bribes offered to the working classes in an attempt to divert them from the higher aims of socialism.

Here, however, powerful feelings were aroused. While it is difficult for men to imagine the suppression of private property, that is, of something that all desire, it is natural to them to compare their condition with that of others; the poorer can easily imagine the uses to which they would put some of the riches of others, and the richer, if once awakened to the condition of the poorer, are bound to feel some remorse on account of their luxuries.

At all times the revelation of poverty has come as a shock to the chosen few: it has impelled them to regard their personal extravagance with a sense of guilt, has driven them to distribute their riches and to mingle with the poor. In every case one knows of in the past, this has been associated with a religious experience: the mind may have been turned to God by the discovery of the poor, or to the poor by the discovery of God: in any case the two were linked, and a revulsion away from riches as evil was always implied.

However, in our century the feeling that has assailed not merely a few spirits but practically all the members of the leading classes has been of a different kind. Upon a society inordinately proud of its ever increasing riches it dawned that "in the midst of plenty," as the saying went, misery was still rife; and this called for action to raise the standard of the poor.

While the discovery of poverty, coupled with an assumption of the impossibility of removing it, had formerly brought about a revulsion against riches, this time a deep-rooted appreciation of worldly goods, coupled with a sense of power, caused an onslaught on poverty itself. Riches had been a scandal in the face of poverty; now poverty was a scandal in the face of riches. (Compare with modern statements[8] the previous identification of poverty with holiness.) To the pace-making middle classes, profoundly committed to the religion of progress, the existence of poverty was not only emotionally but intellectually disturbing: in the same manner as is the existence of evil to the simpler sort of deist. The increasing goodness of civilization, the increasing power of man, were to be finally demonstrated by the eradication of poverty.

Thus, charity and pride went hand in hand. In stressing the role played by pride it is not intended to belittle the part given to charity. Assuredly there are moments in history when the human heart is suddenly mellowed and some phenomenon of this kind occurs. Thus, redistribution was sped on its way by a feeling, or pattern of feelings. How this feeling came to be operative at a given moment is a problem for historians, and is not germane to our topic.

The notions of relief and of lifting working-class standards merged. We must, however, note that redistribution appears as a novelty only in contrast to the practices immediately preceding it and in the choice of its agent, the State. It is inherent in the very notion of society that those in direct want must be taken care of. The principle is applied in every family and in every small community, and in fact went out of practice only a few generations ago as a result of the disruption of smaller communities by the Industrial Revolution. This caused the isolation of the individual, and the new "master" he acquired did not regard himself as bound to him by the same ties as the former lord. It is characteristic that the feasts of consumption of the landed class were feasts *for all*, whereas the consumption of the rich in the new era is purely selfish. It is moreover almost needless to point out that the Church, when it enjoyed enormous gifts from the powerful and the rich, was a great redistributive agency. Between the old customs and the age of the welfare state stretch the "hard times," when the individual was left helpless in his need.

This cannot be ascribed to lack of feeling in generations which were fired with sympathy for slaves, for oppressed nationalities, and with indignation at the news of the "Bulgarian atrocities." One is tempted to conclude that men's powers of sympathy vary in their direction over periods of time, and are somewhat limited at any one moment. However, concern for the least favored was certainly not absent, as Malthus, Sismondi, and many others testify.

The twentieth century offers no more forceful statement of maldistribution than that of John Stuart Mill.[9] But it was assumed that the standard of life of "the people" would be raised by the cheapening of goods, of which the cheapening of salt and spices offered a promising instance. Moreover the relative position of the laborer would be improved by the cheapening of capital. Faith in the benefits of a competitive economy for "the common man" was not ill-grounded, as the American example testifies. But perhaps there was some confusion between two different notions: *one,* that the situation of the "median" worker is best improved by the play of productive forces; and *two,* that there is no call to take care of an unfortunate "rearguard." Such is the "stickiness" of social thinking that as long as emphasis was laid on the raising of the median by the processes of the market, there was reluctance to intervene on behalf of the unfortunate (compare the attitude of the American Federation of Labor in the first years of the Great Depression), while as soon as attention was focused upon this rearguard, it came to be held that the median condition was also to be raised by political measures.

While relief is an unquestionable social obligation which the destruction of neighborliness, of responsible aristocracies and of Church wealth has laid on the State for want of any other agency, it is open to discussion whether policies of redistribution are the best means of dealing with the problem of raising *median* working incomes, whether they can be effective, and whether they do not come into conflict with other legitimate social objectives.

The distinction drawn here is admittedly a difficult one. The two things are confused in practice, and it is not always clear to which end the enormous social machinery set up in our generation is actually working; this creation of ours presents a structure not easily amenable to our intellectual categories. When, through the working of the social services, a man in actual want is provided with the means of subsistence, whether it be a minimum income in days of unemployment, or basic medical care for which he could not have paid, this is a primary manifestation of solidarity. And it does not come under redistribution as we understand it here.

What does come under redistribution is everything which relieves the individual of an expenditure that he could and presumably would have undertaken out of his own purse, and which, freeing a proportion of his income, is therefore equivalent to a raising of this income. A family which would have bought the same amount of food at non-subsidized prices and gets it so much cheaper, an individual who would have sought the same medical services and gets them free, see their incomes raised. And this is what we want to discuss.

As we know, this does not apply only to poorer people: in some countries, especially in England, all incomes are raised in this manner while most incomes are drawn upon to finance the raising. The impact upon incomes of this enormous diversion and redistribution is a very complicated subject with which we are not ready to deal. It is far from being a simple redistribution from the richer to the poorer. And yet it is to a large degree sustained by a belief in the rightness of redistribution from the richer to the poorer and by the belief that this is what the whole process comes to. This basic motivating thought is what we want to deal with.

Indecent low-living and indecent high-living. We propose to deal with redistribution in its pure form: that is, taking from the higher incomes to add to the lower incomes. Such a policy is sustained by a pattern of feelings from which we shall try to extract some implied judgments of value. The urge to redistribute is closely attended by a sense of scandal: it is scandalous that so many should be in dire need, it is also scandalous that so many more should have an inadequate mode of life, which seems to us, in the original sense of the word, indecent. Thus the urge to redistribute is associated more or less with an idea of a *floor* beneath which no one should be left.

In thinking of the higher incomes, we are also conscious of an indecency: the upper modes of life seem to us wasteful of riches which could cover far more legitimate needs. That is, if you will, condemnation by comparison. But there is moreover a certain "way of the rich" which seems to us to call for absolute condemnation. We should in any event have scant sympathy with expenditure in night clubs, casinos, on horse racing and so on.

These two judgments of value are generally fused in the very general feeling which may be termed the "caviar into bread" motive. Not only do we disapprove of the feast of caviar when others lack bread but we disapprove of it absolutely. Therefore when these two feelings are involved, of comparative disapproval and absolute disapproval, no hesitation is felt in pronouncing that the transfer of such surplus is desirable.[10] These illustrations of "silly" expenditure are always uppermost in minds contemplating redistribution.

But of course such judgments upon proper levels of consumption, which we have called "absolute," are relative to a certain society at a certain time. They are in fact the subjective judgments of the policy-making class—in our times of the lower-middle class. In fact the levels of consumption which it deems the suitable minimum and the acceptable maximum are projections of its tastes. It is the class that forms social opinion which also makes up the social standards for what is indecent high-living and indecent low-living.[11]

The floor and the ceiling. Intellectual harmony and financial harmony. We now need a terminology which we shall keep within modest bounds. We call *floor* the minimum income regarded as necessary and the *ceiling* the maximum income regarded as desirable. We call floor and ceiling "intellectually harmonious" in so far as they are the floor and ceiling acceptable to the same mind or minds. Further, we shall call a floor and ceiling "financially harmonious," in so far as there is sufficient surplus to be taken from "above the ceiling" incomes to make up the deficiency in "beneath the floor" incomes. Thus if a is the floor and there are A incomes beneath it which fall short of Aa by the sum L, the ceiling h is financially harmonious with the floor a if the incomes of the class H (the people who have incomes greater than h) are equal or superior to $Hh+L$.

If, on the other hand, a and h are an intellectually harmonious set of floor-and-ceiling and the incomes of the H people who enjoy more than h are $Hh+S$ and S falls short of L, then a and h are not financially harmonious.

Redistributionism is a spontaneous feeling. And in its more naive forms it carries with it an implied conviction that the floor and ceiling which are intellectually harmonious will also prove to be financially harmonious. This, like so many spontaneous assumptions of the human mind, is an error. Questioning members of the western intelligentsia, unfamiliar with income statistics, on the suitable floor and ceiling of incomes, is absorbingly interesting. They always set a and h much too high for financial harmony. The surplus S always falls very far short of the deficiency L to be made up.

The outcome of this exploration comes as something of a surprise. It jolts a widely held belief that our societies are extremely rich and that their wealth is merely maldistributed: a belief unwisely disseminated by the well-meaning abundance-mongers of the 'thirties. What we do find is that such surpluses as we might be willing ruthlessly to take away—always assuming that this would have no effect upon production—are by a long way inadequate to raise our nether incomes to a desirable level. The pursuit of our purpose involves the debasement of even the lower-middle-class standard of life.

Redistributionism was at the outset given its impetus by two absolute disapprovals; the unrightness of underconsumption was matched by the unrightness of overconsumption. What luck if, in order to achieve a worthy purpose, you have to sacrifice nothing of value, if indeed your means to the suppression of an evil are also desirable of themselves! Thus the problem appeared to the intellectual, sitting in judgment upon society. There were bad patterns of life, those of the poor, which he wished to do away with; and he expected that this could be accomplished merely by the suppression of other bad patterns of life, those of the rich. The intellectual (not the artist) is naturally out of sympathy with the extrovert way of life of the rich. There was thus no social loss, in his eyes, implied in redistribution policies. But if the income ceiling is to be brought as low as required to supply the desired floor, then there is a great change. It is now worthy patterns of life which are to be destroyed, standards which the intellectual has been accustomed to and which he holds necessary to the performance of those social functions he most appreciates.

And so, while it still seems right to give, the rightness of taking away is far less obvious. It is easy to say: "Rothschild must forgo his yacht." It is quite another thing to say: "I am afraid Bergson must lose the modest competence which made it possible for him to do his work." Nor is it only a question of unearned income: the executive, the public servant, the engineer, the intellectual, the artist are to be cramped. Is this desirable? Is this right?

There is ample evidence that it is not regarded as desirable or right by the most extreme champions of redistribution. For the remunerations attached to the ever multiplying functions of the redistributing State are far above the ceilings which result from our investigation. No more positive proof could be adduced that such ceilings are not in fact regarded as desirable or acceptable by the advocates of redistribution. Owing, however, to the fallibility of man, it is quite possible that redistributionists are right in advocating redistribution and wrong in providing relatively high incomes for its agents. This may be a concession to surrounding circumstances, a carry-over of inherited notions, an inconsistency. Let us therefore examine without prejudice the possibility that sacrifices from even modest incomes may be justified in order to supplement our minus incomes.

As we now have to weigh the disadvantages of an abnormally low middle-class ceiling as against that of still insufficient working-class incomes, we must seek some criterion of rightness. We are offered the "arithmetic of happiness," the felicific calculus, now coated over with new paint as the economics of welfare.

A discussion of satisfactions. Redistribution started with a feeling that some have too little and some too much. When attempts are made to express this feeling more precisely, two formulae are spontaneously offered. The first we may call objective, the second subjective. The objective formula is based upon an idea of a decent way of life beneath which no one should fall and above which other ways of life are desirable and acceptable within a certain range. The subjective formula is not based upon a notion of what is objectively good for men but can be roughly stated as follows: "The richer would feel their loss less than the poorer would appreciate their gain"; or even more roughly: "A certain loss of income would mean less to the richer than the consequent gain would mean to the poorer."

Here a comparison of satisfactions is made. Can such a comparison be rendered effective? Can we with any precision come to weigh losses of satisfaction to some and gains of satisfaction to others? If so, we may know how to achieve the maximum sum of individual satisfactions capable of being drawn from a given flow of production, which must always be assumed to be unaffected.

The theory of diminishing utility. Not only has maximization of satisfactions played a ruling part in modern economics as developed by Walras and Jevons, but the great tool of generations of economists since the days of these pioneers has been the axiom of diminishing utility. The fact that a given fraction of good a is the less valuable to the holder the more he holds of good a beautifully explains the gain both parties achieve in exchange, each abandoning "last" fractions of that which he has most of in order to gain "first" fractions of that which he has not got. Two sets of goods a and b, at first collected each in one hand, gain in value by the operation of exchange since last fractions of a, of little utility to A, pass into the hands of B, to whom they are more useful, while A acquires B's last fractions of b, which are more valuable to him than to their previous holder.

Two things are to be considered in this operation of exchange. As he abandons his last fraction of a, the holder A loses little, and as he acquires his first fraction of b, he acquires much. Supposing him now so amply provided with $b, c...n$, that he is not tempted to acquire fractions of b, still the abandonment of the last fraction of c is but a small sacrifice. Moreover, for B the acquisition of the first fraction of a is a great gain; this fraction of a by changing hands can still be said to be gaining value in use.

This constitutes the transition from the axiom of diminishing utility to the assumption of diminishing utility of income.

Outstanding economists have found no difficulty in extending the axiom of diminishing utility to income. Thus Professor Pigou: "It is evident that any transference of income from a relatively rich man to a relatively poor man of similar temperament, since it enables more intense wants to be satisfied at the expense of less intense wants, must increase the aggregate sum of satisfactions."[12] This statement, by virtue of its informality, is more readily accepted than Professor Lerner's imposing: "Total satisfaction is maximized by that division of incomes which equalizes the marginal utilities of income of all the individuals in the society."[13]

Marginal utility of income is really a fancy name for the satisfaction or pleasure derived from the last unit of income. Let this be 10 English pounds. Professor Lerner's statement means that income is well distributed when the loss of 10 pounds would cause the same discomfort to any member of the society. Professor Pigou's statement means that the shift of 10 pounds from one individual to another is justified as long as in new hands the £10 will yield more satisfaction than in the former.

Professor Robbins has argued[14] . . . that the stretching of diminishing marginal utility to income is unwarranted, that marginalism in this field involves a comparison of the satisfactions of different persons, and thus falls into the very trap that in its legitimate applications it had sought to avoid. Satisfactions of different persons cannot, he says, be measured with a common rod.

This argument, however, turns out a boon in disguise to the welfarist who had saddled himself with the impossible task of equating the marginal utilities of different individuals. By proving this a stalemate, Professor Robbins unwillingly induces a new move: "The probable value of total satisfactions is maximized by dividing income *evenly*" (Lerner).[15] It is not necessary to dwell upon the highly artificial assumptions that the initial condition is one of equality and that moves away from it are haphazard. The strength of the case for even distribution does not lie in this formal reasoning. It lies in that, as soon as equal distribution is proposed as the solution to the maximization of satisfactions, those who oppose it have laid upon themselves the burden of proving that those who in fact draw the greater incomes have the greater capacity for enjoyment—an undertaking in which they cannot fail to shock every presupposition of a democratic society.

Further points and qualifications. Therefore, in a discussion of the maximization of satisfactions, however the ball is set rolling, it must come to rest on the solution of even distribution. That, however, is on the assumption that the holders of incomes have not developed their lives and tastes in accordance with their incomes, a qualification rightly stressed by Professor Pigou.[16]

It must be granted that a loss of income is a loss of definite satisfactions, while a gain of income beyond a certain proportion is a gain of as yet indefinite satisfactions. What is far more important, the marginalist representation of income as a progression of diminishing terms, the last of which can always be severed without affecting the others, does not hold good all along the line. A certain way of life implies a certain layout of expenditures out of which some "water" can always be "wrung." But when a certain point is reached, the same way of life cannot be maintained, a major readjustment is necessary, there is a fall to another way of life, a fall which involves great dissatisfaction.

Therefore it can be held that the previous discussion of satisfactions failed to do justice to the intensity of dissatisfactions due to loss of income. As we are still ruled by Robbins's principle that satisfactions and dissatisfactions of different persons are not commensurable, one falls back upon the mode of measurement which effectively prevails. It is not to be proven that the sum of individual satisfactions of people benefited is greater than the sum of dissatisfactions of people despoiled. In fact there is every reason to believe that if what is taken from a number of people were distributed among an equal number of people, the latter would gain less total satisfaction than the former were losing. But the fact is that the takings are distributed among a far greater number of people. And there will be more people pleased than displeased, more positive signs than negative: and as the intensity of the values is not to be measured, all one can do is state that there are more positive signs than negative and take the result as a gain; which is what in fact is currently done.

It is, however, generally granted that the intensity of dissatisfactions should not be pushed too far, and the process of reducing upper incomes is therefore to be effected over a period of time.

Discrimination against minorities. The inexpediency of radical levelling in the short run is easily granted. The psychologist warns of the violent, socially disruptive discontent of those suddenly toppled down from their customary modes of life.[17] The economist warns that the conversion to popular use of those productive resources which specifically served the well-to-do will not, in the short run, yield in popular goods and services anything like the value previously yielded in luxury goods and services.

Conceding objections to short run levelling does not weaken the case for long-run levelling. Indeed it strengthens it. For the greater willingness one shows to postpone radical equalization in order to accommodate acquired tastes, the more one implies that differences in subjective wants are a matter of habit, a historic phenomenon. While it would seem excessive to equalize incomes between the men of today, known to us and whom we know to have different needs, it seems plausible to do so in the case of men whose personalities we can imagine to differ less from one another—for the very good reason that they have as yet no personalities. Thereby we can project forward as reasonable what might in reality strike us as absurd.

It is a common behavior of the mind, naturally enamored of simplicity, to build its schemes far away from the annoying complexities of a familiar reality, in the future or in a mythical past, where things have no shapes of their own. After this first operation resulting in a rational scheme, that scheme can be used as a rational model against which the disorderly architecture of today can be measured, and thereby condemned.

Let us however notice a certain consequence of equalization, valid in whatever future we care to place the completion of reform. Let us grant that any differences in tastes due to social habits have been erased. Men will not, however, be uniform in character; some differences in tastes must exist among individuals. Economic demand will not any more be weighted by differences in individual incomes that will have been abolished: it will be weighted solely by numbers. It is clear that those goods and services in demand by greater collections of individuals will be provided to those individuals more cheaply than other goods and services wanted by smaller collections of individuals will be provided to these latter. The satisfaction of minority wants will be more expensive than the satisfaction of majority wants. Members of a minority will be discriminated against.

There is nothing novel in this phenomenon. It is a regular feature of any economic society. People of uncommon tastes are at a disadvantage for the satisfaction of their wants. But they can and do endeavor to raise their incomes in order to pay for their distinctive wants. And this by the way is a most potent incentive; its efficiency is illustrated by the more than average effort, the higher incomes and the leading positions achieved by racial and religious minorities; what is true of these well-defined minorities is just as true of individuals presenting original traits. Sociologists will readily grant that, in a society where free competition obtains, the more active and the more successful are also those with the more uncommon personalities.

If, however, it is not open to those whose tastes differ from the common run to remedy their economic disadvantage by an increase in their incomes, then, in the name of equality, they will be enduring discrimination.

Four consequences deserve notice. Firstly, personal hardship for individuals of original tastes; secondly, the loss to society of the special effort these people would make in order to satisfy their special needs; thirdly, the loss to society of the variety in ways of life resulting from successful efforts to satisfy special wants; fourthly, the loss to society of those activities which are supported by minority demands.

With respect to the latter point, it is a commonplace that things which are now provided inexpensively to the many, say spices or the newspaper, were originally luxuries which could be offered only because some few were willing and able to buy them at high prices. It is difficult to say what the economic development of the West would have been, had first things been put first, as reformers urge; that is, if the productive effort had been aimed at providing more of the things needed by all, to the exclusion of a greater variety of things desired by minorities. But the onus of proving that economic progress would have been as impressive, surely rests with the reformers. History shows us that each successive enlargement of the opportunities to consume was linked with unequal distribution of means to consume.[18]

The effect of redistribution upon society. No one has attempted to draw the picture of the society which would result from radical redistribution, as called for by the logic of reasoning on the maximization of satisfactions.... It would...be one which would exclude the present modes of life of our leaders in every field: whether they are businessmen, public servants, artists, intellectuals or trade-unionists.

We have forbidden ourselves to contemplate any decrease in the activity of anyone, any lowering of production as a whole. But the reallocation of incomes would bring about a great shift in activities. The demand for some goods and services would be increased. The demand for others would drop or disappear.

I for one would see without chagrin the disappearance of many activities which serve the richer, but no one surely would gladly accept the disappearance of all the activities which find their market in the classes enjoying more than £500 of net income. The production of all first-quality goods would cease. The skill they demand would be lost and the taste they shape would be coarsened. The production of artistic and intellectual goods would be affected first and foremost. Who could buy paintings? Who even could buy books other than pulp?

Can we reconcile ourselves to the loss suffered by civilization if creative intellectual and artistic activities fail to find a market? We must if we follow the logic of the felicific calculus. If the two thousand guineas heretofore spent by two thousand buyers of an original piece of historical or philosophical research, are henceforth spent by forty-two thousand buyers of shilling books, aggregate satisfaction is very probably enhanced. There is therefore a gain to society, according to this mode of thought which represents society as a collection of independent consumers. Felicific calculus, counting in units of satisfactions afforded to individuals, cannot enter into its accounts the loss involved in the suppression of the piece of research. A fact which, by the way, brings to light the radically individualistic assumptions of a viewpoint usually labelled socialistic.

In fact, and although this entails an intellectual inconsistency, the most eager champions of income redistribution are highly sensitive to the cultural losses involved. And they press upon us a strong restorative. It is true that individuals will not be able to build up private libraries; but there will be bigger and better and ever more numerous public libraries. It is true that the producer of the book will not be sustained by individual buyers; but the author will be given a public grant, and so forth. All advocates of extreme redistribution couple it with most generous measures of state support for the whole superstructure of cultural activities. This calls for two comments. We shall deal first with the measures of compensation, and then with their significance.

The more redistribution, the more power to the State. Already, when stressing the loss of investment capital which would result from a redistribution of incomes, we found that the necessary counterpart of lopping off the tops of higher incomes was the diversion by the State from these incomes of as much, or almost as much, as they used to pour into investment; the assumption which followed logically was that the State would take care of investment: a great function, a great responsibility, and a great power.

Now we find that by making it impossible for individuals to support cultural activities out of their shrunken incomes, we have devolved upon the State another great function, another great power.

It then follows that the State finances, and therefore chooses, investments; and that it finances cultural activities, and must thenceforth choose which it supports. There being no private buyers left for books or paintings or other creative work, the State must support literature and the arts either as buyer or as provider of *beneficia* to the producers, or in both capacities.

This is a rather disquieting thought. How quickly this State mastery follows upon measures of redistribution we can judge by the enormous progress towards such mastery which has already followed from limited redistribution.

Values and satisfactions. But the fact that redistributionists are eager to repair by State expenditure the degradation of higher activities which would result from redistribution left to itself is very significant. They want to prevent a loss of values. Does this make sense? In the whole process of reasoning which sought to justify redistribution rationally, it was assumed that the individual's satisfaction was to be maximized and that the maximization of the sum of individual satisfactions was to be sought. It was granted for argument's sake that the sum of individual satisfactions may be maximized when incomes are equalized. But in this condition of income equality, if it be the best, must not market values set by the buyers and the resulting allocation of resources be, *ex hypothesi,* the best and most desirable? Is it not in direct contradiction with this whole line of reasoning to resume production of items that are not now in demand?

By our redistribution process we have now, it is assumed, reached the condition of maximum welfare, where the sum of individual satisfactions is maximized. Is it not illogical immediately to move away from it?

Surely, when we achieve the distribution of incomes which, it is claimed, maximizes the sum of satisfactions, we must let this distribution of incomes exert its influence upon the allocation of resources and productive activities, for it is only through this adjustment that the distribution of incomes is made meaningful. And when resources are so allocated, we must not interfere with their disposition, since by doing so we shall, as a matter of course, decrease the sum of satisfactions. It is then an inconsistency, and a very blatant one, to intervene with state support for such cultural activities as do not find a market. Those who spontaneously correct their schemes of redistribution by schemes for such support are in fact denying that the ideal allocation of resources and activities is that which maximizes the sum of satisfactions.

But it is clear that by this denial the whole process of reasoning by which redistribution is justified falls to the ground. If we say that, although people would be better satisfied to spend a certain sum on needs they are more conscious of, we deprive them of this satisfaction in order to support a painter, we obviously lose the right to argue that James's income must go to the mass of the people because satisfaction will thereby be increased. For all we know, James may be supporting the painter.[19] We cannot accept the criterion of maximizing satisfactions when we are destroying private incomes, and then reject it when we are planning state expenditure.

The recognition that maximizing satisfactions may destroy values which we are all willing to restore at the cost of moving away from the position of maximal satisfaction destroys the criterion of maximizing satisfactions.

Are subjective satisfactions an exclusive standard? Indeed, the foregoing discussion reaches beyond a mere refutation of the formal argument for income redistribution. Economists as such are interested in the play of consumer's preferences through the market, and in showing how this play guides the allocation of productive resources so that it comes to correspond with the consumer's preferences. The perfection of this correspondence is general equilibrium. It is perfection of a kind: and it is quite legitimate to speak of such allocation of resources as the best, it being understood that it is the best from the angle of subjective wants, weighted by the actual distribution of incomes. This understanding, however, is often forgotten: many economists . . . have argued that it is not the best, because it is skewed by actual distribution. The peril inherent in this correction is that its champions are apt to forget that the allocation of resources resulting from such distribution of incomes as appears to them most desirable is, precisely as before, the best only from the angle of subjective wants, weighted by the new distribution of incomes. Calling it the best without qualification implies a value judgment which equates the good with the desired, on Hobbesian lines. Now it is quite legitimate for the economist to deal only with the desired and not with the good. But it is not legitimate to treat the optimum in relation to desires as an optimum in any other sense. And that the allocation of resources in relation to desires should fail to be optimal by other standards should not come as a surprise to us.

That a society which we may assume to have maximized the sum of subjective satisfactions should, when we survey it as a whole, strike us as falling far short of a "good society," could have been foreseen by anyone with a Christian background or a classical education.

To the many, however, who were apt to think so much in terms of satisfactions that the "badness" of society seemed to them due to the uneven distribution of satisfactions, it must come as a most useful lesson that the outcome of this viewpoint leads them into an unacceptable state of affairs. The error must then lie in the original assumption that incomes are to be regarded solely as means to consumer-enjoyment. In so far as they are so regarded, the form of society which maximizes the sum of consumer-enjoyments should be best: and yet it is unacceptable. It follows that incomes are not to be so regarded.

Redistributionism the end result of utilitarian individualism. There is no doubt that incomes are currently regarded as means to consumer-enjoyment, and society as an association for the promotion of consumption. This is made clear by the character of the controversy now proceeding on the theme of redistribution. The arguments set against one another are cut from the same cloth. It is fair, some say, to equalize consumer-satisfactions. It is prudent, the others retort, to allow greater rewards to spur production and thereby provide greater means of consumption.

There is an Armenian proverb: "The world is a pot and man a spoon in it." In this image our two sides might choose slogans: an expanding pot with unequal spoons, or a static and possibly declining pot with equal spoons. But perhaps the world is not a pot and surely man is not a spoon. Here we have completely slipped away from any conception of the "good life" and the "good society." It is quite inadmissible to consider the "good life" as a buyer's spree or the "good society" as a suitable queueing up of buyers. And the redistributionist ideal represents a disastrous fall from socialism.

Socialism, before its disastrous decay into a new version of enlightened despotism, was an ethical social doctrine. And as such a doctrine must, to merit the double epithet, it looked to a "good society," which it saw as one wherein men would have better relations with one another, and feel more kindly towards their fellows. This spirit seems to have evaporated from modern reformist tendencies. Redistributionism takes its cue wholly from the society it seeks to reform. An increased consuming power is the promise held out, and fulfilled, by capitalist mercantile society: so is it the promise of the modern reformer. And in fact the choice of right or left is to be finally regarded as not an ethical choice at all, but a bet.... Do we bet that redistributionism with its probable negative effect on economic progress will provide a majority with a higher standard of living than capitalism with its inequality? Or do we put our money—it seems the proper term—on the other horse?

There is no question of ethics here. The end-product of society is anyhow taken to be personal consumption: this is, under socialistic colors, the extremity of individualism. Finally, my probable consumption under one or the other system is to be my criterion. Nothing quite so trivial has ever been made into a social ideal. But it is wrong to accuse our reformers of having invented it: they found it.

What is to be held against them is not that they are utopian, it is that they completely fail to be so; it is not their excessive imagination, but their complete lack of it; not that they wish to transform society beyond the realm of possibility, but that they have renounced any essential transformation; not that their means are unrealistic, but that their ends are flat-footed. In fact the mode of thought which tends to predominate in advanced circles is nothing but the tail-end of nineteenth-century utilitarianism.

Colin Welch

INTELLECTUALS HAVE CONSEQUENCES

The fish, so the French say, decays from the head first. This is what justifies any study of the British left-wing intellectual. By "intellectual" I do not mean an intelligent person, who need not be either left-wing or strictly an intellectual. What I do mean is a person who thinks himself to be moved primarily or solely by his intellect (which may of course be very feeble or very powerful), who regards himself as an intellectual and makes a living thereby or, unable to do so, is influenced by those who do, in the columns of the *New Statesman* and elsewhere. Such people standing as they do in our recent history predominantly on the left, I expect the epithet "left-wing" to be understood wherever I use the word "intellectual"—and "British," too, for I am not qualified to write of others.

And if I pay a lot of attention to comparatively dull dogs like Sidney and Beatrice Webb, Harold Laski, John Strachey, R.H. Tawney, and Anthony Crosland, this is not because I think them more amusing than their wilder sidekicks but because I am sure they and their innumerable followers have had more influence. Despite the fact that only one of those I have mentioned, Mr. Crosland, is still alive,* Britain is still governed by them, perhaps increasingly so. They are still the brains of the ruling Labour Party; they have supplied its dominant prejudices and reflexes as well as the broad mass of its reasoning. Some oaf shrieks, "Shoot the bosses!" or "Make the rich squeal!" It appears to come from the natural promptings of an embittered and unlettered heart. Yet dimly behind such outbursts we are aware of the prompting and blessing of some remote gray ideologue, half forgotten yet still potent.

In trying to describe the intellectual I am daunted to find how much of my work was done for me nearly forty years ago by George Orwell, one of the breed himself for all his percipience and humanity, in *The Road to Wigan Pier.*

The typical socialist is not for him a ferocious worker with a raucous voice; no, it is either a youthful snob Bolshevik or, more typically, a prim little white-collar job man, possibly a teetotaler or vegetarian of nonconformist background, who has no intention of forfeiting his social position: both "unsatisfactory or even inhuman types."

Orwell wonders about the motives of the tract-writing intellectual. Love of the working class, from which he is so far removed? Hard this for Orwell to believe: more likely a "hypertrophied sense of order." He sees in Shaw, for instance, a dull, empty windbag who knows and cares nothing about poverty, who thinks it must be abolished from above, by violence if necessary—perhaps preferably by violence: hence Shaw's worship of "great" men, of dictators fascist or Communist, of Stalin and Mussolini.

Foaming denouncers of the bourgeoisie; book-trained intellectuals who want to throw what remains of our great but half-wrecked civilization down the sink, preferring a mechanized socialist future of "iron and water"; the more-water-in-your-beer reformers, Shaw the prototype; the astute young literary climbers who are Communists because it is fashionable; "and all that dreary tribe of high-minded women and sandal wearers and bearded fruit-juice drinkers who come flocking toward the smell of progress like blue-bottles to a dead cat": all these are the freaks who, in Orwell's view, have brought socialism into disrepute. And, to his bitter regret, socialism is often pictured as a state of affairs in which such "vocal socialists would feel thoroughly at home."

In parentheses it may be added that Orwell's own idea of "a state of affairs worth fighting for" is hardly more alluring. He found it in Barcelona during the Spanish Civil War: the wealthy classes apparently wiped out, the bourgeoisie killed or in flight, almost no "well-dressed" (his quotation marks) people, only rough working-class clothes, blue overalls, various military uniforms.... Here Orwell himself displays in an aberrant form that guilt-ridden mania for drabness and uniformity so characteristic of those he derides. And indeed, for all the vividness of his caricature of the intellectual, there is much that he could not see from the inside, so to speak. A prisoner cannot draw his prison without leaving his cell. Let us quote Orwell once more, and then step outside.

"The world, potentially at least," he cries elsewhere in *The Road to Wigan Pier,* "is immensely rich; develop it as it might be developed and we could all live like princes." Orwell here states, with more qualification than usual, a view common to nearly all intellectuals (see especially William Morris, who for Orwell was another dull windbag). Past and future progress are alike taken for granted. Yet past progress was the fruit of a system they despise and seek to end. How then can they be sure of future progress, or even of maintaining ground already conquered? How on earth would we know of these potential riches if capitalism had not thrust them under our noses? And these intellectuals often describe their mental processes as "scientific"! Does not science proceed with more prudence?

The typical intellectual is like the spoiled child of rich parents. He does not at first wonder why his parents and others are rich; this is for him the normal state of affairs. What bothers him, if he is at all curious, is why some should be poor. He does not see poverty and toil as the natural or original state of affairs, in which capitalism found nearly everybody and from which it has rescued many. No, it is poverty that has to be explained.

Our heir surveys the past and present coldly, without humility, wonder, or gratitude. He is not astonished that islands of wealth and culture should slowly and miraculously have risen from the sea of savagery, but vexed that civilization is not universal and evenly spread. In this respect he is what Tawney called an "intellectual villager," without background, terms of reference, or context. His vanity is often unbounded, typified by Shaw's amazing claim that he knew more about banking than any banker, a remark that reveals him to know even less about banking than the rest of us; contrast Goethe's profound humility in declaring that the invention of double-entry bookkeeping was one of the greatest achievements of the human mind.

Our heir becomes aware of and troubled by his own good fortune; he is often profoundly ignorant of his forebears' struggles, skills, services, and achievements, which are as incomprehensible to him as a watch to a monkey (Tawney's simile, sadly appropriate for his own contemptuous attitude to liberal civilization). Can it be that his forebears stole from the poor what was really theirs, that they enslaved, exploited, and disinherited them, milked them of surplus value? There are hundreds of books from Marx onward to tell him that this—part rubbish, part over-simplification—is so; and thus in self-righteous hatred, rage, and guilt he turns upon his parents and upon the capitalist system that they represent. (Strangely enough, we discern in this idea that the rich have robbed the poor of their birthright, a dim and unacknowledged survival of the golden-age myth, also discernible in William Morris's medieval-ism and elsewhere.)

I have used the word "parents" half metaphorically. Yet surely it is not fanciful to discern among so many British intellectuals an actual dislike, explicit or suppressed, of parents, children, and the family. H.G. Wells, for all too obvious reasons, directed the state to act as parent to all the children engendered by the free love he urged and practiced; and the catastrophist socialists, like the Communist poets of the thirties, urged the overthrow of existing society (including, by definition, of existing families) in the bizarre expectation that something better would emerge. But we also find a dislike for the family among those "moderate," reformist, egalitarian intellectuals like Mr. Crosland who strive, by savage taxation of income during life and of capital at death, as also by inflation, to deprive parents of one of their noblest incentives (another, the purchase of a decent education, Mr. Crosland seeks also to abolish). By such measures they deprive the old of dignity, the young of hope, and all families of the power to stay above mediocrity for more than one generation, and they illegitimate and repress a profound and valuable part of human nature, productive of much past progress.

I suspect that Janus-faced mandarin Keynes in one of his many protean guises has done much to make such depredations respectable. It was he who said that in the long run we are all dead—a remark that would occur to few people with children of their own; he was more consistently egalitarian than he was consistently anything else; and he loudly proclaimed his contempt for the hereditary principle and for the control of wealth by "third-generation men." It is nonetheless odd that an intellectual so cultivated as Keynes should have preferred the first-generation climber to his third-generation successor, who usually has more leisure for thought, learning, art, patronage, and public work. Keynes publicly avowed his preference for the bourgeois "fish" against the proletarian "mud"; yet how on earth can any bourgeoisie arise if it is thrust back into the mud every time the bell tolls?

The intellectual justifies his attacks on hereditary culture by venomous caricatures of the attitudes and interests of the leisured and better-off classes. The American Thorstein Veblen's caricature is the most amusing, but it appears in forms more absurd and solemn in the jeremiads of his English forerunners, contemporaries, and disciples. The Webbs raved against the functionless rich, their futile occupations, licentious pleasures (including luring boys and girls into "concert rooms" for vice), and insolent manners; they were enraged by such gewgaws as the court, titles, soldiers, and diplomats; and they actually declared that "the very existence in any neighborhood of a non-producing rich family, even if it is what it calls well-conducted, is by its evil example a blight on the whole district, lowering the standards, corrupting the morality and to that extent countering the work alike of the churches and the schools." These tirades, it should be added, were financed not only by domestic parsimony but also by Beatrice Webb's unearned annuity of £1,000 a year—a large sum in those days.

Shaw, himself a vast and greedy acquisitor, derided the pleasures of the rich—chocolates, cocktails, silly novels (what about silly plays?), motors, hotels. John Strachey (first a socialist, then a near-fascist, then a Stalinoid Marxist, then a Labour Minister, and rich throughout) denounced Macy's, Harrods, and the Galeries Lafayette, and hoped that privation would restore to the bourgeoisie their former power to think. The patrician Tawney sneered at the common vulgarity and bad manners of businessmen, though when shopgirls were rude he applauded. The moderate and hedonistic Mr. Crosland berates our "illiterate" wealthy classes for their cars and houses, holidays in Cannes, servants, gin (!), and other pleasures to most of which he is no stranger, and even for their failure to stop Georgian buildings from being knocked down. Who on earth does he think built them? And who is knocking them down? London University and local authorities are among the worst villains.

The extinction of such a philistine mob of loafers as is described above would be no loss. Envy is said to demand it, and would in Mr. Crosland's view be assuaged by its accomplishment. If the latter were true, the liquidation of the wealthier classes might arguably be desirable even if the poorer classes were, as I think inevitable, impoverished thereby. But Mr. Crosland and his friends grossly overestimate the present prevalence and virulence of envy (a misjudgment that may be explained by the fact that the only poorer people they know are sour Labour activists, notoriously hostile to everything in any way superior to themselves); they underestimate their own role in fostering and exploiting such envy as exists, thus, incidentally, making themselves objects of envy; they overlook the possibility that, in the relatively equal or "rationally" differentiated society they favor, envy would assume ever more vicious forms and find ever new victims for its malice; and most important of all, they ignore the possibility that the suppression of envy may be essential to the survival of a free capitalist or "mixed" society and that its legitimization (or, by Tawney, virtual canonization) and subsequent triumph will be fatal alike to freedom and prosperity. (For a full treatment of this subject, see Helmut Schoeck's brilliant book *Envy*.)

Now, if the civilized Mr. Crosland took any such threat seriously, he should be genuinely disturbed, for he has ceaselessly proclaimed his devotion to a mixed economy and a free society. What keeps him cheerful (if he still is, which we may doubt) is an almost unbounded optimism, akin to that felt by the classical economists (though far less securely reasoned) and far removed from the destructive and hysterical nihilism of the catastrophists. It expresses itself in a blind and irrational faith in the ability of capitalism somehow to deliver the goods, no matter how emasculated, overburdened, overregulated, diminished, and deprived alike of stick, carrot, confidence, hope, and rational motivation.

In *The Future of Socialism,* written in 1956, Mr. Crosland declared that full employment could be easily achieved and maintained by judicious and timely expansion of domestic demand, that is, by that "continuing mild inflation" that he and other moderates consider tolerable or even beneficial. He ignored the likelihood that inflation, in order to perform the beneficent task he allotted to it, must be less and less mild, more and more rapid and progressive, always a bit more than is expected; for "expected" inflation is discounted in advance and produces no effect on demand. Hence in part our present difficulties, with an unprecedented inflation rate and rising unemployment.

In the same book Mr. Crosland regarded further rapid growth as both essential and certain; no need to bother about it, it can be taken for granted. If it goes on, as it will, material poverty will cease to be a problem. Other problems will indeed remain, fortunately for intellectuals whose lives would be empty without them; not only problems of resentment and envy caused by residual inequalities, but also other problems in the fields of psychology, sociology, divorce reform, and so forth. But economics as the dismal science will have served its turn; prosperity is here to stay; investment incentives will remain buoyant, with high savings, high incomes, and high consumption; adequate capital formation is assured, risks of depreciation much reduced. "We stand in Britain," Mr. Crosland excitedly proclaimed in 1956, "on the threshold of mass abundance." Hey-ho.

"The enjoyment of personal success," Professor Friedrich Hayek has written, "will be given to large numbers only in a society that, as a whole, progresses fairly rapidly," and in which as a consequence more people are rising than falling—and in which indeed most of those falling are falling only relatively though still rising absolutely. It was to such a fortunate society that Mr. Crosland confidently looked forward; and, had his expectations been fulfilled, it is probable that the nit-picking envies and resentments that elsewhere obsess him would fade into insignificance, affording little material for distress or further exploitation.

But alas, at least for the time being, things have turned out very differently. We in Britain find ourselves in a stationary or declining state of society, the former described by Adam Smith as "hard" and "dull" for rich and poor alike, the latter "miserable" and "melancholy." In such states class hatred and bitterness must thrive, together with those who cause, exacerbate, and exploit our miseries. How has this come to pass?

The most important clue lies in Mr. Crosland's extraordinary views about economic incentive and motivation, views that are fully shared not only by other intellectuals but also by successive Labour governments (to which he has been intellectual-in-residence) and their more responsible supporters, and that have clearly guided or justified policy.

"We know too little about incentives," concedes Mr. Crosland at one point, "to make firm statements"—firm statements about whether "equality and rapid growth are hard to reconcile" and about whether "socialist policies must necessarily slow down the rate of growth." Such doubts would induce in other, more modest men, if they valued growth as he does, an extreme caution in enforcing equality, in destroying existing incentives, and in pressing ahead with socialist policies. Not so with Mr. Crosland.

Everywhere in his writings he derides the contribution of financial incentive, competition, profit, and individualism to economic growth; technological and productive advances, in his view, spring rather from "people working on a fixed salary in a large managerial structure." He urges that, if anything, this fixed salary should be lowered, by taxation or other means, for he believes that the spread of income in Britain, though narrower than in the Soviet Union (a country he oddly supposes to be egalitarian), is far too wide. And he thinks that the rewards for saving and investment are far too high, and may be safely reduced.

Mr. Crosland conceded in 1956 that "some danger point must evidently exist at which equality begins to react really seriously on the supply of ability (and also of effort, risktaking, and so on), and hence on economic growth. Where exactly this point lies, no one knows. I do not myself believe we have yet reached it."

Implicit in these remarks is the odd assumption that, once the danger point is reached, we can somehow retrace our steps to safer ground and all will be well again. Yet despite their ignorance of where the danger point lies, or of what to do when they get there, the practice of Mr. Crosland and his friends has been to press ruthlessly on till even they see unmistakable signs that it has been reached. With irresponsible levity they proceed on their mad experiment, like some ignorant peasant cheerfully piling more and more onto a half-starved donkey, or some crazy doctor in a concentration camp using prisoners to find out how much cold the human body can stand.

Without intending it, they may do grave and irreparable damage, and may have already done it; indeed, they might have done it even before Crosland wrote, for, already some twenty years before he wrote, Evan Durbin, one of the most civilized and percipient of intellectuals, had lamented that taxation was too high to permit the continued vigorous survival of the free economy. It was for this reason that Durbin had become a reluctant but convinced socialist.

What are the signs that the danger point has now been reached? With their general contempt for economic motivation, Mr. Crosland and his friends are not likely to be the first to see them. Indeed, like Laski (and like Graham Wallas, who considered, perhaps playfully, that even abnormally strong acquisitive instincts might in the future express themselves in the collection of shells or postage stamps) they prefer to rely on other sorts of motivation to keep the show on the road—the self-identification of business leaders with their firms, professional pride, desire for prestige, public esteem, and greed for power. Why these motives should be preferred is not always clear. Greed for power is not usually regarded as an attractive quality, and Dr. Johnson thought no man so innocently employed as in making money. "Prestige" is often only a pretty word for pompous public relations, for hobnobbing with politicians, in Britain for a hunt for titles, and for conspicuous waste in general.

Nor are all the signs of that danger point particularly easy to spot or quantify. How on earth can one measure such impalpables as effort withheld, enterprise thwarted, hopes blasted, skills unacquired or wasted, idleness preferred? The resultant torpor is not even spread uniformly through the economy; incentives totally inadequate at one point may still elicit effort elsewhere. National economic failure is of course measurable in many ways; we are getting expert at it. But Mr. Crosland is still entitled to debate to what extent measurable failure is due to lack of incentive.

Less debatable, more measurable, and perhaps less reversible is the rising tide of skilled and talented émigrés that I expect will soon become torrential, an exodus that will leave behind a stagnant and impoverished quagmire bereft alike of wealth and culture. But when this exodus becomes apparent to all, it will be too late to stanch the flow; nor will those who have already gone be drawn back by sudden changes of heart or policy in a socialist party that they have grown to mistrust, fear, and hate, that is generally hostile to their interests, and that can never be permanently excluded from office.

Mr. Crosland is still patiently watching the dials, but he does not seem to see what we see: a nation bleeding to death. Nor is this wholly surprising, for in fact one can learn more about human motivations and frustrations, about intentions and despair, by talking to ordinary people in a pub than by poring over the official statistics and surveys that are the intellectual's normal source of information.

Now the present shambles in Britain does not bear much resemblance to the ordered Utopias envisaged by intellectuals like the Webbs, Laski, and Tawney. Yet, if our country is (relatively) poorer, less free, more equal, and less competitive than it was, it is probable that the teachings of such intellectuals have powerfully contributed to these developments, laudable or deplorable as different people may think them.

The Webbs and Laski certainly expected vast material wealth to be produced by the elimination of capitalist "waste" and "inefficiency." They might indeed be disappointed by the results of progress so far achieved, but I presume they would still advise us to press on. Tawney cared less about material wealth than vague spiritual assets like fellowship, and would be distressed less by our drabness than by our morose ill humor and by the class hatred that declining fortune always exacerbates.

But I think all four would kick up a hullabaloo where I have said "less free." "Less free for whom?" they would cry, for like most intellectuals, they muddle the difference between the *freedom* to do something and the *power* to do it. Without power, freedom to them is a mere useless formality, a hollow mockery, like the beggar's freedom to enter the Ritz. Freedom that is enjoyed only by a minority is not to them freedom at all, but a privilege at best to be tolerated, more likely obliterated.

An equal society is thus by definition to them a free society, in which no freedoms exist (or *need* exist) that all do not have the power to enjoy, and in which all can enjoy such freedoms as may exist, if any, and thus be "free." A society of slaves might thus be a free society in their eyes; indeed, I am sure that this philosophical confusion—as well as ignorance, gullibility, callous indifference to suffering, and that hypertrophied sense of order to which Orwell referred—helps to explain the scandalous prostration of British intellectuals before the full horrors of Stalin's tyranny in the thirties and forties. Among those who abased themselves were the Webbs, Laski, John Strachey, Stephen Spender, the Red Dean Hewlett Johnson, and many others, all listed in David Caute's book *The Fellow Travellers*. In some of these cases a harsher term than callous indifference is appropriate, for who does not know, and cannot find in the literature of the thirties if he looks, that positive delight in cruelty and violence from which book-learned ideologues have never been immune?

Beatrice Webb herself wondered why British socialists should be more sympathetic than their Continental counterparts to Russian Communism. I suspect the reason may lie not only in greater ignorance, but also in the complacency bred by distance and by the reassuring presence of the English Channel and the Royal Navy, at that time still formidable; for the Webbs at least were actually timid petty bourgeois, highly respectful of "established expectations" (including their own annuity) and terrified of revolution, which their own inevitable gradualness seems largely designed to avert. Their conversion to Communism, on the face of it incongruous, took place only when disorder had been ferociously suppressed in the Soviet Union and when the risk of disorder in the West, thanks to the Depression, seemed imminent. What they worshiped was always power and success.

People like the Webbs, unable to tell the difference between freedom and power, are obviously very inadequate defenders of freedom, if not actually hostile to it. At best they are coarsely indifferent, at worst harshly inimical, to minority tastes, cultural interests, and moral beliefs, and also to the freedoms that protect them. And in general such intellectuals are totally unable to see the ways in which we all benefit by freedoms that only some of us can enjoy. We may well lack the means or the brains to write the equivalent of Shaw's plays, say, or the Webbs' vast *oeuvre;* but I do not think Shaw or the Webbs are in a good position to deny that we may have benefited from them. Few people could make use of the artistic freedom in Tsarist Russia, and the Webbs would therefore regard that freedom as formal and valueless. Yet the use Tolstoy and Dostoievsky made of their freedom has enriched the lives of millions who lacked the power and now lack the freedom to express themselves fully.

In the same way, Tawney somewhere blandly describes competition as being of value only to those able to compete. What rubbish this is! I do not myself have to be able to compete in order to profit by the competition of rival playwrights, biscuit makers, ideologues, and doctors for my patronage; indeed, as *tertius gaudens,* I profit more obviously than those who compete and fail and may be ruined by their efforts.

Another piece of Tawney nonsense, while we are at it, expresses the moral hatred that he and fellow intellectuals feel for capitalist society. How can people live for service and self-sacrifice, he wails, if society is dominated by ruthless egotism? Why can they not? One may question whether capitalist society is more or less dominated by ruthless egotism than other societies. What cannot so easily be doubted is the freedom it confers on all to live lives of service and self-sacrifice if they so wish. The great classical economists did not say that people *should* be dominated by ruthless egotism. They described men as they are, governed among other motives by an egotism, whether ruthless or enlightened, that may by freedom and wise regulation be turned to public good. If the good life could be lived under Nero, why on earth not under Gladstone?

I described our society today as "less competitive," and here too I think our intellectuals would demur. For one thread running through all their works is that competition, whether desirable or not (it is usually qualified by such epithets as "disorderly," "wasteful," "cutthroat," "unregulated," and so forth), was by the time they wrote dying or dead, being succeeded everywhere by the monopoly that Marx predicted.

Three considerations, to my mind, they entirely overlooked. Baldly stated, without qualifications otherwise desirable, one is that there is no natural or theoretic tendency toward monopoly in an unregulated capitalist system. Another is that those parts of the British and American economies that are monopolistically controlled have not grown much in the past seventy years—except where, in Britain, the government has intervened vigorously either to promote private concentration (as in the thirties) or, as it has done since 1945, to promote monopolistic public corporations. The third is that monopolies should, as Joseph Schumpeter advised, be regarded not only as they are *now,* or at some other particular moment, but also *in time.* What looks like an unassailable monopoly is in fact (unless protected by statute—a very important exception) a fragile structure, its shaky foundations forever washed and eroded by the currents of competition that surge whenever technical advance and new needs make them possible and desirable. For these reasons the wise monopolist is not like the intellectual's caricature of him: he is a timid, not an arrogant man, always behaving as though he were not a monopolist at all. He knows that his position, formidable as it looks to the thoughtless, is in fact constantly menaced by the irresistible forces of modern technological "creative destruction" (Schumpeter's phrase for what the Webbs call "waste").

Thus for the Webbs and their friends there arose no question of preserving or extending competition, which was deservedly moribund. Their task was to devise another and quite different industrial system that would do all that competition had ever done, but more and better. This was the purpose of their vast and all-embracing Babel tower of national and local and municipal boards and public corporations, producing all goods and supplying all services, not for profit but to satisfy measured and objective needs (rather than "appetites"—for some reason a dirty word for them) and to fulfill a majestic public purpose.

It would be quite unjust to accuse them of seeking to impose upon us a uniform tyranny. They wanted to maintain a variety of goods and services (provided profits were excluded), and the whole structure was to be democratically controlled through numberless channels by the "organized" and "informed" criticism of consumers. Yet somehow we doubt their democratic protestations. We note their rapturous submission to the Soviet Union, which forcibly suggests that their devotion to the machinery was far greater than to the democratic spirit that was supposed to inform it. We also note tones of voice, turns of phrase, and manners of speech. Beatrice Webb regarded elections as a device to get the "conscious consent" of the governed. Local government is for Laski merely "educative"—that is, the citizens are there to be instructed, not to control their so-called servants. He quotes with approval Sir Arthur Salter's pompous dictum that "committees are an invaluable instrument for breaking administrative measures onto the back of the public." And Laski is everywhere vexed and alarmed by the possibility that socialist plans might be reversed "by some chance hazard of electoral fortune." At one stage he therefore thought it proper to demand of the Tories, as a condition of their return to office, a pledge that they would repeal no socialist measures.

Nowhere here can we find any genuine respect for democracy. Moreover, throughout the outpourings of all these intellectuals runs an obsession with war and the supposed achievements of arbitrary wartime governments, with their direction of labor, capital, and materials—an obsession particularly ludicrous in people so ovine and unwarlike, and an obsession certainly inimical to democracy and freedom. We find over and over again, particularly in the work of Sir William Beveridge, a socialist in all but name, the view that freedom is a peacetime luxury that we can no longer afford even in peacetime, in which as in war the economy must be directed by what he typically describes as an economic general staff. Those who have actually served in any kind of armed forces are normally less respectful of the extreme efficiency of military methods.

Tawney is more of a democrat, but a peculiarly hectoring one. He is forever demanding that citizens *must* "participate" in committees and industrial boards and local governments and so forth; he considers it not merely a right but also a duty incumbent on us all to be "concerned, self-educated and active." This is a false conception of liberty, a gross invasion of the right to privacy, which indeed is always one of the goods to be "socialized"—that is, destroyed.

Why on earth should we "participate" in all these activities, to many of us profoundly tedious? Why should Evelyn Waugh, say, or

Stravinsky (or even Tawney himself, did he not wish to) bother himself about municipal buses, bakeries, housing, and sewage? We may not think ourselves qualified to meddle with such matters. We may not wish to obtain the qualifications. We may think we have more important things to do, a concept presumably incomprehensible to Tawney, who defined citizenship for the scholar as "knowledge applied to social improvement." No classical scholar, for instance, could by this definition be a citizen.

Yet indeed with the establishment of all the institutions proposed by people like the Webbs, Laski, and Tawney, it might seem to the rest of us at once impossible *and* desperately important to participate in all of them, to prevent them from being dominated by people like the Webbs, Laski, and Tawney, and by all the hordes of qualified scientific socialist experts favored by them, to whom of course these institutions would be infinitely congenial. There would exist what was described by Orwell, quoted above: "a state of affairs in which such vocal socialists would feel thoroughly at home"—yes, indeed, and they alone; for the rest of us would be excluded, by our own decision if not by that of the vocal socialists themselves.

To the vast extent that our economy has been removed from the private to the public sector, we already suffer from a stagnant tyranny of busybodies and bureaucrats. This again was not the Webbs' ideal. One motive force in particular is missing, and that is the supposedly tremendous power of organized consumer criticism to maintain and increase efficiency and to ensure that new processes are promptly introduced and new needs met. Pitiful organs to this end do exist in the ineffective representation of "consumers" on national boards and in Parliament, which is, of course, as the Webbs recognized, totally incapable of controlling the vast and complex functions that it has arrogated to itself. But the Webbs' vast machinery at present lacks the powerful motor and controls they thus devised for it. Would it not go better if consumer wants could be made known?

How could they be? The Webbs envisaged that you and I, or they (it matters not) should collectively as consumers make known what we want and make sure that we get it. At the moment we do this without fuss or palaver, by buying this but not that, by shopping not here but there. Is it seriously suggested that we should turn up in endless tedious committees to argue our preference for New Zealand butter and French burgundy over French butter and Australian burgundy? Perhaps not; more sensible to delegate our choice to some elected manager. But he is only answerable to us as a *mass*. He need not bother about individual or minority preferences; he is not bound to us by the nexus of profit and loss; if he pleases ten, he can afford to ignore nine with impunity.

But so far we deal only with existing wants and known preferences. When we get on to new processes for satisfying existing wants, the difficulties multiply; how am I to know of such processes? Experts may advise me, but experts are notoriously indifferent to considerations of cost; like the Webbs themselves, they tend to prefer the best *technically* to the best *economically,* and to exaggerate the importance of maximum output irrespective of cost.

And when we get on to new wants, what we don't yet want but shall want when we see it, the difficulties multiply at a compound rate. How can I be concerned or active about what I cannot envisage? How can I expect committees and experts to be concerned and active on my behalf? Why should they be? Their life is easier if novelty is suppressed, and no more profitable if it is not.

Like other intellectuals, the Webbs, Laski, and the rest seem wholly incapable of grasping the role of risk-taking and profit- or loss-making in the maintenance of economic efficiency and above all in innovation. If they could have grasped it, they would never have proposed to substitute for it, magically simple and infinitely complex as it is, their foothills and mountain ranges of boards and committees, their swarming hives of bureaucrats and busybodies and experts, their snowstorms of paper, their echoing wastes of gassing and boredom, their pandemonium of ceaseless but sterile controversy.

"We find," wrote de Tocqueville, "an administration almost as numerous as the population, preponderant, interfering, regulating, restricting, insisting upon foreseeing everything, controlling everything, and understanding the interests of those under its control better than they do themselves; in short, in a constant state of barren activity...."

He was writing of French Canada under the *ancien régime.* He might have been writing either of the Webbs' Utopia or of Britain today. In St. Paul's Cathedral, you may find Sir Christopher Wren's tremendous epitaph: *"Si monumentum requiris, circumspice"* (If you seek his monument, look around you). If you seek the Webbs' monument, come to Britain today.

THE CAST

Beveridge, William Henry (1879–1963) was director of the London School of Economics and Political Science from 1919 to 1937, and afterward master of University College, Oxford. Active as a progressive publicist and in government ministries, his wartime report, *Social Insurance and Allied Services* (1942), set down the framework for the postwar welfare state. Beveridge wrote a number of other books, including *Planning Under Socialism* (1936) and *Full Employment in a Free Society* (1944), an influential economic treatise. In 1946 he was made Baron of Tuggal.

Crosland, Anthony (1918–77), who served as Foreign Secretary in the Callaghan government, held many high positions in Labour administrations, among them President of the Board of Trade and Secretary of State for the Environment. Crosland, who taught economics at Trinity College, Oxford, and who was chairman of the Fabian Society, was considered to be one of the most flexible and undoctrinaire leaders of the Labour Party. In *The Future of Socialism* (1956), he outraged the party's "left wing" by arguing against wholesale nationalization, occasionally praising capitalism and market economics, and suggesting that the party was tied too exclusively to the working class. His other books include *Britain's Economic Problem* (1953), *The Conservative Enemy* (1962), and *Socialism Now and Other Essays* (1974).

Johnson, Hewlett (1874–1966), Dean of Canterbury from 1931 to 1963, was known as the "Red Dean" for his frank Communist sympathies. His many books include *Soviet Success* (1947), *China's New Creative Age* (1953), and *The Upsurge of China* (1961). In 1939, after the Soviet Union concluded its nonaggression pact with Germany, Johnson was quoted as saying: "Communism has recovered the essential form of a real belief in God which organized Christianity, as it is now, has so largely lost." He was awarded the Stalin Peace Prize in 1951.

Laski, Harold J. (1893–1950), one of the great theorists of the Fabian Society and the Labour Party, and professor of political science at the London School of Economics from 1926 until his death. Particularly in the 1930s, Laski was strongly influenced by Marxist theory, and saw socialism as the only alternative to fascism, but he wanted to adapt Marxism to Britain's liberal political tradition. He wrote many books, including *Reflections on the Revolution of Our Time*, which was self-consciously patterned after the *Reflections* of Edmund Burke, a man Laski admired. Laski was also deeply interested in the United States; as a young man he taught at Harvard and developed close friendships with Oliver Wendell Holmes, Louis Brandeis, and Felix Frankfurter. Many observers consider Laski's most interesting writing to be his correspondence with Holmes.

Strachey, John (1901–63) was son of the Conservative editor of *The Spectator*, but entered Parliament in 1929 as a follower of radical Labourite Sir Oswald Mosley. In 1931 he left the Labour Party with Mosley, but the two quickly diverged as Mosley became a Fascist and Strachey a Communist in all but party affiliation. Throughout the thirties Strachey wrote a number of Marxist works, including *The Coming Struggle for Power* (1932) and *What Are We to Do?* (1938), intentionally modeled on Lenin's alarum. After the Soviet-Nazi collaboration, Strachey moved away from the Communists; he joined the first postwar Labour government as Food Minister, a post in which he gained a reputation for austerity, and later as War Minister. In 1939 he founded the Left Book Club with Laski and Victor Gollancz.

Tawney, Richard Henry (1880–1962) was an economic historian distinguished for his studies of Britain between 1540 and 1640 and of preindustrial China, as well as for his controversial reworking of the Weber thesis in *Religion and the Rise of Capitalism* (1926). A professor at the London School of Economics, Tawney was active in Labour politics, and he contributed two of the most important works to the canon of British socialist theory: *The Acquisitive Society* (1920) and *Equality* (1931).

Wallas, Graham (1852–1932), a political psychologist, taught at the London School of Economics and was later University Professor of Political Science at the University of London. He joined the Fabian Society in 1886, shortly after George Bernard Shaw founded it, but Wallas resigned in 1904 because he disapproved of Fabian support for tariffs. Wallas's five books include *The Life of Francis Place, Human Nature in Politics,* and *The Great Society* (1914).

Webb, Beatrice (1858–1943) and Webb, Sidney James (1859–1947), leaders of the Fabian Society, also founded *The New Statesman* and the London School of Economics and Political Science to help propagate and refine Fabian ideas. They were tireless researchers and wrote bulky histories of trade unionism and English local government, actually spending their 1892 honeymoon going through trade union records in Glasgow and Dublin. Sidney was active in the Labour Party, becoming President of the Board of Trade and Colonial Secretary; in 1929 he became Lord Passfield. Beatrice is celebrated for her *Minority Report* to the Royal Commission on the Poor, a paper that anticipated the Beveridge Report by thirty-five years. Until 1932 advocates of peaceful reform and of what they called "the inevitability of gradualness," the Webbs visited the Soviet Union that year and were sure they saw the future working. The question mark in the title of their 1935 book *Soviet Communism: A New Civilization?* was omitted from later editions.

Prepared by R. Emmett Tyrrell, Jr., to accompany "Intellectuals Have Consequences" in *The Future that Doesn't Work.*

P. T. Bauer

WESTERN GUILT AND THIRD WORLD POVERTY

Come, fix upon me that accusing eye.
I thirst for accusation.
                              —W.B. Yeats

I

The feeling of guilt has aptly been termed one of America's few remaining surplus commodities. Ubiquitous and repeated allegations that the West is responsible for the poverty of the so-called Third World both reflect and strengthen this feeling of guilt. Yet while such allegations have come to be widely accepted, often as axiomatic, they are not only untrue, but more nearly the opposite of the truth. Their acceptance has nevertheless paralyzed Western diplomacy, both toward the Soviet bloc and toward the Third World, where the West has abased itself before countries which have negligible resources and no real power.

The feeling of guilt toward the Third World has been reinforced by political, emotional, and financial interests. It often goes together with condescension and contempt toward the people of the Third World. On the other hand, it is unaccompanied by a sense of responsibility for the results of the policies it itself inspires—policies which have ironically obstructed development in the Third World, and have contributed to intense and widespread suffering in many parts of it.

Allegations of Western responsibility are usually expressed vaguely and their ostensible grounds shift. But the general thrust is unequivocal.

It is a persistent theme in the United Nations and its numerous affiliates. It is expressed virulently by spokesmen from the Third World and the Communist bloc, and is often endorsed by representatives of the West, especially of the United States. It is sounded continually in the universities, in the churches, and in the media.

Peter Townsend, for example, perhaps the most prominent British writer on poverty, asserts in his much-acclaimed book, *The Concept of Poverty*:

I argued that poverty of deprived nations is comprehensible only if we attribute it substantially to the existence of a system of international social stratification, a hierarchy of societies with vastly different resources in which the wealth of some is linked historically and contemporaneously to the poverty of others. This system operated crudely in the era of colonial domination, and continues to operate today, though more subtly, through systems of trade, education, political relations, military alliances, and industrial corporations.

So too, the late Paul A. Baran of Stanford argues in another widely-used text, *The Political Economy of Growth:* "To the dead weight of stagnation characteristic of pre-industrial society was added the entire restrictive impact of monopoly capitalism. The economic surplus appropriated in lavish amounts by monopolistic concerns in backward countries is not employed for productive purposes. It is neither plowed back into their own enterprises nor does it serve to develop others."

And finally—though of course examples could easily be multiplied[1]—we have the late Dr. Nkrumah, Prime Minister and President of Ghana, perhaps one of the most influential African politicians since World War II, who declares in *Africa Must Unite:*

Thus all the imperialists, without exception, evolved the means, their colonial policies, to satisfy the ends, the exploitation of the subject territories, for the aggrandizement of the metropolitan countries. They were all rapacious; they all subserved the needs of the subject lands to their own demands; they all circumscribed human rights and liberties; they all repressed and despoiled, degraded and oppressed. They took our lands, our lives, our resources and our dignity. Without exception, they left us nothing but our resentment. It was when they had gone and we were faced with the stark realities, as in Ghana on the morrow of our independence, that the destitution of the land after long years of colonial rule was brought sharply home to us.

All these allegations are either misleading or untrue. Thus Professor Townsend cannot be right in saying that the backwardness of poor countries is explicable only in terms of an international social stratification or of colonial domination: the poorest and most backward countries have until recently had no external economic contacts and often have never been Western colonies. Baran's statement is again obviously and wholly untrue since throughout the Third World large agricultural, commercial, and industrial complexes have been built up through profits reinvested locally. Nor does Nkrumah's statement bear much relation to reality. For example, before colonial rule there was not a single cocoa tree in the Gold Coast (Ghana); when colonial rule ended, cocoa exports, entirely from African-owned and operated farms, totaled hundreds of thousands of tons annually—and this was the case with external trade in general.

II

So far from the West having caused the poverty of the Third World, contact with the West has been the principal agent of material progress there. Indeed, the very idea of material progress is Western, especially in the sense of a constant and steadily increasing control over man's environment. People in the Third World did not think in these terms until the arrival of Western man. The materially most advanced societies and regions of the Third World are those with which the West established the most numerous, diversified, and extensive contacts: the cash-crop-producing areas and *entrepôt* ports of Southeast Asia, West Africa, and Latin America; the mineral-producing areas of Africa and the Middle East; and cities and ports throughout Asia, Africa, the Caribbean, and Latin America. The level of material achievement usually diminishes as one moves away from the foci of Western impact: the poorest and most backward are the populations with few or no external contacts, the aborigines being the limiting case.

All this is neither new nor surprising, since the spread of material progress from more to less advanced regions is familiar from economic history. The West was far ahead of the present Third World when it established contact with these regions in recent centuries. It was through these contacts that human and material resources, skills, capital, and new ideas—including the idea of material progress itself— flowed from the West to the Third World.

This process is especially evident in Black Africa. All the foundations and ingredients of modern social and economic life present there today were brought by Westerners, almost entirely during the colonial era. This is true of such fundamentals as public security and law and order; wheeled traffic (sub-Saharan Africa never invented the wheel); mechanized transport (transport powered by steam or gasoline instead of muscle—almost entirely human muscle in Black Africa); roads, railways, and man-made ports; modern forms of money (instead of barter or commodity money, such as cowrie shells, iron bars, or bottles of gin); the application of science and technology to economic activity; towns with substantial buildings, water, and sewerage; public health and hospitals and the control of endemic and epidemic diseases; and formal education.[2]

In short, over the last hundred years or so, contact with the West has transformed large parts of the Third World for the better. Southeast Asia and West Africa provide well-documented examples. For instance, in the 1890s Malaya was a sparsely populated area of hamlets and fishing villages. By the 1930s it had become a country with populous cities, thriving commerce, and an excellent system of roads, primarily thanks to the rubber industry brought there and developed by the British. Again, before the 1890s there was no cocoa production in what is now Ghana and Nigeria, no exports of peanuts or cotton, and relatively small exports of palm oil and palm kernels. These are by now staples of world commerce, all produced by Africans, but originally made possible by European activities. Imports, both of capital goods and of mass consumer goods designed for African use, also rose from negligible amounts at the end of the nineteenth century to huge volumes by the 1950s. These far-reaching changes are reflected in statistics of government revenues, literacy rates, school attendance, public health, infant mortality, and many other indicators, such as the ownership of automobiles and other consumer durables.

Western activities—supplemented at times by the activities of non-Western immigrants, notably Chinese, Indians, and Levantines, whose large-scale migration was, however, made possible by Western initiative—have thus led to major improvements in the material conditions of life in many parts of the Third World. This is not to suggest that there has been significant material progress everywhere in the Third World. Over large areas there have been few contacts with the West. And even where such contacts have been established, the personal, social, and political determinants of economic performance have often proved unfavorable to material advance. But wherever local conditions permitted, contact with the West most often resulted in the elimination of the worst epidemic and endemic diseases, the mitigation or disappearance of famines, and a general improvement in the material standard of living for all.

III

Many of the assertions concerning Western responsibility for poverty in the Third World express or reflect the belief that the prosperity of relatively well-to-do persons, groups, and societies is always achieved at the expense of the less well-off—i.e., that incomes are not generated by those who earn them, but are somehow extracted from others, so that economic activity is akin to a zero-sum game, in which the gains of some are always balanced by the losses of others. In fact, incomes (other than subsidies) are earned by the recipients for resources and services supplied, and are not acquired by depriving others of what they had.

The notion that incomes are extracted rather than earned has been among the most disastrous of popular economic misconceptions or delusions. It has, however, served the purposes of those who expect to benefit from the maltreatment of other people—through, for example, the expropriation or even destruction of relatively prosperous minorities. The notion has been used by medieval rulers and modern demagogues alike, and their victims range from medieval Jewish communities to the ethnic minorities of contemporary Asia and Africa. In Asia and Africa it is widely regarded as axiomatic that poverty reflects exploitation by foreigners, including ethnic minorities who have risen from poverty to prosperity. This belief is encouraged assiduously by local politicians, especially those who promised that political independence under their auspices would herald material prosperity, and is often propagated as well by other influential local groups who also expect to benefit from policies inspired by these ideas.

In recent decades the effectiveness of the notion that incomes are extracted rather than generated has been extended and reinforced by two streams of influence whose operation in this area has been cumulative. The first is Marxist-Leninist ideology, and the second is the spurious belief that the capacities and motivations of people are the same the world over.

In Marxist-Leninist ideology any return on private capital implies exploitation, and service industries are regarded as unproductive. Thus, earnings of foreign capital and the incomes of foreigners or ethnic minorities in the service industries become forms of exploitation. Further, neo-Marxist literature has extended the concept of the proletariat—which in this scheme of things is poor because it is exploited—to the peoples of the Third World (most of whom are in fact small-scale cultivators).

The notion that all individuals and societies are basically alike has also promoted the belief that Western prosperity has been achieved at the expense of the Third World. For if human aptitudes and motivations are substantially the same everywhere and yet some societies are richer than others, then the more prosperous must have oppressed and exploited the rest.

IV

But if the idea that incomes and property are extracted rather than earned is the principal assumption behind the notion of Western responsibility, a number of more specific contentions and suggestions are also heard. Most of these are in effect variants or derivations of the main theme, geared to particular audiences. Perhaps the leading such variant is the argument that the poverty of Asia and Africa can be attributed to colonialism. This idea is axiomatic in much of the Third World and in publications of the UN and its affiliates, and it has great appeal in the United States.

According to General Principle XIV of the first United Nations Conference for Trade and Development (UNCTAD): "The liquidation of the remnants of colonialism in all its forms is a necessary condition of economic development." This passage (which would not have been acceptable to Marx) reflects the Leninist doctrine under which colonialism is by definition exploitative. Leninist doctrine is reflected also in the phrase, "colonialism in all its forms"—a covert reference to foreign investment, which in Leninist ideology is itself a species of external exploitation.

Whatever one thinks of colonialism, however, it is certainly not incompatible with economic development. Some of the richest countries were formerly colonies and were even as colonies already very prosperous (North America, Australia). As I have already stressed, many of the African and Asian colonies of the European powers progressed very rapidly during colonial rule, usually much more so than the independent countries in the same area. And at present one of the few remaining European colonies is Hong Kong. Conversely, some of the materially most backward countries in the world never were colonies (Afghanistan, Tibet, Nepal, Liberia). Ethiopia is perhaps an even more telling example, though it was an Italian colony for a very brief period (six years) in its long history.

The manifest untruth that colonial status must imply poverty, stagnation, and exploitation is sometimes camouflaged by suggestions that without colonialism the peoples of the colonial territories would have created nation states, or developed their own industries, or undertaken economic planning. Yet it is purely fanciful to imagine that such policies would or could have been pursued by the tribal chiefs or local rajahs or sultans who were replaced by colonial governments. And even if they had, such policies would not necessarily have made for progress. Indeed, state subsidies to particular activities or centralized control of economic activity are more likely to perpetuate poverty than to relieve it.

The terms economic colonialism and neo-colonialism have sprung up recently to describe almost any form of economic relation between relatively rich and poor countries, regions, or groups. This terminology confuses poverty with colonial status, a concept which has always been understood to mean lack of political sovereignty. Since the late 1960s, the usage has been extended to cover the activities of multinational corporations in the Third World. In fact, these activities have promoted progress in poor countries by expanding opportunities and raising incomes and government revenues. Thus not only does the new terminology reflect a debasement of language; it also distorts the truth.

The decline of particular economic activities—e.g., the Indian textile industry of the eighteenth century—as a result of competition from cheap imports is sometimes instanced as an example of Western responsibility. This argument identifies the decline of one activity with the decline of the economy as a whole. But except under most peculiar conditions, rarely specified in this context, cheap imports extend the range of choice and of economic opportunities of people in poor countries. These imports are usually accompanied by the development and expansion of other activities: if this were not so, the population would be unable to pay.

V

According to another set of allegations, the West damages the Third World by manipulating the terms of trade so that these are unfavorable to the latter and also deteriorate persistently. This is alleged to have contributed to a decline in the share of the Third World in international trade. A related form of damage is said to be the indebtedness inflicted on the Third World by the West. These allegations are again fictitious, untrue, or irrelevant.

To begin with, the diversity of trading patterns within the Third World renders the aggregation of their terms of trade largely meaningless because the terms of trade of particular Third World countries and groups can move differently and even in opposite directions (the experience of the OPEC countries against other Third World countries is only a recent and familiar example). And except over very short periods, changes in the terms of trade as conventionally measured are of little welfare significance without reference to changes in the cost of production of exports, the range and quality of imports, and the volume of trade.

Insofar as changes in the terms of trade do affect development and welfare, what matters is the amount of imports which can be purchased with a unit of domestic resources, and this cannot be inferred from the ratio of import and export prices. (In technical language, the comparisons relevant to economic welfare and development are the factoral terms of trade and not the crude commodity terms.) Further, expressions such as unfavorable terms of trade are meaningless except by reference to a base period. In recent decades, however, even the crude commodity terms of trade of Third World countries have been exceptionally favorable. When changes in the cost of production, the great improvement in the range and quality of imports, and the huge increase in the volume of trade are taken into account, the external purchasing power of the exports of the Third World in the aggregate is now very favorable, probably more so than ever before. This in turn has made it easier for governments to retain a larger proportion of export earnings through major increases in royalty rates, export taxes, and corporation taxes.[3]

But the terms of trade are in any case irrelevant to the basic causes of Third World poverty. This is obvious, for instance, from the material backwardness of societies and countries with little or no external trade. Changes in the share of the Third World in international trade are also irrelevant to its poverty. A reduction in the share of a country or group of countries in global trade has by itself no adverse economic implications because it often reflects the expansion of economic activity and trade elsewhere, which normally does not damage but benefits those whose relative share has declined. For instance, since the 1950s the large increase in the foreign trade of Japan, the reconstruction of Europe, and the liberalization of intra-European trade have brought about a decline in the share of other groups in world trade, including that of the United States and the United Kingdom. Furthermore, domestic developments and policies unrelated to external circumstances—such as increased domestic use of previously exported products, or domestic inflation, or special taxation of exporters, or the intensification of protectionist policies—frequently reduce the share of a country or group of countries in world trade. (As an aside, I may note that in recent decades the share of the Third World in total world trade has increased and not decreased, notably so since before World War I.)

So far as indebtedness is concerned, the external debts of the Third World reflect resources supplied to it. Indeed, the bulk of the current indebtedness of Third World governments consists of soft loans, often very soft loans, under various aid agreements, frequently supplemented by outright grants. With the worldwide rise in prices, including those of exports of Third World countries, the cost even of these soft loans has diminished greatly. If governments cannot service such soft loans, this reflects either wasteful use of the capital supplied or inappropriate monetary or fiscal policies. It is worth remembering that in the course of their development many rich countries relied extensively on external loans, and hard loans at that.

Nor do persistent deficits in the balance of payments of many Third World countries mean that they are being impoverished by the West. Such deficits are inevitable if the government of a country, whether rich or poor, advancing or stagnating, lives beyond its resources and pursues inflationary policies while attempting to maintain overvalued exchange rates.

It is paradoxical to suggest that external economic relations are damaging to development. They normally benefit people by opening up markets for exports, and by providing a large and diverse source of imports, besides acting as channels for the flow of human and financial resources and for new ideas, methods, and crops. Because of the vast expansion of world trade in recent decades and the development of technology in the West, the material advantages from external contacts are now greater than ever before. The suggestion that these relations are detrimental is not only unfounded but also damaging, because it serves as a specious justification for official restrictions on their volume or diversity.

VI

Yet another batch of arguments holds that the mere presence of the West and the day-to-day activities of its peoples are in themselves harmful to the Third World. One form of such damage is said to derive from the so-called international demonstration effect, brought about by the new availability of cheap consumer goods supplied by the West. This availability supposedly obstructs the material progress of the Third World by encouraging spending there, an argument which of course completely disregards the level of consumption and the extension of choice as criteria of development. Yet these are what

economic development is about. The notion of a damaging international demonstration effect also ignores the role of external contacts as
an instrument of development; it overlooks the fact that the new
consumer goods have to be paid for, which usually requires improved
economic performance, such as more work, additional saving and
investment, and readiness to produce for sale. In short, it overlooks the
obvious consideration that a higher and more varied level of
consumption is both the principal justification (or even the meaning) of
material progress, and also an inducement to further economic
advance.[4]

An updated version of the international demonstration effect
proposes that the eager acceptance of Western consumer goods in the
Third World is a form of cultural dependence engendered by Western
business. (Rather paradoxically this charge is often accompanied by
allegations of the damage to the Third World done by Western patents,
which are said to obstruct the spread of technology.) The implication
here is that the peoples of the Third World have no independent minds,
that they are manipulated at will by foreigners. In fact, however,
Western goods have been selectively and not indiscriminately accepted
in the Third World and have been of massive benefit to millions of
people there.

As was to be expected, allegedly lavish consumption habits and the
pollution of the environment in the West have also been pressed into
ideological service. A standard formulation is that per-capita consumption of food and energy in the U.S. is many times that in India, so that
the American consumer despoils his Indian opposite number on a large
scale—or even, according to Professor René Dumont, is guilty of a kind
of cannibalism (for "in over-consuming meat which wasted the cereals
which could have saved them, we ate the little children of the Sahel, of
Ethiopia, and of Bangladesh"). Apart from everything else, such
formulations fail to note that per-capita production in America exceeds
production in India more than the difference in consumption, allowing
it not only to pay for this consumption, but also to finance domestic and
foreign investment, as well as foreign aid.

The so-called brain drain, the migration of qualified personnel from
the Third World to the West, is again influentially canvassed as an
instance of Western responsibility for poverty in the less-developed
countries. This is a somewhat more complex issue, but it certainly does
not substantiate the charge it is meant to support. As an adverse factor
in Third World development, the voluntary departure of formally
trained people seeking to improve their condition is almost certainly
less important than the enforced exodus of highly educated people and

of others with commercial and administrative skills, or the discrimination of Third World governments against ethnic minorities who remain, or their refusal to employ foreigners. Indeed, many voluntary emigrants leave because their own governments cannot or will not use their services—and not only when they belong to ethnic minorities. Thus their departure does not deprive the society of resources which are productive at present or in the foreseeable future.

Finally, there is the allegation that the West has damaged the Third World by ethnic discrimination. Yet the very countries in which such discrimination occurred were those where material progress was initiated or promoted by contact with the West. The most backward groups in the Third World (aborigines, desert peoples, nomads, and other tribesfolk) were quite unaffected by ethnic discrimination on the part of Europeans, whereas many communities against which discrimination was often practiced—Chinese in Southeast Asia, Indians in parts of Southeast Asia, Asians in Africa, and others—made great material strides forward. In any case, discrimination on the basis of color or race is not a European invention but has been endemic in much of Africa and Asia, notably so in India, for many centuries or even millennia.

VII

The West may indeed be said to have contributed to the poverty of the Third World in two senses. But these differ radically from the familiar arguments.

The changes which have come about in much of the Third World through contact with the West have resulted in a significant decline in mortality and a corresponding increase in life expectation. Many more people survive in the Third World as a result of Western contacts and activities, which means that many more poor people are alive. But this Western contribution to poverty reflects an improvement not a deterioration, since people prefer to survive and to see their children survive. This improvement is obscured in conventional national income statistics as these do not register health, life expectation and the possession of children as components of welfare.

A second sense in which the West may be said to have contributed to the poverty of the Third World is through the politicization of social and economic life—that is, through the tendency to make everything a matter of politics. Thus in the terminal years of British rule extensive and pervasive state economic controls came to be introduced to the colonies, such as widespread licensing of economic activity, and state trading monopolies, including state monopolies over agricultural exports. This last measure was particularly important because it enabled the government to exert direct control over the livelihood of producers, and it has also served as a major source of government finance and patronage. In most British colonies, especially in Africa and in Burma, the ready-made framework of a *dirigiste* or even totalitarian state was handed over to the incoming independent governments.

Inefficient allocation of resources is a familiar result of state controls. Less familiar but more important results of these controls are restrictions on the movement of people between jobs and places, and also on the volume, diversity, and local dispersion of external contacts which are of special significance for the progress of poor countries. Still more important is the exacerbation of social and political tensions. The question of who runs the government has become paramount in many Third World countries, and is often a matter of life and death for millions of people. This is especially so in multiracial societies, like those of much of Asia and Africa. In such a situation the energies and resources of people, particularly the most ambitious and energetic, are diverted from economic activity to political life, partly from choice and partly from necessity. Foreign aid has also contributed substantially to the politicization of life in the Third World. It augments the resources of governments as compared to the private sector; and the criteria of allocation tend to favor governments trying to establish state controls.

Many Third World governments would presumably have attempted such policies even without colonial rule or foreign aid, probably with the help of international organizations. But they could hardly have succeeded without the examples set by colonial governments or the personnel and money provided by Western aid or by international organizations, which in turn are financed largely by the West. Yet far from deploring these policies, the most vocal and influential critics of colonial rule and Western influence, both in the West itself and in the Third World, have usually urged their adoption and extension and have blamed Western governments for not having pursued them sooner and more vigorously.

VIII

I have already indicated my belief that it is the feeling of guilt over material prosperity which accounts for the widespread promotion and acceptance of the bizarre and insubstantial arguments on which allegations of Western responsibility for poverty in the Third World are based. A striking example of much Anglo-Saxon sentiment in this area is an article by the late Cyril Connolly published several years ago in the London *Sunday Times* under the title "Black Man's Burden." Connolly writes:

There is not a single country of which we can truthfully say that its occupation by a European power did it more good than harm.... It is a wonder that the white man is not more thoroughly detested than he is.... In our dealings with every single country, greed, masked by hypocrisy, led to unscrupulous coercion of the native inhabitants and worse, the culture and civilization which we brought was rotten to the core.... Cruelty, greed, uncertainty, and arrogance—the affectation of superiority exemplified by the color bar characterized what can be summed up in one word: exploitation.... We are to blame (I say we for nearly everyone has had some family connection with India, Africa, or the Far East).

This statement by a prominent intellectual is both ludicrous and characteristic. Actually only a tiny fraction of the British population ever had such contacts, and only a fraction of that fraction in any way misconducted itself toward the Third World. The article regards the population of Africa and Asia as much of a muchness ("the black man"), a treatment which is repugnant to millions of people both in the Third World and in the West, and especially so to the great majority of Indians, Chinese, and Arabs. The passage also suggests that incomes are extracted and not earned. And it well expresses the conception of collective guilt which has replaced individual sin in these discussions, thereby exonerating any single identifiable person of responsibility for immoral behavior.

Such feelings help to explain why Western governments support and endorse nonsensical, groundless, and offensive statements by leading Third World politicians, and why the West so often abases itself before governments (usually unrepresentative governments) whose countries are often sparsely populated by relatively small numbers of materially very backward people. It is sometimes suggested that such postures are necessary to keep the Third World outside the Soviet orbit. But with very few and rather doubtful exceptions, these stances have been counter-productive, and have not served the interests of Western political or military strategy (assuming that such a strategy exists). The references to political objectives are unconvincing ex-post-facto rationalizations of anomalous and baffling policies.

IX

But it is not only an unfounded sense of guilt which is reflected in these policies. There is also condescension or even contempt. Economic conditions in the Third World are thought to reflect Western exploitation, compounded by current Western consumption habits, while its economic future supposedly depends on Western aid. Thus it is we and not they who, it is assumed, will largely determine what happens to these societies.

The image of the Third World as a uniform, stagnant mass devoid of distinctive character is another aspect of the same condescension or contempt. The stereotype denies identity, character, personality, and responsibility to the societies and individuals of the so-called Third World. When a distinct independent culture and set of values are recognized, they are often condemned, and their enforced removal is proposed on the ground that they obstruct material progress. For instance, compulsory transformation of man and society is a major theme of Gunnar Myrdal's *Asian Drama*.

The most brutal maltreatment of minorities and the most extensive official discrimination on the basis of color, race, or religion in the Third World are often excused by saying that they have been inspired by the West. In fact, colonial governments have usually protected the minorities and not persecuted them; and discrimination long antedates colonialism. The view that these policies and attitudes have been inspired by the West implies again that the peoples of the Third World have no will or identity of their own and are simply creatures of the West.

Toleration or even support of the brutal policies of many Third World governments, then, seems to reflect a curious mixture of guilt feelings and condescension. Third World governments are not really guilty because they only follow examples set by the West. Moreover, like children, they are not altogether responsible for what they do. In any case, we must support them to atone for alleged wrongs, which our supposed ancestors perpetrated on their supposed ancestors. And economic aid is also necessary to help the children grow up. Similarly, the most offensive and baseless utterances of Third World spokesmen need not be taken seriously, because they are only Third World statements (a license which has been extended to their supporters in the West).

The truth, however, is that the so-called Third World is a vast and diverse collection of societies differing widely in religion, culture, social institutions, personal characteristics and motivations, political arrangements, economic attitudes, material achievement, rates of progress, and many other respects. It is a travesty and not a useful simplification to lump together Chinese merchants of Southeast Asia, Indonesian peasants, Indian villagers, tribal societies of Africa, oil-rich Arabs of the Middle East, aborigines and desert peoples, inhabitants of huge cities in India, Africa, and Latin America—to envisage them all as a low-level uniform mass, a collectivity which moreover is regarded as no more than a copy of Western man, only poorer, and with even this difference the result only of Western responsibility.

The adoption of this stereotype and of the misleading terminology has been made easier by the lack of first-hand public knowledge of conditions in the Third World. Few people in the West know these countries, let alone the diverse policies pursued in them.

Yet had this travesty not suited certain influential interests in the West, it might never have succeeded in establishing itself. These interests have ranged from the churches seeking a new role for themselves to exporters seeking sheltered markets. Two categories may have been specially effective: the personnel and associates of the international organizations, and various disaffected groups who have come to dislike or even hate Western society.

Since World War II the people who work in one way or another for international organizations have come increasingly to consider themselves as agents and representatives of the Third World, a stance which has often suited their political, professional, and personal interests. They have helped to weld together at least superficially the representatives of extremely diverse, conflicting, or even bitterly hostile societies and countries into a bloc, united only by politically and materially profitable enmity to the West. This was achieved by preparing briefs for Third World spokesmen, by organizing meetings for the formulation of positions at international gatherings, and by other similar measures. The ideologies of the Third World and of the United Nations and its associated agencies have become largely interchangeable.

As to the second group—made up of people in the West who are sufficiently disillusioned with their own society to have become disaffected from or even hostile to it—some of them see the Third World as a useful instrument for promoting their cause in what is in essence a civil conflict in the West. The poverty of many Third World countries makes them more akin to instruments than independent allies. But whether as instruments or allies, their usefulness is enhanced if they are regarded as a homogeneous, undifferentiated mass or brotherhood united in opposition to the West.

X

Policies and activities promoted by a sense of guilt and by attitudes and interests related to it do not usually promote the welfare of the people they are supposed to help. Appeasement of guilt has nothing to do with a sense of responsibility. In the present context this is evident in the lack of concern with the conduct of governments which receive economic aid, or with the results of policies ostensibly inspired by humanitarian motives.

Thus the West supports governments whose domestic policies impoverish their own peoples and often inflict extreme hardship both on ethnic minorities and on the indigenous population. President Amin's massive and explicit persecution and expulsion of Asians is only one of many instances. Another is Tanzania (Mr. McNamara's favorite African country, as it has rightly been called) which receives large-scale Western aid while it forcibly herds millions of people into collectivized villages, often destroying their households to make them move.[5] Western aid has conferred respectability on governments like these and helped them conceal temporarily from their own people the economic consequences of their policies.

Commodity agreements for primary products present another anomaly. They are proposed and implemented ostensibly to relieve Third World poverty. Yet these arrangements raise the cost of living in an inflationary world; they benefit the most prosperous countries and groups in the Third World, including expatriates living there; they often benefit Western exporters of the same products or their close substitutes (many rich countries are net exporters of primary products); they provoke political tensions within the exporting countries as well as between them; and they greatly damage some of the poorest groups in many Third World countries, especially people who are barred from producing the controlled products in order to raise their prices. Yet they continue to be advocated and established because any measure which appears to represent a transfer of resources to Third World governments automatically finds favor.

It would be a delusion to believe that the reasoning and evidence produced here, even if accepted as valid, could substantially influence the attitudes of those afflicted by a feeling of guilt or who profit from it, let alone modify the policies which it inspires. Argument and evidence will not affect conduct and measures which are rooted in emotion, often reinforced by the play of personal and political interests. Moreover, the costs and sacrifices of policies inspired by such feelings are rarely borne by those who so warmly advocate their imposition. They are borne instead by ordinary people, mostly of the Third World, who will go on being harmed so long as such feelings, ideas, and policies continue to hold sway.

3
Sexual Equality

Midge Decter

THE LAST TRAIN TO NIHIL

Being a mother...remains, as we are to suppose it has ever been, an arduous undertaking. If it is no longer depleting of health and youth, it nevertheless does draw off great quantities of energy of another kind. If it no longer calls upon the capacity to wrest sheer survival, one's own and that of one's children, from a world abounding in danger and disease, it nevertheless does demand an often wearying kind of artfulness in controlling the daily circumstance of existence. One might therefore imagine—as so many of the movement's male sympathizers seem to do—that women's liberation is merely the latest avatar of an eternal complaint: life is too hard. And so imagining, one might further credit the movement—again, as so many of its sympathizers seem to do—with being merely the latest representation of the age-old aspiration to better the human lot.

But the case of women's liberation does not and cannot rest here—the liberationists themselves would be the first to agree. For in the critique of motherhood lies the very nub of the revolution this movement means to make. Nor is this revolution carelessly so named, despite the fact that we live in a time which has seen the most trivial shift in mood dubbed a "revolution." The movement's demand with respect to motherhood is not simply a demand for the recognition that the modern mother must face a peculiar and unprecedented set of difficulties and for the alteration of a certain number of institutions to help her meet them; it is a demand for nothing less than the radical alteration of nature itself. "Humanity," says Shulamith Firestone, "can no longer afford to remain in the transitional stage between simple animal existence and full control of nature. And we are much closer to a major evolutionary jump, indeed to direction of our own evolution, than we are to a return to the animal kingdom from which we came."[1] The "animal kingdom from which we came" is, of course, that imagined state of submission to brute biology, long ago departed, in which the creatures called humans dumbly and passively reproduced themselves according to the dictates of a blind and accidental nature. The transitional stage that Shulamith Firestone warns us humanity can no longer afford to remain caught in is our present condition—in which those forces which culture has and has not been able to put a hand to are locked in a sometimes uneasy, sometimes even downright hostile, contention. And the "major evolutionary jump"—which women's liberation both prescribes and claims that its very existence predicts—refers to a situation in which the reproduction of the species would cease to entail the necessity of motherhood at all.

This next step in human evolution is characterized variously, and is seen to proceed from a variety of measures, within the same general Liberationist purview. There are those among the movement's spokesmen who embrace the prospect of a world overturned beyond recognition by the continuing researches of the molecular biologists: a world, that is, in which new life might be created and genetically controlled by man-made means in a man-made environment—the so-called test-tube. In such a world women would not only not be pressed with the obligation to have babies, they would be proved an only haphazard and inferior medium for reproduction. Others of the movement's ideologues would content themselves with the somewhat less apocalyptic idea that a woman's specially defined role as mother is to cease after she has given birth. For these, only certain new institutions need be created in order to overturn the slavery that history has made of motherhood. These are the advocates of day-care centers or communal families, in which either the larger or the smaller society into whose domain a baby is born acknowledges the common "ownership" of its young and takes a common and general responsibility for their upbringing. There has, by the way, been a considerable amount of confusion on the question of day-care. The day-care centers of which women's liberation speaks are *not* the inexpensive alternative to individual baby-sitting envisaged by those currently pressing for a greater extension of social-welfare provisions to the working poor. The latter are meant to be only what their name implies, an aid to the working mother that will precisely enable her, while holding a full-time job, to remain a full-time responsible mother. The kind of day-care ideally being demanded by the movement would free every woman entirely from the arbitrary, one-sided responsibility for her children that women's liberation claims society has imposed upon her powerlessness. This kind of "day" care is to be extended aro clock, in homes, or communes, or children's centers, or whateve., to signify officially that the family as we have known it is no more. And in this way, says the movement, not only will women be freed, but children will be freed as well:

> While recognizing that day care is essential for women's liberation, the authors want the Movement to further recognize that day care is essential for the liberation of children. Group child care, in contrast to the more isolating private home environment, has the potential of providing an environment in which children will have more opportunity to develop social sensitivity and responsibility, emotional autonomy and trust, and a wider range of intellectual interests.[2]

Removing children from the overheating and pressure of the nuclear household serves most of all to protect them from the monstrous machine in whose toils they learn to assume the traditional roles assigned their respective sexes. For men and women are both to serve on the staff of the movement-designed day-care center—are both and equally, that is, to embody society's obligation to nurture the young. And so a generation of children may be created who will not automatically be able to associate the aggressive, striving character of work with men nor the tender, humbling ministrations of nurturance with women. The movement's preoccupation with day-care, in other words, is not linked to the need to supplement maternal care but linked rather to a desire to substitute for it a radically new social arrangement—an arrangement, moreover, whose primary virtue would be its capacity to breed what Caroline Bird has so approvingly called "the new androgyny."

Still other liberationists, presumably the least apocalyptic of all—speaking only in the language of a fairer sharing of the burden—mean not so much to remove women from motherhood as to introduce men to it. Such a view need not at first glance seem revolutionary at all, but only an extension of a development that had set in among us at least a generation ago with the Freudian-inspired idea that traditional paternal authority was mankind's major repressive force. The...marriage contract is the prototypical document of this arm of the movement, dividing minute by minute, breath by breath, as it were, between man and woman each and every one of those functions that together spell the daily obligations of mothering. Here again, the purpose served would be twofold: relief of the mother from her onerous and time-consuming job and the creation of a household culture in which maleness and femaleness would be indistinguishable.

Thus, despite what might appear to be a kind of sliding scale from radical to "moderate"—from the enthusiastic anticipation of the time when babies might be produced extra-uterinely, by and at the service of society as a whole, to the putatively equalitarian demand that men take on precisely half the performance of daily maternal duties—the entire movement in the end speaks with a single voice of its true underlying intention. And that is to create a world, or a culture, in which either literally or to all intents and purposes there would be no men and no women. "...the end goal of feminist revolution must be, unlike that of the first feminist movement, not just the elimination of male privilege but of the sex distinction itself: genital differences between human beings would no longer matter culturally."[3] Obviously, the world of test-tube babies is such a world: if there is no birth, there is no gender. Less obviously, but no less inevitably, a world in which mothers, by a mere and inconvenient quirk of biology, were but the vessels of pregnancy, in which motherhood and fatherhood bespoke essentially the same relation to the offspring of a mechanistically apportioned sexual congress, there would also be no gender—except in a sort of uniformly secondary sense of the term.

So with motherhood, as one might expect, women's liberation comes to the crux of its true grievance. Not that women are mistreated, discriminated against, oppressed, enslaved, but that they are—women. I say "as one might expect" because it is in their capacity as mothers that women face the absolute and bedrock of their otherwise finite and adjustable existence. The demands of women's liberation to reorder the workings of career, to renegotiate the terms of sex, and to redefine the basis of marriage might conceivably be taken as a sort of pressure for social melioration that so many of the movement's sympathizers, and some few members of the movement itself, profess them to be. But the demand no longer to be mothers—implied by the liberationist vision of a family that is not a family but a polymorphous mass, and specified outright in the liberationist notion that maternal connection is merely the product of a particular, and noxious, form of social organization— is a demand that goes beyond the basis of a program for altering existing institutions, or even attitudes, and reaches to the heart of what life itself imposes on mortal beings.

For women to claim that they are victims when they are so clearly not is merely an expression of their terror in the face of the harshnesses and burdens of a new and as yet not fully claimed freedom. Such a terror lies behind women's liberation's discussion of work; it is a response not to the experience of exclusion but to the discovery that the pursuit of career is but another form—in some ways more gratifying, in many ways far more bruising—of adult anguish. The equality demanded by the self-proclaimed victim is equality of attribution only: not to be, but to be *deemed*, equal—no matter what.

Similarly, for women to declare that they are female only because men have conspired to make them so is merely an expression of their refusal to confess how much they must depend on others—and, in so confessing, to acknowledge how great is their obligation to others. Such a refusal, precisely, is what lies behind women's liberation discussions of sex and marriage: it is a response not to the experience of exploitation but to the discovery that to be in charge of oneself also requires the courage to recognize the extent of one's frailty and dependence on others. Thus the freedom demanded by those eager to proclaim themselves oppressed when they are not is also a freedom of attribution only: freedom not to receive that which one needs to receive and to give that which is needed of one to give but rather freedom to be relieved—and in the name of some "higher value"—of both.

And finally, for women to announce that their very womanliness results only from a bad and meretricious culture is the expression of a deep hatred for themselves. Such an expression of self-hatred is, indeed, exactly the primary emotion that informs women's liberation's diatribes against the impositions of motherhood. Neither society nor the current organization of the family but the womb itself—that "infirmity in the abdomen"—is ultimately the object of this movement's will to correct, to alter, to extirpate. There is no more radical nor desperately nihilistic statement to issue forth from the lips of humans than that there are no necessary differences between the sexes. For such differences both issue in and do in themselves constitute the most fundamental principle of the continuation of life on earth.

Denial of that principle—no matter how nobly, or on the other hand, how trivially, uttered—becomes the denial of oneself, one's nature and one's true possibilities: becomes, in other words, the denial of life itself. History has provided us with some examples of this impulse. It has spoken to us through false messiahs, through satanic religions, through a love of suicide, and through a variety of cults dedicated to the redefinition of the meaning of being human. As with women's liberation, these messiahs and religions and cults have generally not failed, in their inception anyway, to speak in the language of social justice. And as people learned in the past—and seem to need learn over and over again—should the seeds of such denial take firm root, we shall all of us, men, women, and babes in arms, live to reap the whirlwind.

Catherine H. Zuckert

AMERICAN WOMEN AND
DEMOCRATIC MORALS: *THE BOSTONIANS*

Henry James devoted considerable thought to the character of the American woman. It was not merely, as James sometimes said, that the independent woman was a social novelty worthy of detailed observation and description by the student of manners.[1] Rather, James believed that the development or education of the American woman revealed the possibilities and hidden defects of modern democratic life more clearly than any other social or political phenomenon.

The more we look at American life, the more we see that any social aspect takes its main sense from its democratic connections.... It is therefore what her social climate and air have done, and have failed to do, for the American woman that tell us most about her, and we really approach her nearest in studying her...as...the most confidently "grown" and most fully encouraged plant in our democratic garden.[2]

Thus when James wrote his "American" novel, he focused on the situation of women and the agitation on their behalf. "I wished to write a very *American* tale, a tale very characteristic of our social conditions, and I asked myself what was the most salient and peculiar point in our social life. The answer was: the situation of women, the decline of the sentiment of sex, the agitation on their behalf."[3]

Since James described the circle of reformers in Boston critically and ironically, many readers have taken him to be a conservative opponent of the demand for equal rights. But, as some critics have observed, James treated the major male critic of the women as ironically as he did the feminists.[4] In fact, James was very interested in and sympathetic to the problems of American women.

As for James' interest in feminism in general, what have all his important heroines been to date from Daisy Miller to Isabel Archer but women whose intellects, senses, plans, hopes, are all frustrated simply because they are women.... Henry James was consistently sympathetic to the basic claims of the nineteenth century feminist movement; he is, indeed, one of their unsung heroes.[5]

But James did not, apparently, believe that American women would solve their problems through political action. He may, therefore, provide us with a different view of "the woman question"—both the problem of the relation of the sexes in modern democracy and the proposed solutions to the problem. If he is a conservative, he is not the sort of conservative who either expects or desires a return of the aristocratic order. Rather he wishes to explore the possibilities of democratic life. In his own words, his view

both takes the democratic era unreservedly for granted and yet declines to take for granted that it has shown the whole, or anything like the whole, of its hand. Its inexorability and its great scale are thus converted into a more exciting element to reckon with—for the student of manners at least—than anything actually less absolute that might be put in its place.[6]

We may thus look to *The Bostonians* not only for an analysis of the situation of women but also for an investigation of the problems in general of American political morality.

Structurally, *The Bostonians* is simple: Olive Chancellor (Book 1) and her Southern cousin Basil Ransom (Book 2) wage a contest for the affections of Verena Tarrant which Basil finally wins (Book 3). The plot resembles a traditional love story: Boy meets girl; they become attracted to one another and they marry. Olive's loss to the force of sexual attraction is conventionally predictable. What is harder to understand is why the young couple does not, according to James, "live happily ever after." Yet in the last sentence of the novel, the narrator states: "It is to be feared that with the union, so far from brilliant into which [Verena] was about to enter, these [tears] were not the last she was destined to shed" (p. 464). [7]

The unhappy ending forces the conscientious reader to reconsider James's apparent damnation of the women's movement and Olive as unnatural and perverse. True, Basil might represent merely a bad choice; the institution of marriage and all it implies might not be at issue. But James informs his readers at the very beginning of the novel that Basil "is, as representative of his sex, the most important personage in my narrative" (p. 5). If Basil represents American men and the conventional notion of marriage and if this union promises so little happiness, American women would seem to be more than justified in protesting their fate, according to James. But this protest as represented by Olive promises as little happiness, and, it would seem, the American woman has no alternative choice. Thus the plot leads readers to look back in order to discover the reasons why James thinks that "the most confidently 'grown' and most fully developed plant in our democratic garden" finds no promise of happiness or personal fulfillment in America.

James states the problem at the very beginning of the novel: "It proved nothing of any importance with regard to Miss Chancellor, to say that she was morbid; any sufficient account of her would lie very much to the rear of that. *Why was she morbid, and why was her morbidness typical?*" (p. 11, emphasis supplied). In fact, all the characters in *The Bostonians* represent "types"—Basil is "representative of his sex" while Verena personifies "the situation of women," Olive, "the agitation on their behalf," and Mary Prance, "the decline in the sentiment of sex."[8] No one in the novel actually learns from her or his experience or develops; each almost tragically lives out the fate decreed by her or his weakness.[9] Indeed, it turns out that all these characters fail properly to develop as a result of their commitment to egalitarian political principles and to the efficacy of public education in reforming human beings. Once we understand how egalitarian commitments may stultify personal growth, we will be in a position to look at James's critique of American society in terms of the broader issue of the requirements and character of moral education in a liberal democracy.

Verena embodies the freedom of the American girl. She seems able to choose any life she desires—career, fame, love, marriage, family, friendship, wealth, society. Why then, against the wishes of both friends and parents, does she choose an unhappy marriage? Is it that Verena's character makes her unable to choose well, or, is it that all her "opportunities" prove empty? Or both?

All Verena's opportunities involve "unions" of one kind or another. Matthias Pardon offers Verena marriage and notoriety; he would gladly sacrifice any shred of privacy to the public's "right to know." Verena, however, does not seek to exhibit herself so much as to find appreciation of herself. The problem is that she has no real "self" or "identity"; she is only potential, undefined freedom. When Verena comes to Olive, "She [has] no particular feeling about herself; she only [cares], as yet, for outside things...she has neither a particle of diffidence nor a particle of vanity" (p. 78). Olive seeks to "take possession" of Verena, literally buying her from her parents. But Olive does not touch the core of the girl. Verena admires Olive's dedication and self-sacrifice, but she cannot really join Olive because she does not share her passion. Nor does she recognize the passion that gradually draws her to Basil. She thinks that she likes him because he sees and loves her as she truly is. "The words he had spoken to her...about her genuine vocation, had sunk into her soul and worked and fermented there. She had come at last to believe them.... They had kindled a light in which she saw herself afresh and, strange to say, liked herself better...." (p. 396). It is indeed "strange" that she "liked herself better" because the words Basil spoke were:

You always want to please someone, and now you go to lecturing about the country,...in order to please Miss Chancellor, just as you did it before to please your father and mother. It isn't YOU. ...Ah, Miss Tarrant, if it's a question of pleasing, how much you might please someone else by tipping your preposterous puppet over and standing forth in your freedom as well as in your loveliness! (p. 346).

Even the Southern conservative appeals to personal freedom. Yet the narrator comments, "I know not whether Ransom was aware of the bearing of this interpretation, which attributed to Miss Tarrant a singular hollowness of character; he contented himself with believing that she was as innocent as she was lovely...." (p. 62).

Neither Basil nor Verena (nor Olive for that matter) seems to appreciate the force of physical attraction. Verena does, however, understand that her preference for Basil Ransom over Henry Burrage with his wealth and social position is rooted in her egalitarian political principles and her respect for dedication and self-sacrifice. She reflects, for example, on her preference for walking through the park with Basil to riding in a cab with Burrage:

She had to look down so, it made her feel unduly fine....(p. 330) Walking was much more to her taste.... It came over her that Mr. Ransom had given up his work to come to her at such an hour; people of his kind, in the morning, were always getting their living, and it was only for Mr. Burrage that it didn't matter.... That pressed upon her; she was, as the most good-natured girl in the world, too entirely tender not to feel any sacrifice that was made for her; she had always done everything that people asked (p. 331).

As a result of her upbringing Verena is attracted to the champions of unpopular opinions. Despite her disagreement with Basil's opinions, Verena is touched with pity and a feeling of injustice when she hears that his articles have been rejected. "She remembered, though she didn't mention it, how little success her father had when he tried [getting published]" (p. 342). In the end Verena chooses as her mother had before her. At the price of exile from her family, the daughter of the Boston Greenleafs followed a "quack," a past member of a "free love" community to the altar. Though Mrs. Tarrant bemoans her fall in social position and desires "society" for her daughter, she has an even stronger attachment to the people (democracy) and "ideas" (enlightenment) that she bequeaths to her daughter.

The damning difficulty, however, lies in Verena's inability to distinguish one idea, one will, or one passion, from another; and thus she falls prey, in sequence, to her parents, to Olive, and finally to Basil. "She had kept the consummate innocence of the American girl, that innocence which was the greatest of all, for it had survived the abolition of walls and locks" (p. 124). In the company of her parents Verena has seen many of the ugliest aspects of human life. The young girl's accounts of her past life prompt Olive, however, to ask herself whether "the girl was also destitute of the perception of right and wrong" (p. 111).

Ironically, it is Verena's inability to distinguish one cause from another that makes her a true Bostonian. In her innocence, in her boundless generosity, as in her lack of passion and resentment, she is the heir of Miss Birdseye of whom James wrote:

She belonged to the Short Skirts League, as a matter of course; for she belonged to any and every league that had been founded for almost any purpose whatever. This did not prevent her being a confused, entangled, inconsequent, discursive old woman, whose charity began at home and ended nowhere, whose credulity kept pace with it, and who knew less about her fellow-creatures, if possible, after fifty years of humanitary zeal, than on the day she had gone into the field to testify against the iniquity of most arrangements (p. 27).

And Miss Birdseye is the heir of the Emerson James described: "He had only one style, one manner, and he had it for everything. . . . a kind of universal passive hospitality. . . . It was only because he was so deferential that he could be so detached . . . egotism is the strongest of passions, and he was altogether passionless. It was because he had no personal, just as he had almost no physical wants."[10] The Emersonian moral tradition lacks passion, and lacking passion, it lacks understanding of passion. Its morality, James suggests, consists of a kind of innocence; but an innocence founded upon ignorance must fail when confronted with the facts of human nature. Olive, for example, knows better than to ask Verena to promise that she will never marry, because Olive knows that Verena has not the slightest notion what such a promise might mean. Verena promises easily and then just as easily breaks those promises. Lacking an ego, Verena lacks understanding of the passions that rage if not rule in other human beings. She has no standards; as Basil tells her, she has merely been parroting speeches given her by her parents and Olive. Verena cannot, therefore, judge and choose among men. Indeed, it seems that rather than Verena choosing Basil, Basil chooses her, and she merely gives in to the strongest will (p. 337). So Verena, completely innocent, ends by completely wronging Olive.

Nothing was wanting to make the wrong she should do her complete; she had deceived her up to the very last.... She knew that Olive would never get over the disappointment.... It was a very peculiar thing, their friendship, it had elements which made it probably as complete as any (between women) that had existed. Of course it had been more on Olive's side than on hers; but that, again didn't make any difference... She had lent herself, given herself, utterly, and she ought to have known better if she didn't mean to abide by it (pp. 398–99).

Whereas Verena is the typical American girl, Olive is the exception. James clearly suggests that she is "abnormal," "atypical," "perverted," "unnatural," (but not, like her sister Adeline Luna, artificial). The problem, indeed the "mystery," of the novel, lies in answering the questions the narrator poses as early as page eleven: "why was she morbid, and why was her morbidness typical?"

According to the narrator, Olive "was intelligent enough not to have needed to be morbid, even for purposes of self-defense" (p. 156). Something, therefore, hampers the operation of her intellect. It is her unwillingness or inability to admit any desires on her own part. This unwillingness leads her into fundamental dishonesty even with herself. Olive for example denies herself all personal decoration, yet she lavishes attention on the decor of her long narrow parlor. There she seeks protection from the vulgarity, the push and pull of everyday life. Yet she consistently punishes her dislike of the vulgar by riding in street cars and by associating with reformers in such places as Miss Birdseye's parlor. Why? "By reason of a theory she devotedly nursed, a theory which bade her put off invidious distinctions and mingle in the common life" (p. 23).[11]

Olive sees clearly that there are immense differences among human beings, and she is most repelled by the appalling amount of vulgarity that surrounds her.

With her immense sympathy for reform, she found herself so often wishing that reformers were a little different. There was something grand about Mrs. Farrinder...; but there was a false note when she spoke to her young friend about the ladies in Beacon Street. Olive hated to hear that fine avenue talked about as if it were such a remarkable place, and to live there were a proof of worldly glory. All sorts of inferior people lived there.... It was, of course, very wretched to be irritated by such mistakes" (p. 34).

Both Olive and her sister Adeline Luna draw very definite distinctions among people. Those Adeline draws are false, because they are based on an artificially aristocratic notion of society and no understanding of human nature or dignity. Those Olive draws tend to be true, but are formulated with a bad conscience.

She knew her place in the Boston hierarchy, and...there was a want of perspective in talking to her as if she had been a representative of the aristocracy. Nothing could be weaker, she knew very well, than (in the United States) to apply that term too literally; nevertheless, it would represent a reality if one were to say that, by distinction, the Chancellors belonged to the bourgeoisie—the oldest and the best (p. 35).

Olive recognizes that there is no aristocracy in America. She does not respect social position or wealth or even public prominence (which, she sees, tends to become notoriety). Instead, she admires moral purity.

When Miss Birdseye spoke as if one were a "leader of society," Olive could forgive her even that odious expression, because, of course, one never pretended that she, poor dear, had the smallest sense of the real. She was heroic, she was sublime, the whole moral history of Boston was reflected in her displaced spectacles; but it was part of her originality, as it were, that she was deliciously provincial (p. 35).

Olive recognizes that human beings in fact differ quite substantially, but she seems to believe that they should, nevertheless, be treated equally; and that requires that one be short-sighted.[12] Thus she praises Miss Birdseye for errors of observation and judgment for which she criticizes Mrs. Farrinder. Olive shares the Bostonian view of morality as selflessness if not self-sacrifice. Her character even more clearly than Verena's reveals the destructive consequences of this notion of morality, however, for in Olive's case, self-sacrifice means primarily the sacrifice of intelligence to "moral principle."

Olive exists in a high state of tension, caught by the conflict of her aristocratic nature with her ardently held democratic opinions, which produces the "tragic shyness" and "emotional convulsions" that so characteristically paralyze her. The only compensation she gains is suffering; and a life consisting only of suffering does not seem very appealing. "It would be far easier to abandon the struggle...and, in short, simply expire" (p. 159). But Olive does not want merely to expire. "The most secret, the most sacred hope of her nature [is] that she might some day...be a martyr and die for something" (p. 13). She wants a death with meaning, one in which she would destroy her body and with it the low, while the high, her faith, would remain in the memories of others. Olive thus lives in order to perform a noble deed and at the same time suffers from her ambition to distinguish herself above others.

Olive had often declared before that her conception of life was as something sublime or as nothing at all. The world was full of evil, but she was glad to have been born before it had been swept away, while it was still there to face, to give one a task and a reward. When the great reforms should be consummated, when the day of justice should have dawned, would not life perhaps be rather poor and pale? She had never pretended to deny that the hope of fame, of the very highest distinction, was one of her strongest incitements; and she held that the most effective way of protesting against the state of bondage of women was for an individual member of the sex to become illustrious (pp. 159–60).

Olive wishes to live and die in a crusade to rid the world of evil. Her vision of greatness resembles that of the medieval knight. She has the soul of the nobility of old, with all its pride and rigidity as well as its dedication to high ideals. No wonder Olive envies her brothers' deaths in the Civil War.

But women cannot fight for their country. Moreover, Olive believes, fighting war will not bring justice; fighting produces only more suffering and thus more injustice. Gentle means are required. Women can, indeed, must, lead this new, the only true crusade, for they alone know what it is to suffer.

In the last resort the whole burden of the human lot came upon them...their organism was in itself a challenge to suffering, and men had practiced upon it with an impudence that knew no bounds. As they were weakest most had been wrung from them, and as they were the most generous they had been the most deceived. Olive Chancellor would have rested her case, had it been necessary, on those general facts; and her simple and comprehensive contention was that the peculiar wretchedness which had been the essence of the feminine lot was a monstrous artificial imposition, crying aloud for redress (pp. 195–96).

No wonder Olive "would reform the solar system if she could get hold of it" (p. 7). An order in which the weak are persecuted and the strong protected is completely perverse, completely unnatural. "It was the usual things of life that filled her with silent rage; which was natural enough, inasmuch as, to her vision, almost everything that was usual was iniquitous" (p. 12). Not only does the usual lack distinction by the very fact of its being usual, not only is it completely unjust in general, but it represents an order that prevents Olive from expressing and achieving her own distinction. She has a resentful soul. She would rule, because she believes in the superiority of both her moral character and her intelligence, but her democratic principles deny anyone the right to rule; and Olive knows she is unattractive to the people.

Thus instead of seeking rule she seeks revolution. Olive fervently embraces the women's movement because in it she can unite the two warring elements of her nature—her instincts and her principles—into one passion. Thus far men have ruled on the basis of superior physical strength (force) that makes them brutal, insensitive, and vulgar. Olive can prove her superiority by elevating "daintiness to a religion" and in the process give full if not free rein to her fastidious nature. Women are not superior merely because of their physical daintiness or weakness but also because of the knowledge their weakness provides. They know, as men do not, what it is to suffer; and they will, therefore, be the better rulers, because they will be gentle and peaceful. The fact that they would be the best rulers, but do not rule, proves that the present system of male domination is fundamentally unjust and must be overthrown. Both her democratic principles and her aristocratic instincts are satisfied. Having achieved final, complete reform (or having sacrificed herself in the effort), Olive can expire happily to let her heiress, Verena, live in the New Eden.

At the heart of the passion of this most unprevaricating representative of the most unprevaricating city there lies a fundamental dishonesty. Olive lives emphatically by principle. She decides, for example, that Adeline and Basil ought to marry.

Olive considered all this, as it was her effort to consider everything, from a very high point of view, and ended by feeling sure it was not for the sake of any nervous personal security that she desired to see her two relations in New York get mixed up together. If such an event as their marriage would gratify her sense of fitness, it would be simply as an illustration of certain laws. Olive, thanks to the philosophic cast of her mind, was exceedingly fond of illustrations of laws (p. 164).

Olive seeks to imitate Emerson in a life of "high thinking" and "moral passion" that entails denial of all personal, if not all material needs and comforts. Yet Olive has very great personal needs indeed. Fundamentally, she wishes to be loved and to love, hence she seeks a friend, not an equal but a complement. She cannot allow herself to love or be loved by a man, because that would to her mind constitute an admission of her inferiority, her lack of independence. Thus to Verena she pleads: " 'There is no freedom for you and me save in religiously *not* doing what you will often be asked to do—and I never!' Miss Chancellor brought out these last words with a proud jerk which was not without its pathos. 'Don't promise, don't promise!' she went on. 'I would far rather you didn't. But don't fail me—don't fail me, or I shall die!' " (pp. 140–41). By repressing the needs she finds illegitimate, if not degrading, Olive lives in deep personal insecurity, from which she wants not merely peace, but salvation. For her, feminism is more a source of moral rectitude than political right.

When this young lady, after a struggle with the winds and waves of emotion, emerged into the quiet stream of a certain high reasonableness, she presented her most graceful aspect; she had a tone of softness and sympathy, a gentle dignity, a serenity of wisdom, which sealed the appreciation of those who knew her well enough to like her, and which always impressed Verena as something almost august. Such moods, however, were not often revealed to the public at large; they belonged to Miss Chancellor's very private life (p. 140).

Olive admits she can imagine a man she would like very much, but there are none present. Olive's intelligence and her ambition as well as her more personal needs are frustrated in the first instance by the undistinguished character of the American man, but second and more fundamentally, by her adherence to the typically American convictions that all human beings ought to be free and equal and that freedom consists in economic and personal independence.

Basil Ransom has a distinguished appearance.

He was tall and lean and dressed throughout in black..., his head had a character of elevation...; it was a head to be seen above the level of a crowd, on some judicial bench or political platform...; the eyes especially with...their smouldering fire, might have indicated that he was to be a great American statesman; or...that he came from Carolina or Alabama (pp. 4–5).

In fact, he comes from Mississippi. His Southern origins as well as his economic failure make Basil at first glance a strange "representative of his sex" (p. 5). Would not a "self-made," successful businessman such as James's *The American,* Christopher Newman (literally new man), have been more typical? In the context of American reform movements, James apparently thinks not. Basil's Southern origins associate him with slavery (opposed by the Boston-based abolitionists) and give him aristocratic pretensions, i.e., claims to rule on the basis of differences of birth (in this instance, sexual differences). Some readers have followed Adeline in mistaking Basil for an aristocrat.

[Adeline Luna] delighted in the dilapidated gentry; her taste was completely different from her sister's who took an interest only in the lower class, as it struggled to rise; what Adeline cared for was the fallen aristocracy...; was not Basil Ransom an example of it? was he like a French *gentilhomme de province* after the Revolution? or an old monarchical *émigré* from the Languedoc?" (p. 212).

But James comments: "In reality Olive was distinguished and discriminating, and Adeline was the dupe of confusions in which the worse was apt to be mistaken for the better" (p. 199).

Basil has decidedly Southern manners. "He was addicted with the ladies to the old forms of address and gallantry... (p. 197). His accent always came out strongly when he said anything of that sort—and it committed him to nothing in particular" (p. 203). In any matter of importance to him, Basil's "chivalry" does not determine his action. Before he goes to Marmion to pursue Verena, for example, he reviews the extent of his obligations to Olive:

He was not slow to decide that he owed her none. Chivalry had to do with one's relations with people one hated, not with those one loved. He didn't hate poor Miss Olive, ...and even if he did, any chivalry was all moonshine which should require him to give up the girl he adored in order that his third cousin should see he could be gallant (pp. 403–404).

Like the American South, Basil is more bourgeois than aristocratic; he believes in the importance of economic self-sufficiency and he likes his comfort (pp. 11, 16). Although he cares for the South with "passionate tenderness" (p. 50), after the North wins the war, Basil comes to New York to make money. He will not propose to Verena at first, because he lacks visible means of support.

His scruples were doubtless begotten of a false pride, a sentiment in which there was a thread of moral tinsel, as there was in the Southern idea of chivalry; but he felt ashamed of his own poverty.... This shame was possible to him even while he was conscious of what a mean business it was to practice upon human imbecility, how much better it was even to be seedy and obscure, discouraged about one's self.... [In] spite of the years of misery that followed the war [he] could never rid himself of the belief that a gentleman who desired to unite himself to a charming girl couldn't yet ask her to come and live with him in sordid conditions (p. 275).

His notions of support seem minimal, however, for he thinks the publication of one article in *The Rational Review* constitutes enough promise to propose marriage.

Basil is neither an aristocrat nor, as some have maintained, James's spokesman.[13] James himself states:

I shall not attempt a complete description of Ransom's ill-starred views. ...I shall do them sufficient justice in saying that he was by natural disposition a good deal of a stoic, and that, as a result of a considerable intellectual experience, he was, in social and political matters, a reactionary...with a more primitive conception of manhood than our modern temperament appears to require, and a program of human felicity much less varied (pp. 194–95).

Where Basil has a set, simple view of manhood and the limits of human happiness, James wants to explore the unknown possibilities of the modern age. He does not share the "narrow notions" he attributes to his "hero." Basil contends, for example, that "the masculine tone is passing out of the world; it's a feminine age, an age of hollow phrases and false delicacy and exaggerated solicitudes and coddled sensibilities, which, if we don't soon look out, will usher in the reign of mediocrity.... I don't in the least care what becomes of you ladies" (p. 343). James on the other hand made the "new woman" the center of many of his novels and dwelt on the refinements of "consciousness."

If Basil represents the American man, that man is "narrow" and "primitive" primarily because he has an exceedingly simple and naive view of both the virtues and vices of his fellow human beings (p. 198). Basil prides himself on his insight, but James shows that Basil's view of other people is in fact superficial. For example, he is very proud when he concludes upon seeing Olive that she is "visibly morbid," but the narrator states: "It proved nothing of any importance, with regard to Miss Chancellor, to say that she was morbid; any sufficient account of her would lie very much to the rear of that. Why was she morbid, and why was her morbidness typical? Ransom might have exulted if he had gone back far enough to explain that mystery" (p. 11). Likewise, Basil judges correctly enough that Selah Tarrant represents the worst kind of "carpet-bagger" and that his daughter wants essentially "to please every one who came near her and to be happy that she pleased." He judges correctly because the Tarrants prove to be persons wholly of the surface. When Basil must judge character rather than appearance, he fails abominably, as in his choice of a law partner who proceeds to abscond with the firm's funds. He is, in his own way, as "innocent" as Verena, because he lacks knowledge of good and evil. His "conception of vice was purely as a series of special cases, of explicable accidents" (p. 19).

Basil has a first-rate intelligence, but not much experience (p. 11). Surely the experiences of the Civil War and his trip North should have shown him something about his fellow human beings. The problem lies not so much in what he has or has not seen as in the way he tends to understand his experience. As an example, the narrator presents Basil's reflections after he fails to succeed in law in New York.

He wondered whether he were stupid and unskilled, and he was finally obliged to confess to himself that he was unpractical. This confession was in itself a proof of the fact, for nothing could be less fruitful than such a speculation, terminated in such a way. He was perfectly aware that he cared a great deal for the theory, and so his visitors must have thought when they found him...reading a volume of de Tocqueville. This was the kind of reading he liked; he had thought a great deal about social and economic questions, forms of government and the happiness of peoples (pp. 192–93).

Instead of observing or meditating, Basil loses himself in a book on any occasion (pp. 3, 4, 227); but he does not even remember what he has read (pp. 20, 59, 276). He is neither a careful reader nor a careful observer. He thinks that if he can classify an individual as "impractical" or "morbid" or "pleasing" he has understood him. As a result Basil tends not to learn about human nature from his experience but only to confirm generalizations.

His own views are simple and sweeping: " 'The suffering of woman is the suffering of all humanity,' Ransom returned. 'Do you think any movement is going to stop that—or all the lectures from now to doomsday? We are born to suffer—and to bear it, like decent people' " (p. 238). Basil's view is fundamentally egalitarian—all people suffer, equally. Men are stronger so they should attempt to protect the weaker women; and women should gratefully "accept the lot which men have made for them" (pp. 197–98). His Southern origins seem to be responsible for his rather passive and fatalistic view of human affairs as much as they are responsible for his Southern "manners." "He had seen in his younger years one of the biggest failures that history commemorates, an immense national fiasco, and it had implanted in his mind a deep aversion to the ineffectual" (p. 17). If Basil is conservative, it is not because he believes life in the past was better. He is rather a "realist" who opposes all dreams of human improvement because these idealistic "illusions" merely give rise to more suffering. Because he does not believe that any fundamental improvement in the human condition is possible, Basil does not believe in the efficacy of political action. He does, however, ironically share the women's belief in the efficacy of education: "He, too, had a private vision of reform, but the first principle of it was to reform the reformers" (p. 20).

Basil's only success is in wooing Verena, and the marriage does not promise to be a happy one. Although his highest ambition is to see his "ideas embodied in national conduct" (p. 193), he does not expect to succeed immediately. During the years of waiting he needs the comfort of a wife who seeks only to please him.[14] And pleasing him is apparently to be her only reward (p. 238). But here Basil's "ideas" work against his own vision of domestic bliss. He cannot, in fact, take much comfort in Verena's preference, because he regards Verena as an essentially inferior being and has no respect for her judgment. Verena's sympathy for Basil rests, moreover, not so much on his strength of will or the content of his ideas as on the unpopularity of his cause and his failure to publish. Even during the apparently casual walk in New York she seems unable to keep off the matter of his failure (p. 341). May not allusions to his failures (with an implicit contrast to her own success and greater promise) increase when Verena discovers how little Basil really values her?[15]

Basil is not likely to receive either the comfort or the recognition he expects from his wife; and Verena's resentment is apt to grow. But, in an ironic sense, they belong together. He represents the principle of male domination which is, although neither party in the novel seems to see it, merely the other side of the notion that the goodness of women consists in self-sacrifice. Both are inadequate conceptions of human relations because both abstract from particular characteristics of individuals.

Marriage in a liberal democracy is a matter of personal choice, not merely physical attraction or economic advantage. To conceive marriage in political terms of superiority and inferiority or economic terms of possession is to undermine, if not pervert, the attachment of wife and husband. But Americans, James observes, seem to know no other relations. In his attempt to "possess" Verena (pp. 327, 351), Basil appears heir to the tradition of the slave-holding South. But Olive, the moral heir of the abolitionist lecturers, also seeks to "possess" Verena (pp. 79, 80, 132, 398), and indeed "buys" her from her parents (pp. 117, 176, 421). Both reflect the general American tendency to conceive of human relations in economic terms that constrict the alternatives to possession, if not exploitation (as represented by Selah Tarrant and Matthias Pardon), or independence.[16] Economic relations based on need and exchange are both impersonal and equalizing (by making all things commensurate in terms of their money value) and thus appealing to democrats; but they easily become relations of domination because the value of any person, according to this understanding, does not inhere in the individual (to be discovered, appreciated, and so developed), but consists only in her or his use to the other person, her or his service. Olive.embodies this understanding in her insistent desire not to owe anything to anyone, particularly not to a man (pp. 23, 146). Basil clearly acts from a desire to escape economic debt when he comes North as well as when he considers marrying Adeline for her money; but his leaving his mother and sisters to farm the plantation alone also represents an attempt to transform more personal, familial obligations into economic terms, if only to evade them entirely. His notion of obligations of human beings to each other is minimal; and these obligations exist between the strong and the weak, not between equals. He is as lonely in his pride or independence as Olive is in hers. We never hear him talk to another man. At the middle of the novel we see him consider returning to Mississippi, that "state of despair," not only because he has failed at both law and publishing, but also because he has no one to talk to (p. 192). It is in this isolation and loneliness that he comes to view Verena as a bright, beckoning light. Yet he no more than Olive seeks merely to remedy loneliness with the love and companionship Verena would gladly give. Both seek domination through "possession," because both tend to see any ties to other human beings as qualifications of their own freedom. In friendship or marriage they both therefore seek to be superior for fear of becoming inferior. The alternative to possession or being possessed would thus appear to be solitary living.

Dr. Mary Prance is particularly important, for in her life and person she achieves all the goals of the feminist revolution. She is as independent as Olive and Basil wish everyone to be; not only does she have a career, indeed a profession, so that she need not depend upon anyone for material support, but she also seems able to do without the comforts of the society of other human beings. Her appearance at Miss Birdseye's has nothing to do with any feeling of need on her part for moral reform or personal freedom. "Ransom could see that she was impatient of the general question and bored with being reminded, even for the sake of her rights, that she was a woman—a detail that she was in the habit of forgetting, having as many rights as she had time for. It was certain that whatever might become of the movement at large, Doctor Prance's own little revolution was a success" (pp. 48–49). She and Basil become "friends" as easily and equally as Verena envisions all women and men will in the future become friends. Unlike Olive, Doctor Prance poses no challenge to Basil's masculinity. "She looked like a boy...[although it] was true that if she had been a boy she would have borne some relation to a girl, whereas Doctor Prance appeared to bear none whatever" (p. 41). And she makes no moral or aesthetic demands. All she asks is to be let alone to pursue her studies. She does not practice medicine to alleviate the misery of the poor or to serve humanity, but to learn about human anatomy. Hence she spends her leisure time not on the streets, but in her study with her cadaver.

"Men and women are all the same to me," Doctor Prance remarked, "I don't see any difference. There is room for improvement in both sexes. . . ." And she went on to declare, further, that she thought they all talked too much. . . . "I don't want any one to teach me what a woman can do!. . .she can find out some things, if she tries. . . . I don't know as I cultivate the sentimental side. . . . There's plenty of sympathy without mine. If they want to have a better time, I suppose it's natural; so do men, too, I suppose. But I don't know as it appeals to me—to make sacrifices for it; it ain't such a wonderful time—the best you *can* have!" (pp. 42–43).

In Mary Prance we understand what James means by "the decline of the sentiment of sex." He does not envision the disappearance of sex as a means of propagating the species, although Olive's chastity makes this a relevant question, so much as a decay in personal relations that threatens to destroy the very fabric of society. He is concerned with the forces beyond physical need (economics) which draw human beings together into society—particularly into conversation—and which result in the development of character and intelligence.

All life therefore comes back to the question of our speech, the medium through which we communicate with each other; for all life comes back to the question of our relations with each other. These relations are made possible,. . .are verily constituted by our speech, and are successful. . .in proportion as our speech is worthy of its great human and social function. . . . The more it suggests and expresses the more we live by it—the more it promotes and enhances life. Its quality, its authenticity, its security, are hence supremely important for the general multifold opportunity, for the dignity and integrity, of our existence.[17]

Freedom, morality—all that is distinctively human—inhere in the capacity to speak; and so it is by virtue of her "gift" that Verena is potentially free and Olive confined and tortured in her inability to speak freely. Dr. Prance would substitute action for speech, however; and the action she advocates is study of the body—carried on as well with the dead as with the living. For her, speech is empty; the only realities are the truths of body, matter in motion. Thus she understands women's demands for rights and freedom as a matter of pleasure and pain, "having a better time." And as such, feminism constitutes a false quest, because from a mechanical point of view there is little difference between pleasure and pain; every action brings a reaction, and so there is little to be gained by "sacrificing." All in all, there is no reason to associate with other people beyond need, and for Dr. Prance there is little need. As the good doctor states, she does not "cultivate the sentimental side."

All the characters in the novel misunderstand the demands of the body because each would in her or his own way subordinate nature to the rule of general ideas. Both Basil and Dr. Prance abstract from the particularistic character of the body when they consider physical attraction in terms of laws rather than persons. Olive seeks to deny physical attraction by refusing to recognize its legitimacy or necessity, although she thus implicitly recognizes its existence. And Verena inherits, it appears, her mother's profound ignorance of the strength of physical attraction (p. 74). Although in the end Verena acts, in part, on the basis of physical attraction, it is by no means clear that she recognizes this. Indeed the attachment of all the characters to the moral standard of "innocence" precludes such recognition.

If, as some opponents and proponents have suggested, the goal of the women's movement is to deny the existence of any real difference between the sexes, James has presented this form of the emancipated woman in Dr. Prance. She is neither particularly feminine nor masculine. She is a professional, economically and socially independent. James does not present her, as he does Olive, as unnatural, perverse, or repulsive, but he does not make her particularly attractive either. No one in the novel seems to admire or even to be very interested in her.

Dr. Prance is but one of the circle of typical American reformers who gather in Miss Birdseye's living room. More specifically, she represents one type of person and set of goals to be found in the cluster of groups formed of and on behalf of women in America in the late nineteenth and early twentieth centuries that I have generally labeled the "women's movement." In depicting the variety and complexity of characters, issues, and motives involved in the agitation on behalf of women, James not only counteracts stereotyping of feminists, if ironically, by using stereotypes; but he also invites his readers to consider the problematic relation of these different people and their sometimes contradictory opinions. Dr. Prance and Olive appear, for example, to have many things in common. Both are well educated and live solitary, if not lonely lives. Both befriend Miss Birdseye, though neither much respects the elder lady's opinions. Yet neither particularly likes the other. Indeed, they represent almost opposite poles. Where Dr. Prance suggests that any differences between the sexes are irrelevant, if not nonexistent,

Olive not only reaffirms the essential difference but asserts the superiority of women as well. In presenting this and other contrasts among the women involved in the movement James leads his readers to ask what the significance of the agitation on behalf of women really is.

James pays surprisingly little attention to the historically most effective aspect of the women's movement—the political demand for equal rights. The reason seems to be that the women's movement as represented by Mrs. Farrinder merely constitutes pressure to extend the principles of the existing regime to its constituents. It does not challenge the notion that independence constitutes the apex of human achievement, the notion that the most important thing is to secure one's right to life, liberty, and property. Instead it becomes just another interest group.

Verena and Olive do not seek merely to help women, however; they seek to help everyone by increasing the influence of women so as to counteract if not destroy the self-interested character of American society. Both the critique they embody and their failure to achieve the reform they seek raise questions not merely about the fate of women in America but about the viability and adequacy of the most fundamental principles of American politics.

James agrees with that focus of the women's movement that suggests that independence constitutes an inadequate moral standard. As represented by Dr. Prance, independence is at best unattractive and uninteresting. More important, it constitutes a misunderstanding of the foundations of society, which include not only pleasure and need but also the desire for mutual improvement of character through education. In the case of Basil the desire to be independent tends to be selfish. In the case of Olive, the idea that the good life is an independent life works against the formation of social relations—Olive is often rude and unjust—because to admit to need the company of others implies a certain inadequacy. What is missing from the independent life is human society. But, James observes, democrats such as Olive are suspicious of "society," because "society" involves distinctions that appear artificial and invidious to people who take seriously their nation's declaration that "all men are created equal." Indeed, as James illustrates in Adeline, external social distinctions are false, because in democracies the differences among individuals are not expressed, if they are to be found at all, in differences of dress and manners. But does the fact that social distinctions are false mean that drawing any distinctions among individuals or preferring the company of some individuals to others is necessarily invidious?

James was not the first to see that the most fundamental problem in modern democracies resides in the tendency for individuals to retire into virtual isolation as a result of their mistaken desire for independence and the further tendency for this indifference to others to degenerate into selfishness. Nor was he the first to view women as the source of a possible check on this tendency. In *Democracy in America,* Alexis de Tocqueville outlined the dangers of what he called "individualism" and categorically stated: "No free communities ever existed without morals, and...morals are the work of woman."[18]

Tocqueville's praise of American women has two parts. First, he praised the American girl for her ability to choose her fate intelligently. Unlike her European predecessor, the American girl possessed almost complete freedom before marriage. She had a chance, therefore, to learn the ways of the world through direct experience and exposure; thus if she had to choose a master, she could choose a good one. As for the married woman, Tocqueville admitted that her social seclusion was almost without precedent and that it was based on constraint.

In America the independence of woman is irrevocably lost in the bonds of matrimony.... Religious and trading nations entertain peculiarly serious notions of marriage; the former consider the regularity of woman's life as the best pledge and most certain sign of the purity of her morals; the latter regard it as the highest security for the order and prosperity of the household. The Americans are at the same time a puritanical people and a commercial nation.... Thus in the United States the inexorable opinion of the public carefully circumscribes woman within the narrow circle of domestic interests and duties and forbids her to step beyond it (II:3:x, 212).

Tocqueville was not one to urge simple obedience to or faith in the wisdom of public opinion.

Tocqueville had a deeper reason for praising the willingness of American women to retire into the immediacy and privacy of the family. The democratic family, which allows natural affections to grow and take hold freely, seemed to Tocqueville to be virtually the only sentimental bond holding individuals together and checking the tendency of individualism to become pure selfishness. The natural "ties" of affection Tocqueville stressed, however, are those between father and son, and brother and brother—not those between husband and wife and mother and daughter—because the family does not constitute a free and natural association for the woman, but rather depends upon a "constant sacrifice of her pleasure to her duties" (II: 3: x, 212).

Tocqueville was concerned with women because he was concerned with morals; and he was concerned with morals because he shared the classic understanding that political freedom requires self-control. If one does not govern oneself someone else or external forces will. He saw that the primary source of self-restraint and social obligation in modern democracies is the calculation of one's own future gain or need, "self-interest, rightly understood" (II:2:vii, 129ff). But he also saw that self-interest does not provide an adequate foundation for all social obligations (II:2:ix, 133). He looked first to religion to extend and support the concern of any person for another; but he also saw that religion had an effect in America only insofar as it agreed with the dominant public opinion (II:1:v, 29). He looked finally, therefore, to the example of moral behavior provided by women and only consistently by women in modern materialistic democracies. According to Tocqueville, women demonstrate true self-restraint when they subordinate their pleasures to their duty in order to preserve the family, the only modern democratic association based on free affection rather than calculated self-interest. Tocqueville explicitly recognized that the strict sexual morals of the nineteenth century incorporated commercial notions and were based on economic interests (II:3:xii, 22ff). But he suggested that the behavior of women in submitting themselves to these codes nevertheless provided an example of a higher morality.

James and his characters in *The Bostonians* take up the idea that women can greatly improve democratic life through their example. But James suggests that if self-control were to be understood as self-sacrifice, it would not constitute an adequate understanding of the moral requirements of a free society. In depicting the fates of his two major characters, he criticizes both the proposition that the American woman chooses her fate knowingly and that the excellence of woman consists in her self-sacrifice. Verena represents not only the freedom but the "consummate innocence of the American girl, that innocence which . . . had survived the abolition of walls and locks." According to James, the American girl is, to be sure, exposed; but she does not learn from her exposure. She does not understand what she sees, in part because she has yet to experience passion and so is as yet unable to perceive the cause of much she views. (When Verena does experience passion, her opinions and actions change dramatically as a result of the bit of self-knowledge she attains.) Again, the young woman fails to understand what she sees because there are no societal standards by which she can determine what is true or false, good or bad. She has neither convention nor nature to guide her. She has, in fact, only her family. But Selah Tarrant has no moral standards; and Mrs. Tarrant in her virtual seclusion has had no opportunity to learn more than the most external marks of social distinction. The young girl cannot learn because of her youth and freedom; and her mother cannot teach her, because her mother's seclusion prevents her from enjoying a sufficient variety of relations with other human beings to learn about their myriad ways.

Olive represents, if in exaggerated form, the notion that the morality of the American woman consists of self-sacrifice. As Tocqueville himself observed, this ideal is not altogether appealing. "I am aware that an education of this kind is not without danger; I am sensible that it tends to invigorate the judgment at the expense of the imagination and to make cold and virtuous women instead of affectionate wives and agreeable companions to man" (II:3:ix, 211). There is, moreover, a further problem with the notion of morality as self-sacrifice that Olive herself recognizes. If women achieve their superior moral status not merely by the fact and knowledge of suffering (everyone suffers to some extent) but by sacrificing themselves—their pleasure and interests—to others (husband and children first but not solely) and accepting this deprivation and suffering silently (thus becoming martyrs), they lose that moral superiority if they protest their lot in public and try to remedy it. If they remain silent, however, they perpetuate a fundamentally unjust system for the sake of their own moral purity. The solution proposed by the women's movement is to put women forward publicly as examples of virtue. Olive, the martyr, appears to follow logically from this moral syllogism—she does sacrifice her "self" or her ego—but the logic is self-defeating. Once unconscious selflessness becomes conscious sacrifice of self, it is no longer attractive. Nor is it understood. It appears to be merely absurd self-righteousness. When forced into public by circumstances at the end of the novel, Olive necessarily sacrifices all her standards by making a direct appeal to an undiscriminating public who, lacking her standards, fails to recognize her sacrifice and before whom, therefore, she looks ridiculous rather than noble. Public exposure—whether of others or of oneself—can produce only shame, or worse, shamelessness; it cannot produce morality any more than innocence can. Indeed, exposure constitutes merely the negative side of the tendency to understand virtue as innocence of all vice.

The source of the popular notion of morality as selflessness is relatively apparent because the selfishness and ugly aspects of American society are so prominent. Further, it is appealing because selflessness threatens no one. That constitutes the first defect of this idea of morality: it makes morality perfectly ineffective. Second, since this innocence constitutes ignorance of the fundamental fact of human nature—that it is passionate—it not only leaves the moral person defenseless against passion, both in her/himself and in others, but it also produces a narrow, blunt view of life that works in the end to cut its adherents off from all other human beings whom she or he must condemn as selfish. This conception of morality thus furthers the isolation of one individual from another which in turn degenerates into a kind of selfishness.

Natural affection cannot effectively check the evils of democratic society, James suggests, because nature will be affected in its operation by all social conditions—including the democratic—although it will not be destroyed. James suggests, for example, that the attraction of the sexes is natural. But that attraction can become distorted and deformed into domination and resentment, as we have every reason to expect it will in the marriage of Basil and Verena, as a result of understanding marriage in economic terms. "Nature" can become misguided if she is not educated.

Americans do need a moral education, according to James; but not the "self-sacrificing" kind the women's movement proposes. They need to learn not only self-control but also the reasons why it is necessary to control both themselves and others in order to really be able to control one's own fate. They need to learn the passion, the pleasures and pains, virtues and vices of which human beings are capable. And they need to learn that social relations are not merely economically based relations of domination or possession but that the society of others is the only means through which individuals can develop their personal potential.

Public idolization of "innocence" works against this knowledge; so do public "campaigns." As all American political thinkers since the authors of *The Federalist* have observed, the rule of public opinion may become the tyranny of the majority—the worst tyranny in history because it threatens to be more pervasive, more lasting, and more arbitrary than the tyranny of any single man in the past. If the rule of public opinion may be more arbitrary, it would seem that it might also be freer and hence more moral than previous kinds of rule. One need only educate the public; so political programs in America tend to become programs of moral reform. But moral reform as a public program, James suggests, involves a contradiction in terms. In public one must appeal to general principles or the lowest common denominator, to what all people hold in common, their bodily needs. Public opinion is not, therefore, really arbitrary or free; it is rather very much tied to basic needs defined in physical or economic terms to which it will tend to reduce all else. Society may also be a basic need; in Olive, at least, the desire for friendship as well as recognition seems to be the source of her attachment to the women's movement. But democratic people do not recognize the desire for friendship (or any other psychic need) as such; they regard society merely as mutual, if necessary, dependence, to be avoided as much as possible. By mounting a public campaign based on "impersonal principles," the women's movement only furthers the basic thrust of American society toward autonomy and sameness; and in its impersonal lack of concern for the individual as an individual, it is as immoral as the society it would reform.

Indeed, James believes, the women's movement would destroy the root of a superior morality in women—their personal concerns. This is precisely what is needed in modern democracies. True, women are often criticized most for precisely this trait, which may produce gossip, but need not do so if the concern is not to expose the defects of others but to develop, learn, and appreciate their individual turns of character. If, in a word, women can keep their interest truly personal and not public. Such a personal concern can, as in the case of Adeline, become too familiar, insinuating and insulting to the integrity of the individual. For this reason as well as her ideological commitment to the equality of all, Olive tries to suppress such a personal interest in herself and others. Unlike Verena, Olive does know how to distinguish among individuals; but as a result she seeks a refuge even more cloister-like than the marriage described by Tocqueville. Because she sees not only the distinctions among individuals, but also the complete lack of public guidance and support for drawing such distinctions in a society characterized by its easy tolerance and democratic creed, Olive becomes afraid precisely where the more ordinary American woman grows, albeit unconsciously, bold.[19] Olive has character because she has pride, which she tries to suppress, however, because her democratic principles tell her all human beings are equal and pride is therefore unjustified. She is afraid to talk to others both because of what the conversation may reveal about her and because the others may not as a result give her the recognition she desires and does, yet does not, deserve. That is the importance of Olive—why she is morbid and why her morbidity is typical. Of all the characters in *The Bostonians*, she has the finest nature, both morally and intellectually; and that nature is most perverted by her democratic surroundings and education.

All three leading characters in *The Bostonians*, in fact, present us with exceptional natures which are stultified if not perverted in their development as a result of their service to "ideas" rather than attention to individual persons. Basil has a "first-rate intelligence" but his theories prevent him from ever gaining the experience, that is, the knowledge of human nature, he needs to develop it. Verena never learns to distinguish service to one set of ideas from service to another, whereas Olive is psychologically destroyed. None of the characters fails because she or he lacks opportunity in the obvious sense of deprivation of social position or wealth. Nor do they lack education in the formal sense. Rather they suffer from the wrong kind of education; and it is not merely that they learn from books rather than people, but that they read the wrong kind of books. None of the three gives one any reason to think she or he would be an avid, even a casual reader of Henry James, for example. All three would consider such novels frivolous. They read primarily history and philosophy in search of general laws of economic and social behavior whereby they would not merely understand but reform first their compatriots, and finally humanity.

James suggests through practice rather than precept that the novel can provide the kind of moral education Americans need. The novelist can give her or his readers the "experience" Verena and Basil lack by showing them different ways not only of living but also of thinking about living; and she or he can educate readers about the inmost recesses of her or his characters without engaging in journalistic exposure (p. 195). Publicity à la Matthias Pardon, as the phrase goes, "leaves nothing to the imagination"; as a result it destroys all personal integrity, and with integrity the ground of morality. Only through the imagination can one come to know the souls of others and yet protect them from either exposure or shamelessness; through the imagination one can extend oneself to others, moreover, without threat of domination. The novelist not only can supply the knowledge of character social conversation once provided and public preaching cannot, but he can also show the "interest" in the life and thought of the individual who is constantly threatened with extinction by the external sameness of modern industrial life. By portraying the interest, complexity, and beauty of individual consciousness, James performs a very important political function, if in an unpolitical fashion, by giving expression and thus support to the fundamental proposition of American political life—the value of the individual. Tocqueville observed:

The language, the dress, and the daily actions of men in democracies are repugnant to conceptions of the ideal.... This forces the poet constantly to search below the external surface which is palpable to the sense, in order to read the inner soul; and nothing lends itself more to the delineation of the ideal than the scrutiny of the hidden depth in the immaterial nature of man (II, 80).

James's novels, including *The Bostonians*, present criticisms of American intellectual and moral traits, but these criticisms are grounded in a thoroughly liberal commitment to the importance of individual development and fulfillment. By depicting the defects of modern life in terms of the individualistic values of liberal democracy, James reaffirms and refines those values. The moral education his novels provide thus has profound political meaning. Nor was James unaware of the moral character of his art. Rather, he once wrote, "the greater imagination [is] the imagination of the moralist."[20]

4

"Remedies" for Inequality: School Busing and "Reverse" Discrimination

Robert F. Sasseen

AFFIRMATIVE ACTION AND THE PRINCIPLE OF EQUALITY

I

This country has long prided itself on the equality of opportunity which is present here. The fact has been real, and the pride has been warranted. At the same time, thoughtful citizens have been disturbed by the apparent lack of opportunity existing for certain groups in our society, especially for the descendents of conquered peoples and former slaves. Similarly, this country has long condemned discrimination and unequal treatment on the grounds of race, religion, or national origin; but many Americans view such discrimination as a continuing cause of persistent inequalities. The fact that such discrimination has persisted in the social and economic spheres despite its prohibition in the law, however, is not proof that the condemnation is hypocritical as many claim, but suggests instead the recalcitrance of human nature to reason and the foundation of such discrimination in a powerful and perhaps natural inclination. The condemnation has been no less persistent than the discrimination. It has formed many of our laws and has its ultimate ground in the no less powerful and persistent American belief that "all men are created equal." This belief that men are equally "endowed by their creator with certain unalienable rights" underlies our conviction that such distinctions as birth, wealth, race, origin, and religion ought not at all to exist in the law as qualifications for public office and, so far as possible, ought not to count in the competition of life.

It has always been recognized, however, that such distinctions do, as a matter of fact, count in life's competitions. There is a sense in which the sins of the father are necessarily visited on the son. There is no escaping the fact, for example, that the beloved son of a virtuous father has a greater opportunity in the race of life than the neglected offspring of a vicious man. This inescapable fact leads, upon reflection, to the conclusion that there are limits to what the law should attempt in an effort to promote equal opportunity. For the differences in opportunity which originate in the distinctions of birth, wealth, race, or religion cannot be eliminated short of an omnipotent rule bent on an absolute equalization of conditions, which would be simply antithetical to liberty and the security of rights. Indeed, such differences cannot even then be entirely eliminated if the counting of such distinctions has a natural foundation and so long as governments are run by men. In short, the limits of politics place many of the factual inequalities in social and economic opportunity beyond the direct reach of government and law.

A similar conclusion also emerges from a more direct reflection on the principle of equality. First announced for us in the Declaration of Independence, the principle has its origin in the natural rights doctrine of Hobbes and Locke. The principle of equality does not mean that men are, or ought to be, the same in every respect or in most respects. Nor does it mean that men are, or ought to be, the same in birth, talent, strength, virtue, dignity, wealth, or condition. Rather, the principle of equality means that no man is naturally entitled to rule another man in the right to his life, liberty, and the fruits of his labor. It means that all men are naturally and equally the subjects of "certain unalienable rights" among which are "life, liberty and the pursuit of happiness," and that "to secure these rights, Governments are instituted among men, deriving their just powers from the consent of the governed."

This familiar language of the Declaration of Independence entails a comprehensive view of the origin, nature, and purpose of government. According to this view, life and liberty belong by nature to each individual equally, but both life and liberty are naturally insecure. Men are naturally led by their indefeasible and individual pursuit of happiness into an inevitable, even deadly conflict. This perennial conflict is too often resolved by a partisan victory in which the weak are subjected to the pleasures of the strong. Government is necessary for men to overcome the natural insecurity of their rights, but government is also itself prone to the perhaps greater evils attending the rule of the strong in their own interest. According to this view, then, the problem of government is to render individuals secure in their life and liberty by overcoming anarchy and avoiding despotism. In the view of our founding fathers, this end requires a government which is republican in form, democratic in character, and essentially limited in its purpose to the security of rights and the protection of liberty. Government must be democratic in order to avoid the despotism of the few, republican in order to avoid the folly and tyranny of the many, and thus limited in its purpose in order to avoid both of those evils and also to free men for the conquest of nature and the amelioration of the human condition. In short, the principle of equality requires a republican constitution and limitation of government for the sake of political, civil, and individual liberty.[1] Thus it may be said that, if equality is the principle of republican government, liberty is its proper end. The principle of equality establishes a regime of liberty.

In this context it becomes clear that the equal opportunity characteristic of a republican regime consists not in the equalization of wealth or condition but in the political and civil liberty guaranteed by the laws. The principle of equality means that neither wealth, nor birth, nor family, nor race, nor religion constitutes a natural title to rule, that such distinctions should not be legally or constitutionally recognized as a qualification for political office, and that political rule should be impartial with respect to the various claims and disputes arising from these distinctions.[2] But in this and in the requirement of liberty, the principle of equality implies that these distinctions will continue to exist and to be consequential in the lives and affairs of men. Equal opportunity does not consist in the elimination of these distinctions or in the reduction of men to a condition of social and economic equality. Rather, equal opportunity consists in the moderation of the effects of such distinctions through the impartiality of the law and its refusal to sanction them as rightful claims to special privilege under the law.[3]

Contrary, then, to a widespread belief, equal opportunity does not mean that men are equal at the starting line in the race of life, or that government should attempt to make them so. Equal opportunity is, so to speak, more of a by-product of the regime than a direct object of its legislation. It is a beneficial consequence of the regime's liberty and the law's impartiality with respect to the claims naturally arising from distinctions of wealth, birth, race, religion, or national origin. In short, equal opportunity consists in, as it arises from, equal treatment under the law.

II

Affirmative action has its origin in a governmental effort to ensure equal treatment in employment everywhere. It is a policy developed within the federal bureaucracy—in the Department of Labor and the Department of Health, Education and Welfare—in response to

Executive Order 11246. The order applies to all employers with federal contracts in excess of $10,000 and, as amended, declares that:

> the contractor will not discriminate against any employee or applicant for employment *because of* race, color, religion, sex or national origin. The contractor will take *affirmative action to ensure* that applicants are employed and that employees *are treated* during their employment *without regard to* their race, color, religion, sex or national origin.[4]

Affirmative action was developed as a means to the legitimate end of the executive order and is properly to be judged in terms of its compatibility with equal treatment and its consistency with the principle of equality. This judgment requires a precise understanding of the character of the policy, which can be gained only through a careful examination of what the policy requires. For the true character of a policy is to be known not from the rhetoric of its advocacy or the intention explicit in its origin but from the aim implicit in its requirements. To understand the true character of a policy it is necessary to know what the policy specifically requires.

Executive Order 11246 forbids discrimination, commands equal treatment, and requires positive action to eliminate the one and accomplish the other. In its statement of the policy developed to enforce this order, HEW—which has responsibility for the compliance of colleges and universities—explains that "nondiscrimination requires the elimination of all existing discriminatory conditions *whether purposeful or inadvertent.*" A discriminatory condition is any employment practice or policy which *"operate(s) to the detriment* of any persons on grounds of race, color, religion, sex or national origin." An employer, therefore, "must carefully and systematically examine all its employment policies" and revise them as necessary to remove their discriminatory effects. It is not enough, however, for an employer to revise his policy and practice to make them neutral. He must "do more than ensure employment neutrality with regard to race, color, religion, sex or national origin." An employment policy of "benign neutrality" would "tend to perpetuate the *status quo ante* indefinitely" and thus fail "to overcome the effects of systemic institutional forms of exclusion and discrimination." Accordingly, an employer must *"make additional efforts to recruit, employ and promote* qualified members of groups formerly excluded, *even if that exclusion cannot be traced to particular discriminatory actions* on the part of the employer." Finally, though an employer must not discriminate against anyone, his affirmative action in developing a nonneutral employment policy must be "designed to further employment opportunity," not for everyone but specifically for "women and minorities"—indeed, not for every minority but specifically for "Negroes, Spanish-surnamed, American Indians and Orientals."[5] Affirmative action thus appears as a federal policy bureaucratically designed to force employers everywhere, under penalty of the loss of federal funds, to do what is necessary "to recruit, employ and promote" more women and minority persons.

This design is transparent in many of the policy's directives concerning specific employment practices. For example, "nepotism rules," which forbid the employment of close relatives in the same department, commonly originated in the recognition of the troubles such proximity too often creates. Since, however, in American culture the husband is considered the primary breadwinner and the wife is expected to follow his job, more wives than husbands have been affected by the application of the policy. The policy can thus be seen as a "discriminatory condition" which "operates to the detriment" of women in its tendency "to limit the opportunities available to women more than men" and must, therefore, be revised as necessary to remove the hindrance it poses to their employment.[6] Childbearing is another and obvious example of a condition affecting employment which "tends to limit the opportunities" of women more than men. An employment policy which makes no provision for maternity leaves, clearly "operates to the detriment" of women and can thus be viewed as a "discriminatory condition" which the employer is bound to correct. "Childbearing must be considered as a justification for a leave of absence for a female employee regardless of marital status," even "if the employer has no leave policy."[7] Similarly, childraising is a condition which, in American culture, "tends to limit" the employment opportunities of women more than men. Accordingly, "an employer should, as part of his affirmative action program, encourage child care programs" and thereby "contribute significantly to (his) affirmative action profile."[8]

The affirmative action policy, of course, is also designed to secure the employment and advancement of minority persons throughout the country. But one of the chief obstacles to this end is the fact that more members of the preferred minority groups are less skilled and less educated than are the others with whom they must compete for jobs and promotions. This fact, however, can be made to serve the desired end, since—given this fact—the application of employment standards may operate to exclude minority persons more than others. Thus, an employer's practice in this respect can be made to appear as a "discriminatory condition" which "operates to the detriment of... persons on the grounds of race, color, religion, sex or national origin."

Such a practice "must be subjected to rigorous examination and its discriminatory effects eliminated."[9] Similarly, an employer's "policies and practices on promotion should be...administered to ensure that women and minorities are not at a disadvantage."[10] His "job category assignments and treatment of individuals within a single job classification" must also be reviewed, since "experience shows that individuals of one sex or race frequently tend to be 'clustered' in certain job classifications, or in certain departments" which "most often...tend to be lower paid, and have less opportunity for advancement than those to which non-minority males are assigned."[11]

Affirmative action seeks the advancement of women and minority persons through an attack on employment practices which can be made to appear as "discriminatory conditions." Earlier drafts of the policy seemed to take a different approach and required that employers without enough women or minorities simply hire "qualifiable" persons from the preferred groups or hire those with qualifications equal to the least qualified of the employees in a particular job. But now the policy speaks only of hiring "qualified" persons; and HEW emphatically denies that it sanctions lower standards, differential treatment, or "reverse discrimination" in the required effort to advance individuals from the preferred groups.[12] Prevailing job standards and qualification requirements may remain unchallenged unless more individuals in the preferred groups than others fail to meet the standards or to possess the required qualifications. In that event, the standards and qualifications would obviously "limit the opportunities" of women and minority persons more than others and can be treated as "discriminatory conditions" which "operate to the detriment" of persons "on grounds of their race, sex or national origin." Affirmative action requires that such standards and qualifications be eliminated, or else be shown to be "valid predictors of job performance." They must be eliminated "unless the contractor can demonstrate that such criteria are conditions of successful performance" on the job in question. Similarly, the policy requires "the validation of all criteria for promotion."[13] It is a question, certainly, whether reasonable standards of employment or promotion can all be scientifically validated as "job related"; but, there can be no doubt that a narrow definition of "validation" and "job related" will be sought, since the policy's approach is to eliminate "discriminatory conditions" whenever and wherever possible.[14]

Clearly transparent in all of this is the overriding aim of the policy to force employers "to recruit, employ and promote" more women and minority persons. This design of the policy is equally transparent in its directives concerning the efforts an employer must make to overcome his "underutilization" of persons in the preferred groups. Underutilization is "having fewer women or minorities in a particular job than would reasonably be expected by their availability" in an employer's labor market.[15] If an employer has too few, he must act affirmatively to get more. This obligation does not depend on the specific cause of the underutilization. Having too few of the preferred persons, for example, may be the result of real discrimination or of an employer's nondiscriminatory application of till-now unquestioned standards of employment; or, it may be the result of the failure of minorities to apply in sufficient numbers, or of the insufficient presence of minorities in an employer's recruitment channels. Whatever its cause, underutilization must be corrected.

To correct this "deficiency," an employer must "develop...specific goals and timetables designed to overcome that underutilization." He must make every effort to employ more, and the "achievement of goals"—though "not the sole measurement of a contractor's compliance"—is an indispensable measure of his good faith efforts. The achievement of numerical employment goals within the timetable is "a primary threshold for determining...whether an issue of compliance exists." If an employer fails to set goals and timetables, or if he fails to achieve the goals within the specified timetable due to "inattention" to the affirmative action policy, he "may be found out of compliance" and lose his federal funds.[16]

The affirmative action policy thus requires an employer to make a statistical analysis of his work force by department and job classification, broken down into sex and race. The employer must also make a similar statistical analysis of his employment market. He must then compare the two analyses. The comparison is for the purpose of locating "deficiencies." An employer is "deficient" if the proportion of women and minority persons in his work force, or perhaps in any particular job classification or department, is less than the proportion of "qualified" women and minority persons in his labor market. He is "deficient" if he is statistically out of proportion with respect either to the rate or the proportion of women and minority persons recruited, employed, or promoted. If "deficient," the employer must establish numerical goals and take affirmative action to overcome this statistical discrimination within a specific time period. The employer must then make every good faith effort to meet his affirmative action goals, to bring the preferred groups into a proper proportionality. In short, the affirmative action policy requires an employer to develop:

a set of specific and *result-oriented* procedures.... An acceptable affirmative action program *must* include an analysis of areas within which the contractor is deficient in the utilization of minority groups and women, and further, goals and timetables to which the contractor's good faith efforts must be directed to correct the deficiencies and, thus, to *increase materially the utilization of minorities and women.*[17]

Affirmative action thus appears in its naked aspect. The true character of a policy is to be known not from the rhetorical language in which it is dressed but from what the policy specifically requires. Though clothed in the language of "nondiscrimination" and "equal opportunity," the policy can be seen for what it is through its particular directives. Affirmative action is nothing more or less than a forced employment policy designed overall "to increase materially the utilization of minorities and women." Its overriding aim is to compel employers everywhere "to recruit, employ and promote" more of these preferred persons. Under the guise of enforcing an executive order and through a sophistical manipulation of the concepts of "discrimination" and "equal opportunity," the affirmative action policy has transformed a legitimate order to ensure equal treatment into a wilful command to hire more members of the preferred groups. Affirmative action is simply and overall a preferential policy of proportional employment.

III

The advocates of the policy will object that this is either a deliberate distortion or an innocent misunderstanding—but, in any event, a reprehensible misrepresentation of the true character and aim of affirmative action. They claim that it is an antidiscrimination policy aimed at genuinely equal opportunity. They insist that affirmative action is a necessary, reasonable, and effective means to overcome discrimination, to establish equality, and to remedy the effects of past discrimination. "Unless positive action is undertaken to overcome the effects of past discrimination, a benign neutrality in employment practices will tend to perpetuate the *status quo ante* indefinitely."[18] In short, without affirmative action there can be no real progress to full equality.

There can be no doubt that this defense has powerful rhetorical appeal. It deserves careful examination to determine whether it succeeds in demonstrating both the necessity of the policy and the error in understanding affirmative action to be a preferential policy of proportional employment. This examination may properly begin at the beginning with the practical problem faced by the compliance agencies in fulfilling their responsibility under the executive order prohibiting discrimination and commanding "affirmative action to ensure" the treatment of all employees "without regard to their race, color, religion, sex or national origin." The compliance agencies were faced with the practical problem of how to administer and enforce that command. In particular, they were faced with the tough question of how they were to determine whether an employer actually discriminates or is acting affirmatively to ensure equal treatment.

The answer given to this proper question is ironic, but seems to have all the propriety of the Biblical statement that "by their fruits ye shall know them." The policy answers that the compliance agency can know whether there is discrimination or equal treatment by the results of employment practice. The compliance agency can know by the easily ascertainable fact of whether there exists statistical underutilization and whether *effective* efforts are made to employ more members of the preferred groups. The irony of this answer consists in its begging of the original question. To the problem of discovering real discrimination, the policy's solution is to give up the attempt—an employer must conscientiously strive "to recruit, employ and promote qualified members of groups formerly excluded, *even if that exclusion cannot be traced to particular discriminatory actions* on the part of the employer."[19] To the problem of demonstrating positive action to ensure equal treatment, the solution is to look for effective effort to overcome underutilization, to achieve proper proportionality in the employment of members of the preferred groups. The simplicity of this solution makes it an attractive answer to a complex practical problem. But it is an answer which altogether begs the question and transforms both the executive order and the civil rights legislation into a preferential policy of proportional employment.

The denial of this transformation is based on the assertion that the policy is a necessary and reasonable means to the legitimate end intended by the executive order. Here the end of nondiscrimination and equal treatment is unquestionably legitimate. At issue is the relation to this end of the requirements imposed on employers everywhere by the affirmative action policy. To require that "underutilized" employers hire more women and minority persons is another and quite different thing. The problem is to understand the connection between the one and the other, between treating equally and hiring more. There must be an intrinsic and valid connection, or else the policy cannot be justified as a necessary and reasonable means to the legitimate end intended by the executive order. Indeed, without such a connection the policy has no legal foundation whatsoever.

It may be thought that the necessary connection is to be found in the assertion that a policy of "benign neutrality" will merely "perpetuate the *status quo ante* indefinitely," that without affirmative action there can be no real progress towards genuinely equal opportunity. If this pure assertion were true, it would be impossible to account for the undeniable progress which had occurred before affirmative action was so recently conceived in the womb of the federal bureaucracy. But this pure assertion fails to justify affirmative action not only because it is false but because it also assumes the point at issue here. National security, for example, is certainly a legitimate end, but that end does not justify everything a bureaucrat might wish to do in the belief that otherwise victory would be delayed indefinitely. The bureaucrats in HEW and the Department of Labor mean to compel employers to hire and promote more women and minority persons, but there is neither legal nor Constitutional authority for such compulsion unless hiring more is intrinsically and validly connected to the legitimate requirement of equal treatment. This necessary link between means and end, if it can be found at all, is to be found only in the concept of "underutilization."

In the name of equal treatment, the policy requires an employer to determine underutilization and to correct it. Its understanding of underutilization, however, is quite unusual. Ordinarily, "underutilization" is a concept used in economic analysis and refers to the relation between persons and jobs. A person is said to be underutilized when employed in a job beneath his actual capacity. A company would have a problem of underutilization to the extent that it employed persons beneath their capacity, and—conversely—it would have no such problem if each person were employed to the level of his capacity. Similarly, in the perspective of the whole, an economy could be characterized by underutilization if a significant portion of its work force were employed in jobs well beneath their actual capacity. Strictly speaking, "underutilization" is an economic concept referring to persons and to functions; it is a matter essentially of skills and jobs.

In the affirmative action policy, however, underutilization is a different matter altogether. It is essentially a matter of representation. It is a matter of the relation between the composition of an employer's work force and the composition both of his labor market and, by naturally inevitable extension, of the general population. The extension is inevitable because naturally we think of representation in terms of population, because the labor market will itself be seen as "underutilized" if the preferred groups are not represented therein proportionately, and because the demand to remedy past injustice will apply to the market no less than to the factory. Anyhow, in the affirmative action policy underutilization is simply underrepresentation. It "is...'having fewer women or minorities in a particular job than would reasonably be expected by their availability.' "[20] Any employer—even one whose employees were all situated commensurate to their capacity in an economy in which all such persons were similarly employed—has a problem of underutilization to the extent his work force is not proportionately representative of the preferred groups in his labor market. "Underutilization" is here nothing else but "under-representation," and such underrepresentation is said to be a "deficiency" which the employer is bound to correct in the name of equality.

Now underutilization implies—indeed, it is intelligible only by reference to—a concept of proper utilization. The employment of persons beneath their actual capacity can be thought of as *under*utilization only if the employment of persons commensurate to their capacity is understood to be normal or natural utilization. Moreover, underutilization as such cannot be understood as a "problem" unless employment commensurate to capacity is thought to be proper utilization, the level of utilization required by the nature and purpose of an economy. Similarly, underrepresentation implies—indeed, it is intelligible only by reference to—a concept of proper representation. A disproportionate representation of groups in an employer's work force can be thought of as *under*representation only if the proportionate representation of groups is thought to be the normal or natural representation. Moreover, underrepresentation in employment cannot as such be understood to be an inequity unless equality is thought both to consist in arithmetic proportionality and naturally to result in the proportionate representation of groups in employment. Thus it can be said that underrepresentation is a "deficiency" which must be corrected in the name of equality, in fulfillment of a command to ensure equal treatment in employment everywhere.

This central concept of "underutilization" reveals the true character of the affirmative action policy and, at the same time, demonstrates the failure of its defense as a necessary and reasonable means to enforce the command of equal treatment. Underutilization is the policy's focus of concern and point of attack. The underrepresentation of particular groups triggers action under the policy. Action is required to overcome the underrepresentation of women, blacks, Spanish-surnamed ·individuals, American Indians, and Orientals. Most groups, however, are not included in this focus of concern—not Poles, Italians, Slavs, Irish, Swedes, Portuguese, Hindus, Mormons, Jews, Catholics, Seventh-Day Adventists, atheists, homosexuals, Communists, conservatives, Republicans, nor any of the other minority groups composing American society. Affirmative action is required to overcome the underrepresentation of only the select groups, and the required action must be effectively designed to overcome that underutilization—that is, to represent them proportionately. Clearly, affirmative action is simply, precisely, and truly characterized as a preferential policy of proportional employment. A race-conscious employment policy thus preferring some groups to others must surely breed a race-conscious employment practice preferring individuals from the preferred groups over individuals from the other groups. A step beyond employment neutrality is necessarily a step into discrimination in employment. Through the concept of "underutilization," a legitimate order to ensure equal treatment has been transformed into a wilful command to recruit, employ, and promote more members of the preferred groups.

The concept of "underutilization," moreover, fails to supply the link between means and end which is necessary to justify the policy. Proportional employment is not the same thing as equal treatment and cannot be connected to equal treatment as a necessary or reasonable means except through a particular and erroneous understanding of the principle of equality. The requirement to overcome underutilization can be validly connected to the command to treat equally only if equal treatment means no underutilization. Affirmative action can be justified in the name of equality only if equality naturally involves proportional employment and requires the distribution of jobs in arithmetic proportion among the groups composing society. This can be seen in the logic of the policy's defense. Indeed, it is the internal logic of the policy itself and can be stated in almost syllogistic form:

Equality requires equal employment.
Equal employment is proportional employment.
Therefore, equality requires proportional employment.

Further:

The preferred groups do not have proportional employment.
                                        (They are "*under*utilized.")
But equality requires proportional employment.
                                        (It requires "proper" utilization.)
Therefore, the preferred groups do not have equality.

Finally:
Affirmative action requires equality for the preferred groups.

Equality requires proportional employment.

　　　　　　　　　　(It requires "proper" utilization.)

Therefore, affirmative action requires proportional employment
of the preferred groups.

　　　　　　　　　(It requires the elimination of "*under*utilization.")

　　This statement of the policy's logic reveals the real premise of
affirmative action. That premise is the understanding of equal
opportunity to be a matter primarily of social or economic condition
and equal treatment to consist in the distribution of jobs—hence wealth
and status—in arithmetic proportion among the groups composing
society. Without this premise there is no intrinsic relation between
means and end, no valid connection between the affirmative action
requirement to overcome employment underrepresentation and the
legitimate command of the executive order for employers to take
positive measures to ensure equal treatment. Simply stated, hiring
proportionately can be considered equal treatment only if underutilization necessarily means unequal treatment. Similarly, underutilization is necessarily a sign of unequal treatment only if proportional
employment is naturally the result of treating equally. Clearly, only
such an understanding of equality can supply the necessary link
between the means of hiring more and the end of treating equally.

　　This premise of affirmative action, however, is a false understanding
of the principle of equality which thus vitiates the policy and invalidates
its defense. The principle of equality does not imply that, if all men were
treated equally, property would naturally be distributed in arithmetic
proportion among the groups composing society. The freedom born of
the principle naturally precludes such a result. Nor does the principle
imply that the task of government is to make individuals or groups
equal to one another in jobs, wealth, or status. Quite to the contrary, the
principle of equality implies a limited government whose task is
impartially to secure individuals in their rights and protect them in the
exercise of their liberty. To denigrate this understanding of government
as a posture of "benign neutrality" contrary to the requirements of the
times is to undermine the understanding of equality which is the
foundation of our convictions that discrimination is wrong and equal
treatment is right. Without that understanding and those convictions,
no real progress is even conceivable, let alone possible.

　　At this point partisan, angry, impatient, or practical persons may
object to the apparently abstract irrelevance of this analysis. They have
scarcely any tolerance for such "ego trips" since, in their view, the

situation is entirely clear and affirmative action is unquestionably legitimate. There can be no doubt that blacks, Chicanos, and women are in an inferior and unequal condition. It must be believed that this unequal condition is unjust, the result of unequal treatment and past discrimination. To think otherwise is at bottom a form of racism which blames the victim for his oppression. Clearly, the situation is simply unjust and no longer tolerable. Affirmative action is a modest attempt to remedy the effects of terrible wrongs. Without it there can be no real progress. Decent men everywhere should set aside their sterile doubts and at once begin the difficult task of making the policy work. It is time that justice were done!

This rhetorical appeal has power enough to still the tongues even of many persons whom it cannot persuade. But their doubts persist. Their compassion leads them to deplore the wretched condition of the truly disadvantaged. Their sense of justice underlies their belief in equal treatment, supports their wish for everyone to enjoy equal opportunity, and makes them anxious to correct past wrongs. But their sense of reality leads them to reject so simple-minded an explanation of the cause of present inequalities, and that sense of justice itself makes them altogether suspicious of a preferential policy of proportional employment. Indeed, it is simple slander contemptuously to reject such misgivings as the product of self-interest or the effect of "unconscious" racism. Such slander and contempt may suggest that righteous indignation and moral outrage have other roots than the desire for justice.

The desire for justice, no matter how pure, is by itself insufficient for the determination of what is just and effective policy. Affirmative action has transformed a legitimate policy of equal treatment into a wilful policy of preferential and proportional employment. This policy is grounded in a radical and false understanding of the principle of equality, and its defense in terms of that false understanding thus fails to justify the policy. Now, in a desperate appeal to compassion and decent prejudice, the preferential policy of proportional employment is to be justified as a remedy for the effects of past discrimination.

The persuasive power of this rhetorical argument requires that it be taken more seriously than perhaps it deserves. In the first place, even were it granted that underrepresentation is simply the effect of past discrimination, it does not follow that a preferential policy of proportional employment is its proper remedy. Precisely speaking, not the effect but the action producing the effect is the injustice in the question—not the statistical underrepresentation, but the discrimination and unequal treatment alleged as its cause. The proper remedy of that precise wrong is the policy perverted by affirmative action—the policy originally intended to ensure nondiscrimination and equal treatment. For proportional representation to be a proper remedy, underrepresentation must be thought wrong not only as an effect but in and of itself. But underrepresentation cannot be understood as such a wrong except in terms of that false understanding of equality which is the real premise of affirmative action.

In the second place, even in the perspective of the restitution required by justice and on the supposition that underrepresentation is simply an effect of past discrimination, it does not follow that a preferential policy of proportional employment is proper restitution. Of course, individual justice requires the restoration to a person of a good of which he was wrongfully deprived and to which he was rightfully entitled. But a restitution to a group is a difficult matter both to understand and to accomplish. Apart from the fact that under affirmative action particular individuals are to receive particular jobs of which they were individually not wrongfully deprived at the expense of other individuals and from institutions which may have done them no wrong, the general good which this policy attempts to restore is proportional representation in employment. To conceive of proportional representation as the matter of group restitution is to suppose it a good to which the group was naturally entitled and wrongfully deprived. But this presupposes that false understanding of equality which is the real premise of the policy.

Finally, it is not true that underrepresentation is simply an effect of past discrimination. This pure assertion is yet another illustration of an American propensity to "devil theories" which would explain a recalcitrant social problem in terms of some devil and attempt to solve the problem by declaring the devil illegal. This assertion presupposes a simplistic theory of social causality which, as Professor Edward C. Banfield has demonstrated, seriously distorts the nature of our problems and makes them even more recalcitrant to amelioration.[21] To understand present disproportions in terms of past discrimination is no more tenable on its face than the contrary attempt to account for them in terms of a theory of natural inequality. For this reason it is unwise and even dangerous to insist upon this simplistic understanding of a complex social problem. The former theory now prevails in public opinion, but this fact is not merely a result of the triumph of its truth over the falsity inherent in the presently unpopular theories of natural inferiority. The present victory of the one theory over the other is as much a consequence of the other factors which form and sustain public opinion. A reflection on this fact should give pause to the partisans of affirmative action. The no less plausible but equally false theory of natural inequality waits to be held as self-evident truth the moment its acceptance suits the mood of the public, the interest of the majority, or the circumstances of the times.

Truth to tell, the pure assertion that underrepresentation is an effect of past discrimination and has its proper remedy in affirmative action derives from that false understanding of equality which is once again revealed as the true premise of this preferential policy of proportional employment. Underrepresentation can be seen as simply the effect of improper discrimination only if proportional representation is understood to be the proper or natural effect of the principle of equality. Proportional employment can be asserted as a proper remedy only if equality is thought to consist in employment on the basis of arithmetic proportionality. This radical theory of equality is the true foundation of the policy, and the acceptance of the policy necessarily entails the establishment of that theory as the principle of public law and policy. The ultimate establishment of this false principle of equality will fundamentally alter the character of the republic, and that prospect makes affirmative action a truly revolutionary public policy.

IV

Abraham Lincoln once said: "in this and like communities, public sentiment is everything. With public sentiment, nothing can fail; without it nothing can succeed. Consequently he who molds public sentiment, goes deeper than he who enacts statutes or pronounces decisions. He makes statutes and decisions possible or impossible to be executed." In another place, Lincoln noted that "our government rests on public opinion. Whoever can change public opinion can change the government practically just so much. Public opinion, on any subject, always has a 'central idea' from which all its minor thoughts radiate. That 'central idea' in our political public opinion...is 'the equality of men.' "[22]

The true character of affirmative action has been demonstrated through an examination of its requirements and of its defense in the name of equality. It is simply a preferential policy of proportional employment which has transformed a legitimate order to ensure equal treatment into a wilful command to recruit, employ, and promote properly proportionate numbers of women and minority persons. The true premise of the policy and of its perversion of the executive order is a false theory of equality which radically changes "the central idea" in our laws and opinion, and thereby threatens the foundation and character of our country. This is the most fundamental aspect of affirmative action, and it is this which makes the policy so essentially reprehensible. Acceptance of the policy entails the public establishment of an altogether false and pernicious understanding of the principle of equality.

As was noted at the outset, the principle of equality properly refers to the equality of men in their natural possession of certain unalienable rights. It does not imply a society in which all men are or ought to be equal in social status and economic condition. Nor does it imply a society free from the conflicts and injustices which naturally arise from the liberty of citizens and their differences with respect to wealth, birth, race, religion, or national origin. But the principle of equality does imply a government impartial regarding the conflicting claims originating in these differences, and limited in what the law should attempt in mitigation of the inequalities inevitable in a free society. The principle of equality implies that the equalization of conditions and the assimilation of differences are not direct or proper objects of legislation, but indirect and beneficial effects of both the law's impartiality as well as the political equality and civil liberty of the people. Genuine equality of opportunity consists in this liberty of citizens and their equal station under the law.

The affirmative action policy, however, teaches that genuine equality is primarily a matter of social status or economic condition and that no group possesses genuinely equal opportunity unless jobs, wealth, and status are distributed in arithmetic proportion among all groups equally. The policy makes this end a proper object of government and, in so doing, legitimizes a passion both characteristic of democracy and capable of destroying it. This passion for equal status and condition is antithetical to freedom and has long been recognized as the mortal disease of democratic government. The effort to gratify this passion, as Alexis de Tocqueville noted in his *Democracy in America*, leads inevitably to an accelerating concentration of political power, centralization of administration, and, finally, to a new form of Caesarism.[23]

The affirmative action policy, through its disingenuous manipulation of the concept of equal opportunity and its sophistical defense in the name of equality, sets the federal government directly to the task of forcing in employment a dramatic equalization of economic conditions for a selected portion of our society. Were the courts to sanction and the people to acquiesce in this astonishing expansion of federal authority, executive prerogative, and bureaucratic direction, the principle of our country and the character of our government will have been changed decisively. The aim of the republic will have been changed from the security of rights and the preservation of liberty to the equalization of conditions. In the last analysis the forced equalization of conditions requires despotic power, and the decisive change introduced through affirmative action is thus pregnant with that possibility.

But the affirmative action policy needs to be understood in still another light. As was said at the beginning, this country has long prided itself on the equality of opportunity present here; yet, thoughtful citizens have long been disturbed by the persistent disadvantages suffered by blacks and others in our society. The cherished dream of full integration seems no nearer realization still, and affirmative action has perhaps arisen in a desperate effort to make that dream come true. Affirmative action, however, is a fundamental betrayal of that dream. In its effort to force the proportional employment of persons identified by their race or national origin, the policy writes racial distinctions into law and declares that, after all, race *should* count in the competitions of life and in the distribution of the benefits of society. In so doing, the policy sanctions the eventual establishment of an American form of apartheid.

Finally, what is indeed reprehensible in affirmative action is its arrogant contempt for Americans generally, but especially its contempt for blacks and the other pretended beneficiaries of the policy. In effect, this paternalistic policy announces their perpetual inferiority and makes them to be special wards of the state. No one, whatever his race or origin, can accept such dependency without loathing and self-contempt; but, if someone can, then his spurious equality must render him contemptible in the eyes of his fellow citizens. Such a policy might force proportional employment across the land. It cannot turn wards into citizens or foster a society integrated on the foundation of true independence and genuine equality. We cherish our dream of such a society, and it would be folly now to betray the long struggles of our people—men and women alike, of all races and every origin—to make that dream come true. It is a true dream, and the realization of its truth requires fidelity to the principle of equality and its regime of liberty. Only by such fidelity shall we overcome the injustices we abhor and realize our wish for all Americans everywhere to enjoy the fruits of equal opportunity and the blessings of liberty.

Nathan Glazer

IS BUSING NECESSARY?

It is the fate of any social reform in the United States—perhaps anywhere—that, instituted by enthusiasts, men of vision, politicians, statesmen, it is soon put into the keeping of full-time professionals. This has two consequences. On the one hand, the job is done well. The enthusiasts move on to new causes while the professionals continue working in the area of reform left behind by public attention. But there is a second consequence. The professionals, concentrating exclusively on their area of reform, may become more and more remote from public opinion, and indeed from common sense. They end up at a point that seems perfectly logical and necessary to them—but which seems perfectly outrageous to almost everyone else. This is the story of school desegregation in the United States.

For ten years after the 1954 Supreme Court decision in *Brown v. Board of Education*, little was done to desegregate the schools of the South. But professionals were at work on the problem. The NAACP Legal Defense Fund continued to bring case after case into court to circumvent the endless forms of resistance to a full and complete desegregation of the dual school systems of the South. The federal courts, having started on this journey in 1954, became educated in all the techniques of subterfuge and evasion, and in their methodical way struck them down one by one. The federal executive establishment, reluctant to enter the battle of school desegregation, became more and more involved.

The critical moment came with the passage of the Civil Rights Act in 1964, in the wake of the assassination of a President and the exposure on television of the violent lengths to which Southern government would go in denying constitutional rights to Negroes. Under Title IV of the Civil Rights Act, the Department of Justice could bring suits against school districts maintaining segregation. Under Title VI, no federal funds under any program were to go to districts that practiced segregation. With the passage of the Elementary and Secondary Education Act in 1965, which made large federal funds available to schools, the club of federal withdrawal of funds became effective. In the Department of Justice and in the Department of Health, Education and Welfare, bureaucracies rapidly grew up to enforce the law. Desegregation no longer progressed painfully from test case to test case, endlessly appealed. It moved rapidly as every school district in the South was required to comply with federal requirements. HEW's guidelines for compliance steadily tightened, as the South roared and the North remained relatively indifferent. The Department of Justice, HEW, and the federal courts moved in tandem. What the courts declared was segregation became what HEW declared was segregation. After 1969, when the Supreme Court ordered, against the new administration's opposition, the immediate implementation of desegregation plans in Mississippi, no further delay was to be allowed.

The federal government and its agencies were under continual attack by the civil-rights organizations for an attitude of moderation in the enforcement of both court orders and legal requirements. Nevertheless, as compared with the rate of change in the years 1954 and 1964, the years since 1964 have seen an astonishing speeding-up in the process of desegregating the schools of the South.

Yet the desegregation of schools is once again the most divisive of American domestic issues. Two large points of view can be discerned as to how this has happened. To the reformers and professionals who have fought this hard fight—the civil-rights lawyers, the civil-rights organizations, the government officials, the judges—the fight is far from over, and even to review the statistics of change may seem an act of treason in the war against evil. Indeed, if one is to take committed supporters of civil rights at their word, there is nothing to celebrate. In 1970 the Civil Rights Commission, the independent agency created by the Civil Rights Act of 1957 to review the state of civil rights, attacked the government in a massive report on the civil rights enforcement effort. "Measured by a realistic standard of results, progress in ending inequity has been disappointing. . . . In many areas in which civil-rights laws afford pervasive legal protection—education, employment, housing—discrimination persists, and the goal of equal opportunity is far from achievement." And the report sums up the gloomy picture of

Southern school segregation, sixteen years after *Brown:* "Despite some progress in Southern school desegregation...a substantial majority of black school children in the South still attend segregated schools."[1] Presumably, then, when a majority of Negro children attended schools in which whites were the majority, success by one measure should have been reported. But in its follow-up report one year later, this measure of success in Southern school desegregation was not even mentioned. The civil-rights enforcement effort in elementary and secondary schools, given a low "marginal" score for November 1970 (out of four possibilities, "poor," "marginal," "adequate," and "good"), is shown as having regressed to an even *lower* "marginal" score by May 1971, after HEW's most successful year in advancing school integration!

But from the point of view of civil-rights advocates, desegregation as such in the South is receding as a focus of attention. A second generation of problems has come increasingly to the fore: dismissal or demotion of black school principals and teachers as integration progresses and their jobs are given to whites; expulsions of black students for disciplinary reasons; the use of provocative symbols (the Confederate flag, the singing of "Dixie"); segregation within individual schools based on tests and ability grouping; and the rise of private schools in which whites can escape desegregation.

But alongside these new issues, there is the reality that the blacks of the North and West are also segregated, not to mention the Puerto Ricans, Mexican Americans, and others. The civil-rights movement sees that minorities are concentrated in schools that may be all or largely minority, sees an enormous agenda of desegregation before it, and cannot pause to consider a success which is already in its mind paltry and inconclusive. The struggle must still be fought, as bitterly as ever.

There is a second point of view as to why desegregation, despite its apparent success, is no success. This is the Southern point of view, and now increasingly the Northern point of view. It argues that a legitimate, moral, and Constitutional effort to eliminate the unconstitutional separation of the races (most Southerners now agree with this judgment of *Brown*), has been turned into something else—an intrusive, costly, painful, and futile effort to regroup the races in education by elaborate transportation schemes. The Southern Congressmen who for so long tried to get others to listen to their complaints now watch with grim satisfaction the agonies of Northern Congressmen faced with the crisis of mandatory, court-imposed transportation for desegregation. On the night of November 4, 1971, as a desperate House passed amendment after amendment in a futile effort to stop busing, Congressman

Edwards of Alabama said:

Mr. Chairman, this will come as a shock to some of my colleagues. I am opposing this amendment. I will tell you why. I look at it from a rather cold standpoint. We are busing all over the First District of Alabama, as far as you can imagine. Buses are everywhere...people say to me, "How in the world are we ever going to stop this madness?" I say, "It will stop the day it starts taking place across the country, in the North, in the East, in the West, and yes, even in Michigan."

And indeed, one of the amendments had been offered by Michigan Congressmen, long-time supporters of desegregation, because what had been decreed for Charlotte, North Carolina; Mobile, Alabama; and endless other Southern cities was now on the way to becoming law in Detroit and its suburbs.

As a massive wave of antagonism to transportation for desegregation sweeps the country, the liberal Congressmen and Democratic Presidential aspirants who have for so long fought for desegregation ask themselves whether there is any third point of view: whether they must join with the activists who say that the struggle is endless and they must not flag, even now; or whether they must join with the Southerners. To stand with the courts in their latest decisions is, for liberal Congressmen, political suicide. A Gallup survey in 1971 revealed that 76 percent of respondents opposed busing, almost as many in the East (71 percent), Midwest (77 percent), and West (72 percent), as in the South (82 percent); a majority of Muskie supporters (65 percent) as well as a majority of Nixon supporters (85 percent). Even more blacks oppose busing than support it (47 to 45 percent). But if to stand with the further extension to all the Northern cities and suburbs of transportation for desegregation is suicide, how can the liberal Congressmen join with the South and with what they view as Northern bigotry in opposing busing? Is there a third position, something which responds to the wave of frustration at court orders, and which does not mean the abandonment of hope for an integrated society?

How have we come from a great national effort to repair a monstrous wrong to a situation in which the sense of right of great majorities is offended by policies which seem continuous with that once noble effort? In order to answer this question, it is necessary to be clear on how the Southern issue became a national issue.

After the passage of the Civil Rights Act of 1964, the first attempt of the South to respond to the massive federal effort to impose desegregation upon it was "freedom of choice." There still existed the black schools and the white schools of a dual school system. But now whites could go to black schools (none did) and the blacks could go to white schools (few dared). It was perfectly clear that throughout the South "freedom of choice" was a means of maintaining the dual school system. In 1966 HEW began the process of demanding statistical proof that substantially more blacks were going to school with whites each year. The screw was tightened regularly, by the courts and HEW, and finally, in 1968, the Supreme Court gave the coup de grâce, insisting that dual school systems be eliminated completely. There must henceforth be no identifiable black schools and white schools, only schools.

But one major issue remained as far as statistical desegregation was concerned: the large cities of the South. For the fact was that the degree of segregation in the big-city Southern schools was by now no longer simply attributable to the dual school systems they, too, had once maintained; in some instances, indeed, these schools had even been "satisfactorily" (by some federal or court standard) desegregated years before. What did it mean to say that their dual school systems must also be dismantled "forthwith"?

Contrast, as a concrete instance, the case of rural New Kent County in Virginia, where the Supreme Court declared in 1968 that "freedom of choice" would not be accepted as a means of desegregating a dual school system. Blacks and whites lived throughout the county. There were two schools, the historic black school and the historic white school. Under "freedom of choice," some blacks attended the white school, and no whites attended the black school. There was a simple solution to desegregation, here and throughout the rural and small-town South, and the Supreme Court insisted in 1968, fourteen years after *Brown*, that the school systems adopt it: to draw a line which simply made two school districts, one for the former black school, and one for the former white school, and to require all children in one district, white and black, to attend the former black school, and all children in the other, white and black, to attend the former white school.

But what now of Charlotte, Mobile, Nashville, and Norfolk? To draw geographical lines around the schools of these cities, which had been done, meant that many white schools remained all white, and many black schools remained all black. Some schools that had been "desegregated" in the past—that is, had experienced some mix of black and white—had already become "resegregated"—that is, largely black or all black as a result of population movements rather than any official action.

If there were to be no black schools and no white schools in the city, one thing at least was necessary: massive transportation of the children to achieve a proper mix. There was no solution in the form of geographical zoning.

But if this was the case, in what way was their situation different from that of Northern cities? In only one respect: the Southern cities had once had dual school systems, and the Northern cities had not. (Even this was not necessarily a decisive difference, for cities outside the Old South had also maintained dual systems until 1954. Indiana had a law permitting them until the late 1940s, and other cities had maintained dual systems somewhat earlier.) Almost everything else was the same. The dynamics of population change were the same. Blacks moved into the central city, whites moved out to the suburbs. Blacks were concentrated in certain areas, owing to a mixture of formal or informal residential discrimination, past or present, economic incapacity, and taste, and these areas of black population became larger and larger, making full desegregation by contiguous geographical zoning impossible. Even the political structures of Southern and Northern cities were becoming more alike. Southern blacks were voting, liberal candidates appealed to them, Southern blacks sat on city councils and school boards. If one required the full desegregation of Southern cities by busing, then why should one not require the full desegregation of Northern cities by busing?

Busing has often been denounced as a false issue. Until busing was decreed for the desegregation of Southern cities, it was. As has been pointed out again and again, buses in the South regularly carried black children past white schools to black schools, and white children past black schools to white schools. When "freedom of choice" failed to achieve desegregation and geographical zoning was imposed, busing sometimes actually declined. In any case, when the school systems were no longer allowed to have buses for blacks and buses for whites, certainly the busing system became more efficient. After 1970, busing for desegregation replaced the busing for segregation.

But this was not true when busing came to Charlotte, North Carolina, and many other cities of the South, in 1971, after the key Supreme Court decision in *Swann v. Charlotte-Mecklenburg County Board of Education*. The City of Charlotte is 64 square miles, larger than Washington, D.C., but it is a part of Mecklenburg County, with which it forms a single school district of 550 square miles, which is almost twice the size of New York City. Many other Southern cities (Mobile, Nashville, Tampa) also form part of exceptionally large school districts. While 29 per cent of the schoolchildren of Mecklenburg County are black, almost all live in Charlotte. Owing to the size of the county,

24,000 of 84,500 children were bused, for the purpose of getting children to schools beyond walking distance. School zones were formed geographically, and the issue was, could all-black and all-white schools exist in Mecklenburg County, if a principle of neighborhood school districting meant they would be so constituted?

The Supreme Court ruled they could not, and transportation could be used to eliminate black and white schools. The Court did not argue that there was a segregative intent in the creation of geographical zones—or that there was not—and referred to only one piece of evidence suggesting an effort to maintain segregation, free transfer. There are situations in which free transfer is used by white children to get out of mostly black schools, but if this had been the problem, the Court could have required a majority-to-minority transfer only (in which one can only transfer from a school in which one's race is a majority, and to a school in which one's race is a minority), as is often stipulated in desegregation plans. Instead the Court approved a plan which involved the busing of some 20,000 additional children, some for distances of up to 15 miles, from the center of the city to the outer limits of the county, and vice versa.

Two implications of the decision remain uncertain, but they may lead to a reorganization of all American education. If Charlotte, because it is part of the school district of Mecklenburg County, can be totally desegregated with each school having a roughly 71-29 white-black proportion, should not city boundaries be disregarded in other places and larger school districts of the Mecklenburg County scale be created wherever such action would make integration possible? A district judge has already answered this question in the affirmative for Richmond, Virginia.

But the second implication is: If Charlotte is—except for the background of a dual school system—socially similar to many Northern cities, and if radical measures can be prescribed to change the pattern that exists in Charlotte, should they not also be prescribed in the North? And to that question also a federal judge, ruling in a San Francisco case, has returned an affirmative answer.

San Francisco has a larger measure of integration probably than most Northern cities. Nevertheless de facto segregation—the segregation arising not from formal decisions to divide the races as in the South, but from other causes, presumed to be social and demographic—has long been an issue in San Francisco. In 1962, the NAACP filed suit against the school board, charging it with "affording, operating, and maintaining a racially segregated school system within the San Francisco Unified School District, contrary to and in violation of the equal protection and due process clause of the Fourteenth Amendment of the Constitution of the United States." As John Kaplan has written:

The history of this suit is a short and strange one. The Board of Education retained for its defense a distinguished local attorney, Joseph Alioto ([later] the mayor), who was primarily an anti-trust specialist. Alioto started discovery proceedings and the heart seemed to go out of the plaintiffs.

In any case, after admitting in depositions that the Board had no intention to produce a condition of racial imbalance; that it took no steps to bring about such a condition; that its lines were not drawn for the purpose of creating or maintaining racial imbalance; that there was no gerrymandering; and finally that the Board was under no obligation to relieve the situation by transporting students from their neighborhoods to other districts, the plaintiffs' attorney allowed the suit to be dismissed for want of prosecution on December 2, 1964.

It was assumed that this disposed of the legal issue. Meanwhile the San Francisco school system continued to struggle with the problem. After a long series of censuses, disputes, and studies, the school board proposed to set up two new integrated complexes, using transportation to integrate, one north and one south of Golden Gate Park. They were to open in 1970. When, however, one was postponed because of money problems, suit was brought once again by integration-minded parents, this time charging de jure segregation on the ground that the school board's failure to implement the two integrated school complexes amounted to an official act maintaining the schools in their presently segregated state.

Judge Stanley Weigel, before whom the matter was argued, very sensibly decided to wait for the Supreme Court's ruling in the Charlotte-Mecklenburg County case which, he and many others thought, might once and for all settle the question of whether de facto segregation was no less unconstitutional than de jure segregation. Although one may doubt from certain passages in the Charlotte-Mecklenburg decision that the Supreme Court did indeed mean to outlaw de facto segregation, Judge Weigel seems to have decided that it did. "The law is settled," he declared, "that school authorities violate the constitutional rights of children by establishing school attendance boundary lines knowing that the result is to continue or increase substantial racial imbalance."

But in ordering the desegregation of the San Francisco schools by transportation, Judge Weigel did not simply rest the matter on de facto segregation; he also listed acts of commission and omission which he believed amounted to de jure school segregation.

Now one can well imagine that a school board which does not or did not recently operate under state laws that required or permitted segregation could nevertheless through covert acts—which are equally acts under state authority—foster segregation. It could, for example, change school-zone lines, so as to confine black children in one school and permit white children to go to another school. It could build schools and expand them so that they served an all-black or all-white population. It could permit a transfer policy whereby white children could escape from black schools while blacks could not. It could assign black teachers to black schools and white teachers to white schools.

Judge Weigel charged all these things. The record—a record made by a liberal school board, appointed by a liberal mayor, in a liberal city, with a black president of the school board—does not, in this layman's opinion, bear him out, unless one is to argue that any action of a school board in construction policy or zone-setting or teacher assignment that precedes a situation in which there are some almost all-black schools (there were no all-black schools in San Francisco) and some almost all-white schools (there were no all-white schools in San Francisco) can be considered de jure segregation.

Under Judge Weigel's interpretation, there is no such thing as de facto segregation. All racial imbalance is the result of state actions, either taken or not taken. If not taken, they should have been taken. De facto disappears as a category requiring any less action than de jure.

This is the position of many lawyers who are arguing these varied cases. I have described the San Francisco case because it led to a legal order requiring desegregation by transportation of the largest Northern or Western system so far affected by such an order. But massive desegregation had also been required by a district judge in Denver, who had then had his judgment limited by the Circuit Court of Appeals.*
.... Simultaneously, Detroit and the surrounding counties and the state of Michigan were put under court order to come up with a plan that permits the desegregation of the schoolchildren of Detroit by busing to the neighboring suburbs, and a federal judge moved toward the same result in Indianapolis.**

The hardy band of civil-rights lawyers now glimpses—or glimpsed, before the two latest appointments to the Supreme Court—a complete victory, based on the idea that there is no difference between de facto and de jure segregation, an idea which is itself based on the larger idea that there is no difference between North and South. What is imposed on the South must be imposed on the North. As Ramsey Clark, a former Attorney-General of the United States, puts it, echoing a widely shared view:

In fact, there is no *de facto* segregation. All segregation reflects some past actions of our governments. The FHA [Federal Housing Administration] itself required racially restrictive convenants until 1948. But, that aside, the consequences of segregated schooling are the same whatever the cause. Segregated schools are inherently unequal however they come to be and the law must prohibit them whatever the reason for their existence.

In other words, whatever exists is the result of state action. If what exists is wrong, state action must undo it. If segregated schools were not made so by official decisions directly affecting the schools, then they were made so by other official decisions—Clark, for example, points to an FHA policy in effect until 1948—that encouraged residential segregation. Behind this argument rests the assumption, now part of the liberal creed, that racism in the North is different, if at all, from racism in the South only in being more hypocritical. All segregation arises from the same evil causes, and all segregation must be struck down. This is the position that many federal judges are now taking in the North— even if, as Judge Weigel did, they try to protect themselves by pointing to some action by the school board that they think might make the situation de jure in the earlier sense as well.

II

I believe that three questions are critical here. First, do basic human rights, as guaranteed by the Constitution, require that the student population of every school be racially balanced according to some specified proportion, and that no school be permitted a black majority? Second, whether or not this is required by the Constitution, is it the only way to improve the education of black children? Third, whether or not this is required by the Constitution, and whether or not it improves the education of black children, is it the only way to improve relations between the races?

These questions are in practice closely linked. What the Court decides is constitutional is very much affected by what it thinks is good for the nation. If it thinks that the education of black children can only be improved in schools with black minorities, it will be very much inclined to see situations in which there are schools with black majorities as unconstitutional. If it thinks race relations can only be improved if all children attend schools which are racially balanced, it will be inclined to find constitutional a requirement to have racial balance.

This is not to say that the courts do not need authority in the

Constitution for what they decide. But this authority is broad indeed and it depends on a doctrine of judicial restraint—which has not been characteristic of the Supreme Court and subordinate federal courts in recent years—to limit judges in demanding what they think is right as well as what they believe to be within the Constitution. Indeed, it was in part because the Supreme Court believed that Negro children *were* being deprived educationally that it ruled as it did in *Brown.* They were being deprived because the schools were very far from "separate and equal." But even if they were "equal," their being "separate" would have been sufficient to make them unconstitutional: "To separate them from others of similar age and qualifications simply because of their race generates a feeling of inferiority as to their race and status in the community that may affect their hearts and minds in a way unlikely ever to be undone."

While much has been made of the point that the Court ruled as it did because of the evidence and views of social scientists as to the effects of segregation on the capacity of black children to learn, the fact is that the basis of the decision was that distinctions by race had no place in American law and public practice, neither in the schools, nor, as subsequent rulings asserted, in any other area, whether in waiting rooms or golf courses. This was clearly a matter of the "equal protection of the laws." It was more problematic as to what should be done to insure the "equal protection of the laws" when such protection had been denied for so long by dual school systems. But remedies were eventually agreed upon, and the Court has continued to rule unanimously—as it did in *Brown*—on these remedies down through *Swann v. Charlotte-Mecklenburg Board of Education.*

Inevitably, however, the resulting increase in the freedom of black children—the freedom to attend the schools they wished—entailed a restriction on the freedom of others. In "freedom of choice," the freedom of white children was in no way limited. In geographical zoning to achieve integration, it was limited, but no more than that of black children. But in busing to distant schools, white children were in effect being conscripted to create an environment which, it had been decided, was required to provide equality of educational opportunity for black children. It was perhaps one thing to do this when the whites in question were the children or grandchildren of those who had deprived black children of their freedom in the past. But when a district judge in San Francisco ruled that not only white children but Chinese children and Spanish-speaking children must be conscripted to create an environment which, he believed, would provide equality of educational opportunity for black children, there was good reason for wondering whether "equal protection of the laws" was once again being violated, this time from the other side.

We are engaged here in a great enterprise to determine what the "equal protection of the laws" should concretely mean in a multi-racial and multi-ethnic society, and one in which various groups have suffered differing measures of deprivation. The blacks have certainly suffered the most, but the Chinese have suffered too, as have the Spanish-speaking groups, and some of the white ethnic groups. Is it "equal protection of the laws" to prevent Chinese-American children from attending nearby schools in their own community, conveniently adjacent to the afternoon schools they also attend? Is it "equal protection of the laws" to keep Spanish-speaking children from attending schools in which their numerical dominance has led to bilingual classes and specially trained teachers? Can the Constitution possibly mean that?

One understands that the people do not vote on what the Constitution means. The judges decide. But it is one thing for the Constitution to say that, despite how the majority feels, it must allow black children into the public schools of their choice; and it is quite another for the Constitution to say, in the words of its interpreters, that some children, owing to their race or ethnic group alone, may not be allowed to attend the schools of their choice, even if their choice has nothing to do with the desire to discriminate racially. When, starting with the first proposition, one ends up with the second, as one has in San Francisco, one wonders if the Constitution can possibly have been interpreted correctly.

Again and again, reading the briefs and the transcripts and the analyses, one finds the words "escape" and "flee." The whites must not escape. They must not flee. Constitutional law often moves through strange and circuitous paths, but perhaps the strangest yet has been the one whereby, beginning with an effort to expand freedom—no Negro child shall be excluded from any public school because of his race—the law has ended up with as drastic a restriction of freedom as we have seen in this country in recent years. No child, of any race or group, may "escape" or "flee" the experience of integration. No school district may facilitate such an escape. Nor may it even (in the Detroit decision) fail to take action to close the loopholes permitting anyone to escape.

Let me suggest that, even though the civil-rights lawyers may feel that in advocating measures like these they are in the direct line of *Brown*, something very peculiar has happened when the main import of an argument changes from an effort to expand freedom to an effort to restrict freedom. Admittedly the first effort concerned the freedom of blacks, the second in large measure concerns the freedom of whites (but not entirely, as we have seen from the many instances in the South where blacks have resisted the elimination of black schools, and in the North where they have fought for community-controlled schools). Nevertheless, the tone of civil-rights cases has turned from one in which the main note is the expansion of freedom, into one in which the main note is the imposition of restrictions. It is ironic to read in Judge Stanley Weigel's decision, following which every child in the San Francisco elementary schools was placed in one of four ethnic or racial categories and made subject to transportation to provide an average mix of each in every school, an approving quotation from Judge Skelly Wright:

The problem of changing a people's mores, particularly those with an emotional overlay, is not to be taken lightly. It is a problem which will require the utmost patience, understanding, generosity, and forbearance from all of us, of whatever race. But the principle is that we are, all of us, freeborn Americans, with a right to make our way, unfettered by sanctions imposed by man because of the work of God.

That was the language of 1956. One finds very little "patience, understanding," etc., in Judge Weigel's own decision, which required the San Francisco School District to prepare a plan to meet the following objectives:

Full integration of all public elementary schools so that the ratio of black children to white children will then be and thereafter continue to be substantially the same in each school. To accomplish these objectives the plans may include:
    a. Use of non-discriminatory busing if, as appears now to be clear, at least some busing will be necessary for compliance with the law.
    b. Changing attendance zones whenever necessary to head off racial segregation.

According to Judge Weigel, the law even requires: "avoidance of the use of tracking systems or other educational techniques or innovations without provision for safeguard against racial segregation as a consequence." Can all this be in the Constitution too?

A second issue that would seem to have some constitutional bearing is whether those who are to provide the children for a minority black environment are being conscripted only on the basis of income. The prosperous and the rich can avail themselves of private schooling, or they can "flee" to the suburbs. And if the Richmond and Detroit rulings should be sustained, making it impossible to "escape" by going to the suburbs, the class character of the decisions would become even more pronounced. For while many working-class and lower-middle-class people can afford to live in suburbs, very few can afford the costs of private education.

Some observers have pointed out that leading advocates of transportation for integration—journalists, political figures, and judges—themselves send their children to private schools which escape the consequences of these legal decisions. But even without being ad hominem, one may raise a moral question: if the judges who are imposing such decisions, the lawyers who argue for them (including brilliant young lawyers from the best law schools employed by federal poverty funds to do the arguing), would not themselves send their children to the schools their decisions bring into being, how can they insist that others poorer and less mobile than they are do so? Clearly those not subject to a certain condition are insisting that others submit themselves to it, which offends the basic rule of morality in both the Jewish and Christian traditions. I assume there must be a place for this rule in the Constitution.

A key constitutional question with which the Supreme Court will now finally have to do deal is whether de facto segregation is really different from de jure segregation, and if so, whether lesser remedies can be required to eradicate it.

Is there really a meaningful difference between a 100 percent black school under a law that prohibits blacks from going to school with whites, and a 100 percent black school that is created by residential segregation? The question has become even subtler: is there a difference between a majority black school in a city which once had de jure segregation, and such a school in a city which did not? I believe that the answer to the second question is no. But in the first case the distinction was meaningful when the Supreme Court handed down *Brown* and is meaningful today. In the de facto situation, to begin with, not all schools are 100 percent segregated. Indeed, none may be. A child's observation alone may demonstrate that there are many opportunities to attend integrated schools. The family may have an opportunity to move, the city may have open enrollment, it may have a voluntary city-to-suburb busing program. The child may conclude that if one's parents wished, one could attend another school, or that one could if one lived in another neighborhood—not all are inaccessible economically or because of discrimination—or could conclude that the presence of a few whites indicated that the school was not segregated.

Admittedly social perception is a complicated thing. The child in a 100 percent black school as a result of residential concentration and strict zoning may see his situation as identical to that of a child in a 100 percent black school because of state law requiring separation of the races. But the fact is that a black child in a school more than 47 percent black (the San Francisco definition of "segregation") may also see himself as unfairly deprived. Or any black child at all, in view of his history, and the currently prevailing interpretation of his position, even if he is the only black child in a white school, may so conclude. Perception is not only based on reality, a reality which to me makes the de facto segregated school a very different thing from the de jure segregated school. Perception can turn the lovely campuses of the West Coast into "jails" which confine young people, and can turn those incarcerated by courts for any crime into political prisoners. If we feel a perception is wrong, one of our duties is to try to correct it, rather than to assume that the perception of being a victim must alone dictate the action to be taken. False perceptions are to be responded to sympathetically, but not as if they were true.

If one finds segregation of apparently de facto origin, what is the proper remedy?

In some cases, one can show that it is not really de facto by pointing to actions that the school board took with a segregatory intent—for example, changing a school-zone line when blacks moved into an area to keep a school all or mostly black or another one all or mostly white. I do not think this was demonstrated in the case of San Francisco, but it was the crucial issue in the first Northern school desegregation case, that of New Rochelle, which was never reviewed by the Supreme Court, and in Pontiac, Michigan, and for some schools in Denver. In districts with a hundred or more schools and a long history, with perhaps scores of school-zone lines changed every year, it would be unlikely if one could not come up with some cases that seemed to show this. Sometimes it was done under pressure of local white parents. Finding this, a court might require something as simple as that the zone line be changed back (this, of course, by the time it came to court would hardly matter since the black residential area would almost certainly have expanded and both zone lines would probably be irrelevant). Or it might require that no zone line be set in the future which had the effect of maintaining segregation. Or that no parental wishes of this sort be taken into account. In cases where segregatory zone lines were commonly or regularly set (Pontiac), more radical relief would be more appropriate.

But there is a basic and troubling question here. School boards are either elected, or appointed by elected officials. They are thus directly or indirectly responsible to citizens. One can well understand the constitutional doctrine which asserts that no elected or appointed board, no governmental official, may deny constitutional rights—e.g., allowing a Communist to speak in a school building—regardless of the wishes of its constituency. But in the case of schooling and school-zone boundary-setting, a host of issues is involved: convenience of access, quality of building, assumed quality of teaching staff, racial composition of students, etc. A board is subject to a hundred influences in making such a decision. It is not as simple a matter as proving this Communist was not allowed to speak because of mass pressure. Nor is the motivation of parents and boards ever unmixed.

In Boston, the school board opened a new school in a black section. It tried to save the state aid that would be lost if it did not take some action to desegregate, and it zoned children living at some distance away into the new school. The white parents protested and eventually the board succumbed to their pressure and allowed them to send their children to their old nearby schools. To the minds of most enforcers of school desegregation, state and national, the board condemned itself for a segregatory act. One of the things the boycotting parents said was that they were afraid their children would get beaten up going through the area they had to traverse in order to get to school. Who is to say that this was pure fantasy, in the conditions of the modern city, and that what the white parents really meant was that they did not want their children to go to a mostly black school? It is this kind of determination on the intent and effect of hundreds of school-board decisions that judges are now required to make. When one reads cases such as those in Indianapolis, Detroit, and elsewhere, the mind reels with the complexity of numerous school-zoning and construction decisions. Briefs, hearing transcripts, exhibits run to thousands of pages. And at least one conclusion that this reader comes to is that no judge can or ought to have to make decisions on such issues, and the chances are that whatever decision he makes will be based on inadequately analyzed information.

Is it the law—and, not being a lawyer, I do not know—that if a segregatory intent plays *any* part in school decisions, then *every* measure of relief, no matter how extensive, is justified? If so, from a non-legal point of view it seems odd that one uncertain act with an uncertain effect on the social and racial patterns of an entire city should justify massive measures to reconstruct a school system.

Perhaps the most serious constitutional issue in a line of cases erasing the distinction between de jure and de facto segregation and also erasing the political boundaries between school districts in order to achieve a racial balance in which every black student is in a minority in every school (and presumably, as the cases develop, every Spanish-speaking student, and so on) is that all this makes impossible one kind of organization that a democratic society may wish to choose for its schools: the kind of organization in which the schools are the expression of a geographically defined community of small scale and regulated in accordance with the democratically expressed views of that community. This is the point Alexander Bickel has argued so forcefully. We have had a good deal of discussion in recent years of "decentralization," "community control," and "parental control" of schools. There were reasons for "community control" long before the issue exploded in New York in the late 1960s, and there were reasons for "parental control" long before the educational voucher scheme was proposed. Now the new line of cases makes the school ever more distant from the community in which it is located and from the parents who send their children to it.

While busing schemes vary, in some, children from a number of different areas are sent to a single school and children from one area are sent to a number of schools. It becomes hard for parental or community concerns to be exercised on the particular school to which one's children go. Thus, in San Francisco, in the Mission district, owing to the effective work of the Mission Coalition (a Saul Alinsky–style community organization), the local community has considerable influence on public programs in the area. With a wide base of membership, this organization can help determine what is most effective in the local schools. But if it wants to create an atmosphere in the school best suited to the education of Spanish-speaking children, what sense does this make when the schools are filled with children from distant areas? And how can it influence the education the Mission children receive in the distant schools to which many of them are now sent?

In effect, the new line of cases gives enormous control to central school bureaucracies, who will make decisions subject only to the courts and the federal government on the one hand, and the mass opinion of a large area dominated by the inevitable slogans which can create majorities on the other. Clearly this is one way of reducing the influence of people over their own environment and their own fate. I believe indeed that the worst effect of the current crisis is that people already reduced to frustration by their inability to affect a complex society and a government moving in ways many of them find incomprehensible and undesirable, must now see one of the last areas of local influence taken from them in order to achieve a single goal, that of racial balance.

The one reason for community control that has recently been considered most persuasive is that the inadequate education of black children may be improved under a greater measure of black community control. This may or may not be the case, but I believe that all people, black and white, have the right to control as much of their lives as is possible in a complex society, and the schools are very likely the only major function of government which would not suffer—and might even benefit—from a greater measure of local control. In education, there are few "economies of scale." It has always seemed fantastic that educators, in proposing "complexes" for 20,000 elementary-school children for purposes of desegregation, could also argue that schools of that size would also be more "efficient." Interestingly, lawyers and judges, in their effort to find de jure segregatory intent in the acts of Northern school boards, will sometimes claim that schools were deliberately made small to lessen the chances of integration. Thus in Detroit, one charge against the school board, accepted by Judge Roth, was that the board built small schools of 300 in order to contain the population and make desegregation more difficult. Paul Goodman and many others would argue that even schools of 300 are probably too large. In San Francisco, on the other hand, the argument was that schools were expanded to "contain" the black and white population. The Detroit judge, it seems, would have preferred the large San Francisco schools, and the San Francisco judge would have preferred the small Detroit schools, if one takes their arguments at face value. But one may be allowed to suspect that if the situations had been reversed, they would still both have found "de jure" segregation in their respective cities.

One consequence of this transfer of power to the center when one transports for racial balance is that there is no local pressure to build a school to serve a local population, since one cannot know what the effect of any local school will be. Thus all decisions on school building revert to the hands of the central school authorities, only affected, as I have already pointed out, by judges and the federal government on the one hand, and a mass opinion unrelated to local district needs on the other. I am skeptical as to whether this will improve school-construction policies. Federal civil-rights agencies and judges have not as yet shown themselves very perceptive in their criticism of local school-construction policies. One piece of evidence of de jure segregation cited by the San Francisco judge, was the building of a new school in Hunter's Point, a black area. The school authorities had resisted building there. The local people insisted on a new school. Just about everyone who supports desegregation in San Francisco supported the local people, even though they knew that the school would be segregated. The local NAACP also supported the building of the new school. The judge, in his decision, cited the building of this school as a sign of the "segregatory" policies of the San Francisco school authorities. To the judge, the black people of Hunter's Point were being "contained," when they should have been sent off elsewhere, leaving their own area devoid of schools (or perhaps any other facilities). But for the people of the area who demanded the school, they were being served. That their school would be, to a federal judge's mind, "segregated" did not seem to them a good reason for all city facilities to be built only in white or Spanish-speaking or Chinese areas.

The attempt of judges and civil-rights lawyers to argue that this or that school was built to be "segregated" for whites or blacks is in any case often naive. The dynamics of population movements in the cities have been too rapid (the black population of San Francisco increased from 5,000 in 1940 to 96,000 in 1970) and the process of school-building too slow, for any such intention to be easily demonstrated or realized in Northern cities. One of the schools cited in the San Francisco case as "segregated" black (64 percent black in 1964), had been cited as recently as 1967 in the Civil Rights Commission's report on *Racial Isolation in the Public Schools* as having been built in order to foster the "segregation" of whites, since it had opened in 1954 with a student body that was almost all white. Presumably, at least for the intervening period, it must have been integrated.

The crucial point is: do federal courts have the right to impose a school policy that would deprive local communities and groups, white and black, of power over their schools? Some of them seem quite sure that they do. Judge Roth in Detroit is critical of the blacks of that city for contributing to what he considers "segregation" by demanding black principals and teachers:

In the most realistic sense, if fault or blame is to be found it is that of the community as a whole, including of course the black components. We need not minimize the effect of the actions of federal, state, and local governmental officers and agencies...to observe that blacks, like ethnic groups in the past, have tended to separate from the larger group and associate together. The ghetto is a place of confinement and a place of refuge. There is enough blame for everyone to share.

We would all agree with Judge Roth that the ghetto must not be a place of confinement and that everything possible must be done to make it as easy for blacks to live where they wish as it is for anyone else. But why should it be the duty or the right of the federal government and the federal judiciary to destroy the ghetto as a place of refuge if that is what some blacks want? Judge Roth is trying to read into the Constitution the crude Americanizing and homogenizing which is certainly one part of the American experience, but which is just as certainly not the main way we in this country have responded to the facts of a multi-ethnic society. The doctrines to which Judge Roth lends his authority would deny not only to blacks, but to any other group, a right of refuge which is quite properly theirs in a multi-ethnic society built on democratic and pluralist principles.

I do not speak here of limiting what communities may freely choose to do in order to integrate their schools. I speak only of the judicial insistence that they *must* do certain things. Much busing for desegregation is engaged in by school boards independently of court decisions, because the board feels this is good for education; or because it is under pressure from blacks and white liberal citizens who demand such measures; or because it is required or is under pressure to do so from state education authorities—who, in the major Northern and Western states, and in particular in Massachusetts, New York, Pennsylvania, and California, require local school districts to eliminate racial imbalance defined in various ways. More than 50 percent black is racial imbalance in Massachusetts, and 15 percent more or less of each group in each school than the proportion of that group in the entire district is racial imbalance in California. (It was on the basis of the 15 percent rule that more than 47 percent black was considered segregated in San Francisco, for the proportion of black students in the schools was 32 percent.) Thus, the City of Berkeley has been transporting its children to achieve integration for three years now, without any court or federal action. Riverside has done the same. Many cities have implemented, independently of court action, some degree of transportation for integration. Many of these actions have been attacked in the courts from the other side—that is, by white parents charging that for racial reasons alone they were being assigned to schools far from their homes. All these challenges have been struck down in the courts, in spite of state laws (such as New York's) which declare transportation for desegregation illegal. Interestingly enough, while the San Francisco school board was under attack from one side for having failed to implement one of its integration-through-busing school complexes, it was under attack from the other side for having implemented the one it had. It was of course the first of the two attacks that was supported by the district judge.

It is not this kind of action-to-integrate—undertaken by elected school boards, or by school boards appointed by elected officials, for educational or political reasons—that is under discussion here. Unless a political decision is clearly unconstitutional it should stand. Indeed, it is very likely that decisions to achieve racial balance taken by school boards not under judicial or federal order but because the political forces in that district demand it, have better effects than those undertaken under court order by resentful school administrations. In the first case, the methods of reducing racial imbalance have been worked out through the processes of political give-and-take, the community and teachers and administrators have been prepared for the change by the political process, the parents who oppose it have lost in what they themselves consider a fair fight. The characteristics of judge-imposed decisions are quite different.

III

There is, then, considerable room for doubt as to whether the Constitution actually mandates a system whereby every school shall have a black minority and no school shall have a black majority. Nevertheless present-day judges, with whom the doctrine of judicial restraint is not especially popular, seem able to find constitutional warrant for whatever policies they feel are best for the society. And so we come to the other crucial questions raised by the new line of cases: Is school desegregation the only way to improve the education of black children and/or the relations between the races?

Without rehearsing the terrible facts in detail, we know that blacks finish high school in the North three or more years behind whites in achievement. We also know with fair confidence that this huge gap is not caused by differential expenditures of money. Just about as much is spent on predominantly black schools outside the South as on predominantly white ones. Classes in black schools will often be smaller than classes in white ones—because the black schools tend to be located in old areas with many school buildings, while white schools tend to be in newer areas with fewer and more crowded school buildings. Blacks will often have more professional personnel assigned, owing to various federal and other programs. There are, to be sure, lower teacher salaries in the predominantly black schools, because they usually have younger teachers with less seniority and fewer degrees. Anyone who believes this is a serious disadvantage for a teacher has a faith in experience and degrees which is justified by no known evidence. (It is quite true that the big cities spend much less on their schools, white and black, than the surrounding suburban areas, which are almost entirely white. Regardless of the fact that spending more is unlikely to do much to improve education—it tends mostly to improve teachers' salaries and fringe benefits—it is quite unconscionable that more public money should be spent on the education of those from prosperous backgrounds than on those from poorer families. But this is quite separate from the issue of whether within present school districts less is spent on the education of black children, and whether spending more would reduce the gap in achievement.)

If money is not the decisive element in the gap between white and black, what is? In 1966 the Coleman report on *Equality of Educational Opportunity* reviewed the achievement of hundreds of thousands of American school children, black and white, and related it to social and economic background, to various factors within the schools, and to integration. In 1967, another study, *Racial Isolation in the Public Schools,* analyzed the effects of compensatory-education programs and reviewed the data on integration. Both studies—as well as subsequent experience and research—suggested that if anything could be counted on to affect the education of black children, it was integration. However, the operative element was not race but social class. The conclusion of the Coleman report still seems the best statement of the case: "The apparent beneficial effect of a student body with a high proportion of white students comes not from racial composition per se, but from the better educational background and higher educational aspirations that are, on the average, found among white students."

On the other hand, if such integration did have an effect, it was not very great. The most intense reanalysis of Coleman's data[2] concludes: "Our findings on the school racial composition issue, then, are mixed...the initial *Equality of Educational Opportunity* survey overstressed the impact of school social class.... When the issue is probed at grade 6, a small independent effect of schools' racial composition appeared, but its significance for educational policy seems slight."

The study of these issues has reached a Talmudic complexity. The finding that integration of different socioeconomic groups favors the achievement of lower socioeconomic groups apparently stands up, but the effect is not large. One thing, however, does seem clear: integrating the hapless and generally lower-income whites of the central city with lower-income blacks, particularly under conditions of resentment and conflict, as in San Francisco, is likely to achieve nothing, in educational terms.

In San Francisco, the number of children enrolled in elementary schools dropped 6,519 against a projected drop of 1,508 (a 13 percent decline against a projected 3 percent decline) in response to Judge Weigel's decision. The junior-high-school enrollment, not yet subjected to full-scale busing, declined only 1 percent, and high-school enrollment remained the same. In Pasadena, California, there was a 22 percent drop in the number of white students in the school system between 1969—before court-imposed busing—and 1971. In Norfolk, Virginia, court-imposed busing brought a drop of 20 percent. If, as seems probable, it is the somewhat better-off and more mobile who leave the public-school system when busing is imposed, the effect on the achievement of black children is further reduced.

It is in response to such facts as these and in the light of such findings as Coleman's that judges in Detroit and Indianapolis and elsewhere now call for combining the central city and the suburb into unified school districts. But if this elaborate reorganization of the schools is being undertaken so that the presumed achievement-raising effect of socioeconomic integration may occur, we are likely to be cruelly disappointed. There is little if any encouragement to be derived from studies, published and unpublished, of voluntary busing programs even though such busing takes place under the most favorable circumstances (with motivated volunteers, from motivated families, and with schools acting freely and enthusiastically). Indeed, much integration through transportation has been so disappointing in terms of raising achievement that it may well lead to a revaluation of the earlier research whose somewhat tenuous results raised what begin to look like false hopes as to the educational effects of socioeconomic integration.

IV

There is yet a final argument. One will hear it in Berkeley, which underwent full desegregation by busing three years ago, and which has seen no particular reduction of the white-black achievement gap. The argument is that school integration will improve relations between the races and that in view of the extremity of interracial tensions in this country, anything that improves these relations must be done. In Berkeley, a liberal community with an elected school board which voluntarily introduced transportation for racial balance and was not turned out for doing so, one can perhaps make this argument. But race relations are not ideal even in Berkeley, as Senator Mondale's committee discovered in 1971 when it conducted hearings there on the most successful American case of racial balance through transportation.

The Mondale committee discovered, for example, that after the schools were fully integrated, a special program for blacks— Black

House—was established at the high-school level from which non-black students and teachers were excluded. (Berkeley High School, the only one in the city, has always been integrated.) The committee discovered, when it spoke to students—selected, one assumes, by the school authorities because they would give the best picture of integration—that students of different groups had little to do with one another. The black president of the senior class said: "...the only true existence of integration of Berkeley High is in the hallways when the bell rang everybody, you know, pass [sic] through the hallways, that is the only time I see true integration in Berkeley High." Senator Brooke probed deeper. Since the young man was black and a majority of his classmates were white, had they not voted for him? "The whites didn't even participate in voting.... They felt the student government was a farce." (The opposing candidate was also black.) What about social activities? "Like we have dances, if there is a good turnout you see two or three whites at the dances...." Intramural sports? "The basketball team is pretty integrated, the crew team is mainly white, soccer team mainly white, tennis team mainly white." Did this mean, Senator Brooke asked, "that blacks don't go out for these teams that are white and whites don't go out for those teams that are all black?" The class president guessed that "whites like to play tennis and blacks like to play basketball better." Still, he did think integration was a good idea, as did a Japanese girl who told the Senators: "I think like the Asian kids at Berkeley High go around with Asian kids."

A Chicano student testified:

I think the integration plan is working, started to work in junior high, it is different levels, the sixth graders go up to seventh grade now. I think now the Chicanos and blacks, they do hang around in groups. Usually some don't, I admit, like I myself hang around with all Chicanos but I am not prejudiced. I do it because I grew up with them, because they were my school buddies when there were segregated schools.

A black girl in elementary school said: "About integration, I don't think it is too integrated, but it is pretty well integrated. I have a lot of white friends...." She lives in an integrated neighborhood. A white girl from the high school testified:

Integration, ideally, as far as I can see it isn't working. I mean like as far as everybody doing things together...I have one class where there are only two whites in it. I being one of them, you know, like I don't have any problems there, but outside...[with other blacks] we just do different things. I am not interested in games. I couldn't care less. I don't know anything about Berkeley as far as the athletics go. . . . I wear very short skirts and walking down the halls I get hassled enough by all the black Dukes, you know. . . .

Senator Brooke was surprised she wasn't hassled by the white boys too and suggested that they might use a different technique.[3]

This is about the most positive report one can make on school integration. Why should anyone be surprised? There is a good deal of hanging around in groups, and there is some contact across racial lines, but the groups seem to have different interests and different social styles. The younger children have more in common than the older ones. It would be hard to say whether this commonality of interest will continue through high school—a popular Berkeley theory—or whether differences will assert themselves as the children grow older even though they were exposed to integration earlier than those now in high school. In other communities which have been studied, black children who are bused tend to become more anti-white than those who are not bused. One can think of a number of reasons for this.

If, then, the judges are moving toward a forcible reorganization of American education because they believe this will improve relations between the races, they are acting neither on evidence nor on experience but on faith. And in so acting on faith they are pushing against many legitimate interests: the interest in using tax money for education rather than transportation; the interest of the working and lower-middle classes in attending schools near their homes; the interest of all groups, including black groups, in developing some measure of control over the institutions which affect their lives; the interest of all people in retaining freedom of choice wherever this is possible.

There is unfortunately a widespread feeling, strong among liberals who have fought so long against the evil of racial segregation, that to stop now—before busing and expanded school districts are imposed on every city in the country—would be to betray the struggle for an integrated society. They are quite wrong. They have been misled by the professionals and specialists—in this instance, the government officials, the civil-rights lawyers, and judges—as to what integration truly demands, and how it is coming about. Professionals and specialists inevitably overreach themselves, and there is no exception here.

It would be a terrible error to consider opposition to the recent judicial decisions on school integration as a betrayal of the promise of *Brown*. The promise of *Brown* is being realized. Black children may not be denied admittance to any school on account of their race (except for the cases in which courts and federal officials insist that they are to be denied admittance to schools with a black majority simply because they are black). The school systems of the South are desegregated. But more than that, integration in general has made enormous advances since 1954. It has been advanced by the hundreds of thousands of blacks in Northern and Western colleges. It has been advanced by the hundreds of thousands of blacks who have moved into professional and white-collar jobs in government, in the universities, in the school systems, in business. It has been advanced by the steady rise in black income which offers many blacks the opportunity to live in integrated areas. Most significantly, it has been advanced because millions of blacks now vote—in the South as well as the North—and because hundreds of blacks have been elected to school committees, city councils, state legislatures, the Congress. This is what is creating an integrated society in the United States.

We are far from this necessary and desirable goal. It would be a tragedy if the progress we made in achieving integration in the 1960s were not continued through the 70s. We can now foresee within a reasonable time the closing of many gaps between white and black. But I doubt that mandatory transportation of schoolchildren for integration will advance this process.

For, so far as the schools in particular are concerned, the increase in black political power means that blacks—like all other groups—can now negotiate, on the basis of their own power, and to the extent of their own power, over what kind of school systems should exist, and involving what measure of transportation and racial balance. In the varied settings of American life there will be many different answers to these questions. What Berkeley has done is not what New York City has done, and there is no reason why it should be. But everywhere black political power is present and contributing to the development of solutions.

There is a third path for liberals now agonized between the steady imposition of racial and ethnic group quotas on every school in the country—a path of pointlessly expensive and destructive homogenization—and surrender to segregation. It is a perfectly sound American path, one which assumes that groups are different and will have their own interests and orientations, but which insists that no one be penalized because of group membership, and that a common base of experience be demanded of all Americans. It is the path that made possible the growth of the parochial schools, not as a challenge to a common American society, but as one variant within it. It is a path that, to my mind, legitimizes such developments as community control of schools and educational vouchers permitting the free choice of schools. There are as many problems in working out the details of this path as of the other two, but it has one thing to commend it as against the other two: it expands individual freedom, rather than restricts it.

One understands that the Constitution sets limits to the process of negotiation and bargaining even in a multi-racial and multi-ethnic setting. But the judges have gone far beyond what the Constitution can reasonably be thought to allow or require in the operation of this complex process. The judges should now stand back, and allow the forces of political democracy in a pluralist society to do their proper work.

5
The Roots of
Contemporary Egalitarianism

Irving Kristol

ABOUT EQUALITY

There would appear to be little doubt that the matter of equality has become, in these past two decades, a major political and ideological issue. The late Hugh Gaitskell proclaimed flatly that "socialism is about equality," and though this bold redefinition of the purpose of socialism must have caused Karl Marx to spin in his grave—he thought egalitarianism a vulgar, philistine notion and had only contemptuous things to say about it—nevertheless most socialist politicians now echo Mr. Gaitskell in a quite routine way. And not only socialist politicians: in the United States today, one might fairly conclude from the political debates now going on that capitalism, too, is "about equality," and will stand or fall with its success in satisfying the egalitarian impulse. To cap it all, a distinguished Harvard professor, John Rawls, recently published a serious, massive, and widely-acclaimed work in political philosophy whose argument is that a social order is just and legitimate *only* to the degree that it is directed to the redress of inequality. To the best of my knowledge, no serious political philosopher ever offered such a proposition before. It is a proposition, after all, that peremptorily casts a pall of illegitimacy over the entire political history of the human race—that implicitly indicts Jerusalem and Athens and Rome and Elizabethan England, all of whom thought *in*equality was necessary to achieve a particular ideal of human excellence, both individual and collective. Yet most of the controversy about Professor Rawls's extraordinary thesis has revolved around the question of whether he has demonstrated it with sufficient analytical meticulousness. The thesis itself is not considered controversial.

One would think, then, that with so much discussion "about

equality," there would be little vagueness as to what equality itself is about—what one means by "equality." Yet this is not at all the case. I think I can best illustrate this point by recounting a couple of my editorial experiences at the journal, the *Public Interest*, with which I am associated.

It is clear that some Americans are profoundly and sincerely agitated by the existing distribution of income in this country, and these same Americans—they are mostly professors, of course—are constantly insisting that a more equal distribution of income is a matter of considerable urgency. Having myself no strong prior opinion as to the "proper" shape of an income-distribution curve in such a country as the United States, I have written to several of these professors asking them to compose an article that would describe a proper redistribution of American income. In other words, in the knowledge that they are discontented with our present income distribution, and taking them at their word that when they demand "more equality" they are not talking about an absolute leveling of all incomes, I invited them to give our readers a picture of what a "fair" distribution of income would be like.

I have never been able to get that article, and I have come to the conclusion that I never shall get it. In two cases, I was promised such an analysis, but it was never written. In the other cases, no one was able to find the time to devote to it. Despite all the talk "about equality," no one seems willing to commit himself to a precise definition from which statesmen and social critics can take their bearings.

As with economists, so with sociologists. Here, instead of income distribution, the controversial issue is social stratification—i.e., the "proper" degree of intergenerational social mobility. The majority of American sociologists seem persuaded that the American democracy has an insufficient degree of such mobility, and it seemed reasonable to me that some of them—or at least one of them!—could specify what degree would be appropriate. None of them, I am sure, envisages a society that is utterly mobile—in which *all* the sons and daughters of the middle and upper classes end up in the very lowest social stratum, where they can live in anticipation of *their* sons and daughters rising again toward the top—and then of their grandsons and granddaughters moving downward once again! On the other hand, there is much evident dissatisfaction with what social mobility we do have. So why not find out what pattern of social mobility would be "fair" and "just" and "democratic"?

I regret to report that one will not find this out by consulting any issue of the *Public Interest*. I further regret to report that nowhere in our voluminous socioligical literature will one find any such depiction of the ideally mobile society. Our liberal sociologists, like our liberal economists, are eloquent indeed in articulating their social discontents, but they are also bewilderingly modest in articulating their social goals. Now, what is one to infer from this experience? One could, of course, simply dismiss the whole thing as but another instance of the intellectual irresponsibility of our intellectuals. That such irresponsibility exists seems clear enough—but *why* it exists is not clear at all. I do not believe that our intellectuals and scholars are genetically destined to be willfully or mischievously irresponsible. They are, I should say, no more perverse than the rest of mankind, and if they act perversely there must be a reason—even if they themselves cannot offer us a reason.

I, for one, am persuaded that though those people talk most earnestly about equality, it is not really equality that interests them. Indeed, it does not seem to me that equality per se is much of an issue for anyone. Rather, it is a surrogate for all sorts of other issues—some of them of the highest importance; these involve nothing less than our conception of what constitutes a just and legitimate society, a temporal order of things that somehow "makes sense" and seems "right."

A just and legitimate society, according to Aristotle, is one in which inequalities—of property, or station, or power—are generally perceived by the citizenry as necessary for the common good. I do not see that this definition has ever been improved on, though generations of political philosophers have found it unsatisfactory and have offered alternative definitions. In most cases, the source of this dissatisfaction has been what I would call the "liberal" character of the definition—i.e., it makes room for many different and even incompatible kinds of just and legitimate societies. In some of these societies, large inequalities are accepted as a necessary evil, whereas in others they are celebrated as the source of positive excellence. The question that this definition leaves open is the relation between a particular just and legitimate society and the "best" society. Aristotle, as we know, had his own view of the "best" society—he called it a "mixed regime," in which the monarchical, aristocratic, and democratic principles were all coherently inter-mingled. But he recognized that his own view of the "best" regime was of a primarily speculative nature—that is to say, a view always worth holding in mind but usually not relevant to the contingent circum-stances (the "historical" circumstances, we should say) within which actual statesmen have to operate.

Later generations found it more difficult to preserve this kind of philosophic detachment from politics. The influence of Christianity, with its messianic promises, made the distinction between "the best" and "the legitimate" even harder to preserve against those who insisted that *only* the best regime was legitimate. (This, incidentally, is an assumption that Professor Rawls makes as a matter of course.) The Church tried—as an existing and imperfect institution it had to try—to maintain this distinction, but it could only do so by appearing somewhat less Christian than it had promised to be. When the messianic impulse was secularized in early modernity, and science and reason and technology took over the promise of redemptive power—of transforming this dismal world into the wonderful place it "ought" to be—that same difficulty persisted. Like the Church, all the political regimes of modernity have had to preserve their legitimacy either by claiming an ideal character which in obvious truth they did not possess, or by making what were taken to be "damaging admissions" as to their inability to transform the real into the ideal.

The only corrective to this shadow of illegitimacy that has hovered threateningly over the politics of Western civilization for nearly two millennia now was the "common sense" of the majority of the population, which had an intimate and enduring relation to mundane realities that was relatively immune to speculative enthusiasm. This relative immunity was immensely strengthened by the widespread belief in an afterlife—a realm in which, indeed, whatever existed would be utterly perfect. I think it possible to suggest that the decline of the belief in personal immortality has been the most important *political* fact of the last hundred years—nothing else has so profoundly affected the way in which the masses of people experience their worldly condition. But even today, the masses of people tend to be more "reasonable," as I would put it, in their political judgments and political expectations than are our intellectuals. The trouble is that our society is breeding more and more "intellectuals" and fewer common men and women.

I use quotation marks around the term "intellectuals" because this category has, in recent decades, acquired a significantly new complexion. The enormous expansion in higher education, and the enormous increase in the college-educated, means that we now have a large class of people in our Western societies who, though lacking intellectual distinction (and frequently lacking even intellectual competence), nevertheless believe themselves to be intellectuals. A recent poll of American college teachers discovered that no fewer than 50 percent defined themselves as "intellectuals." That gives us a quarter of a million American intellectuals on our college faculties alone; if one adds all those in government and in the professions who would also lay claim to the title, the figure would easily cross the million mark! And if one also adds the relevant numbers of college students, one might pick up another million or so. We are, then, in a country like America today, talking about a mass of several millions of "intellectuals" who are looking at their society in a highly critical way and are quick to adopt an adversary posture toward it.

It is this class of people who are most eloquent in their denunciations of inequality, and who are making such a controversial issue of it. Why? Inequality of income is no greater today than it was twenty years ago, and is certainly less than it was fifty years ago. Inequality of status and opportunity have visibly declined since World War II, as a result of the expansion of free or nearly-free higher education. (The percentage of our leading business executives who come from modest socioeconomic backgrounds is much greater today than in 1910.) Though there has been a mushrooming of polemics against the inequalities of the American condition, most of this socioeconomic literature is shot through with disingenuousness, sophistry, and unscrupulous statistical maneuvering. As Professor Seymour Martin Lipset has demonstrated, by almost any socioeconomic indicator one would select, American society today is—as best we can determine—*more* equal than it was one hundred years ago. Yet, one hundred years ago most Americans were boasting of the historically unprecedented equality that was to be found in their nation, whereas today many seem convinced that inequality is at least a problem and at worst an intolerable scandal.

The explanation, I fear, is almost embarrassingly vulgar in its substance. A crucial clue was provided several years ago by Professor Lewis Feuer, who made a survey of those American members of this "new class" of the college-educated—engineers, scientists, teachers, social scientists, psychologists, etc.—who had visited the Soviet Union in the 1920s and 1930s, and had written admiringly of what they saw. In practically all cases, what they saw was power and status in the possession of their own kinds of people. The educators were enthusiastic about the "freedom" of educators in the USSR to run things as they saw fit. Ditto the engineers, the psychologists, and the rest. Their perceptions were illusory, of course, but this is less significant than the wishful thinking that so evidently lay behind the illusions. The same illusions, and the same wishful thinking, are now to be noticed among our academic tourists to Mao's China.

The simple truth is that the professional classes of our modern bureaucratized societies are engaged in a class struggle with the business community for status and power. Inevitably, this class struggle is conducted under the banner of "equality"—a banner also raised by the bourgeoisie in *its* revolutions. Professors are genuinely indignant at the expense accounts which business executives have and which they do not. They are, in contrast, utterly convinced that *their* privileges are "rights" that are indispensable to the proper workings of a good society. Most academics and professional people are even unaware that they are among the "upper" classes of our society. When one points this out to them, they refuse to believe it.[1]

The animus toward the business class on the part of members of our "new class" is expressed in large ideological terms. But what it comes down to is that our *nuovi uomini* are persuaded they can do a better job of running our society and feel entitled to have the opportunity. This is what *they* mean by "equality."

Having said this, however, one still has to explain the authentic moral passion that motivates our egalitarians of the "new class." They are not motivated by any pure power-lust; very few people are. They clearly dislike—to put it mildly—our liberal, bourgeois, commercial society, think it unfit to survive, and seek power to reconstruct it in some unspecified but radical way. To explain this, one has to turn to the intellectuals—the real ones—who are the philosophical source of their ideological discontent.

Any political community is based on a shared conception of the common good, and once this conception becomes ambiguous and unstable, then the justice of any social order is called into question. In a democratic civilization, this questioning will always take the form of an accusation of undue privilege. Its true meaning, however, is to be found behind the literal statements of the indictment.

It is interesting to note that, from the very beginnings of modern bourgeois civilization, the class of people we call intellectuals—poets, novelists, painters, men of letters—has never accepted the bourgeois notion of the common good. This notion defines the common good as consisting mainly of personal security under the law, personal liberty under the law, and a steadily increasing material prosperity for those who apply themselves to that end. It is, by the standards of previous civilizations, a "vulgar" conception of the common good—there is no high nobility of purpose, no selfless devotion to transcendental ends, no awe-inspiring heroism. It is, therefore, a conception of the common good that dispossesses the intellectual of his traditional prerogative— which was to celebrate high nobility of purpose, selfless devotion to transcendental ends, and awe-inspiring heroism. In its place, it offered the intellectuals the freedom to write or compose as they pleased and then to sell their wares in the marketplace as best they could. This "freedom" was interpreted by—one can even say experienced by— intellectuals as a base servitude to philistine powers. They did not accept it two hundred years ago; they do not accept it today.

The original contempt of intellectuals for bourgeois civilization was quite explicitly "elitist," as we should now say. It was the spiritual egalitarianism of bourgeois civilization that offended them, not any material inequalities. They anticipated that ordinary men and women would be unhappy in bourgeois civilization precisely because it was a civilization of and for the "common man"—and it was their conviction that common men could only find true happiness when their lives were subordinated to and governed by uncommon ideals, as conceived and articulated by intellectuals. It was, and is, a highly presumptuous and self-serving argument to offer—though I am not so certain that it was or is altogether false. In any case, it was most evidently not an egalitarian argument. It only became so in our own century, when aristocratic traditions had grown so attenuated that the only permissible anti-bourgeois arguments had to be framed in "democratic" terms. The rise of socialist and Communist ideologies made this transition a relatively easy one. A hundred years ago, when an intellectual became "alienated" and "radicalized," he was more likely to move "Right" than "Left." In our own day, his instinctive movement will almost certainly be to the "Left."

With the mass production of "intellectuals" in the course of the twentieth century, traditional intellectual attitudes have come to permeate our college-educated upper-middle classes—and most especially the children of these classes. What has happened to the latter may be put with a simplicity that is still serviceably accurate: they have obtained enough of the comforts of bourgeois civilization, and have a secure enough grip upon them, to permit themselves the luxury of reflecting uneasily upon the inadequacies of their civilization. They then discover that a life that is without a sense of purpose creates an acute experience of anxiety, which in turn transforms the universe into a hostile, repressive place. The spiritual history of mankind is full of such existential moments, which are the seedbeds of gnostic and millenarian movements—movements that aim at both spiritual and material reformations. Radical egalitarianism is, in our day, exactly such a movement.

The demand for greater equality has less to do with any specific inequities of bourgeois society than with the fact that bourgeois society is seen as itself inequitable because it is based on a deficient conception of the common good. The recent history of Sweden is living proof of this proposition. The more egalitarian Sweden becomes—and it is already about as egalitarian as it is ever likely to be—the more *enragés* are its intellectuals, the more guilt-ridden and uncertain are its upper-middle classes, the more "alienated" are its college-educated youth. Though Swedish politicians and journalists cannot bring themselves to believe it, it should be obvious by now that there are *no* reforms that are going to placate the egalitarian impulse in Swedish society. Each reform only invigorates this impulse the more—because the impulse is not, in the end, about equality at all but about the equality of life in bourgeois society.

In Sweden, as elsewhere, it is only the common people who remain loyal to the bourgeois ethos. As well they might—it is an ethos devised for their satisfaction. Individual liberty and security—in the older, bourgeois senses of these terms—and increasing material prosperity are still goals that are dear to the hearts of the working classes of the West. They see nothing wrong with a better, bourgeois life—a life without uncommon pretensions, a life to be comfortably lived by common men. This explains two striking oddities of current politics: 1) The working classes have, of all classes, been the most resistant to the spirit of radicalism that has swept the upper levels of bourgeois society; and 2) once a government starts making concessions to this spirit—by announcing its dedication to egalitarian reforms—the working class is rendered insecure and fearful, and so becomes more militant in *its* demands. These demands may be put in terms of greater equality of income and privilege—but, of course, they also and always mean greater inequality vis-a-vis other sections of the working class and those who are outside the labor force.

Anyone who is familiar with the American working class knows—as Senator McGovern discovered—that they are far less consumed with egalitarian bitterness or envy than are college professors or affluent journalists. True, they do believe that in a society where so large a proportion of the national budget is devoted to the common defense, there ought to be some kind of "equality of sacrifice," and they are properly outraged when tax laws seem to offer wealthy people a means of tax avoidance not available to others. But they are even more outraged at the way the welfare state spends the large amounts of tax monies it does collect. These monies go in part to the non-working population and in part to the middle-class professionals who attend to the needs of the non-working population (teachers, social workers, lawyers, doctors, dieticians, civil servants of all descriptions). The "tax rebellion" of recent years has been provoked mainly by the rapid growth of this welfare state, not by particular inequities in the tax laws— inequities, which, though real enough, would not, if abolished, have any significant impact on the workingman's tax burden.

Still, though ordinary people are not significantly impressed by the assertions and indignations of egalitarian rhetoric, they cannot help but be impressed by the fact that the ideological response to this accusatory rhetoric is so feeble. Somehow, bourgeois society seems incapable of explaining and justifying its inequalities—seems incapable of explaining and justifying how these inequalities contribute to or are consistent with the common good. This, I would suggest, derives from the growing bureaucratization of the economic order, a process which makes bourgeois society ever more efficient economically, but also ever more defenseless before its ideological critics.

For any citizen to make a claim to an unequal share of income, power, or status, his contribution has to be—and has to be seen to be—a human and personal thing. In no country are the huge salaries earned by film stars or popular singers or professional athletes a source of envy or discontent. More than that: in most countries—and especially in the United States—the individual entrepreneur who builds up his own business and becomes a millionaire is rarely attacked on egalitarian grounds. In contrast, the top executives of our large corporations, most of whom are far less wealthy than Frank Sinatra or Bob Hope or Mick Jagger or Wilt Chamberlain, cannot drink a martini on the expense account without becoming the target of a "populist" politician. These faceless and nameless personages (who is the president of General Electric?) have no clear title to their privileges—and I should say the reason is precisely that they are nameless and faceless. One really has no way of knowing what they are doing "up there," and whether what they are doing is in the public interest or not.

It was not always so. In the nineteenth century, at the apogee of the bourgeois epoch, the perception of unequal contributions was quite vivid indeed. The success of a businessman was taken to be testimony to his personal talents and character—especially character, than which there is nothing more personal. This explains the popularity of biographies of successful entrepreneurs, full of anecdotes about the man and with surprisingly little information about his economic activities. In the twentieth century, "entrepreneurial history," as written in our universities, becomes the history of the firm rather than the biography of a man. To a considerable extent, of course, this reflects the fact that most businessmen today are not "founding fathers" of a firm but temporary executives in a firm—the bureaucratization of modern society empties the category of the bourgeois of its human content. To the best of my knowledge, the only notable biography of a living businessman to have appeared in recent years was that of Alfred

P. Sloan, who made his contribution to General Motors a good half century ago.

Nor is it only businessmen who are so affected. As the sociological cast of mind has gradually substituted itself for the older bourgeois moral-individualist cast of mind, military men and statesmen have suffered a fate similar to that of businessmen. Their biographies emphasize the degree to which they shared all our common human failings; their contributions to the common good, when admitted at all, are ascribed to larger historical forces in whose hands they were little more than puppets. They are all taken to be representative men, not exceptional men.

But when the unequal contributions of individuals are perceived as nothing but the differential functions of social or economic or political roles, then only those inequalities absolutely needed to perform these functions can be publicly justified—and the burden of proof is heavy indeed, as each and every inequality must be scrutinized for its functional purport. True, that particular martini, drunk in that place, in that time, in that company, might contribute to the efficiency and growth of the firm and the economy. But would the contribution really have been less if the executive in question had been drinking water?[2]

So this, it appears to me, is what the controversy "about equality" is really about. We have an intelligentsia which so despises the ethos of bourgeois society, and which is so guilt-ridden at being implicated in the life of this society, that it is inclined to find even collective suicide preferable to the status quo. (How else can one explain the evident attraction which totalitarian regimes possess for so many of our writers and artists?) We have a "new class" of self-designated "intellectuals" who share much of this basic attitude—but who, rather than committing suicide, pursue power in the name of equality. (The children of this "new class," however, seem divided in their yearnings for suicide via drugs, and in their lust for power via "revolution.") And then we have the ordinary people, working-class and lower-middle-class, basically loyal to the bourgeois order but confused and apprehensive at the lack of clear meaning in this order—a lack derived from the increasing bureaucratization (and accompanying impersonalization) of political and economic life. All of these discontents tend to express themselves in terms of "equality"—which is in itself a quintessentially bourgeois ideal and slogan.

It is neither a pretty nor a hopeful picture. None of the factors contributing to this critical situation is going to go away—they are endemic to our twentieth-century liberal-bourgeois society. Still, one of the least appreciated virtues of this society is its natural recuperative powers—its capacity to change, as we say, but also its capacity to preserve itself, to adapt and survive. The strength of these powers always astonishes us, as we anticipate (even proclaim) an imminent apocalypse that somehow never comes. And, paradoxically enough, this vitality almost surely has something to do with the fact that the bourgeois conception of equality, so vehemently denounced by the egalitarian, is "natural" in a way that other political ideas—egalitarian or anti-egalitarian—are not. Not necessarily in all respects superior, but more "natural." Let me explain.

The founding fathers of modern bourgeois society (John Locke, say, or Thomas Jefferson) all assumed that biological inequalities among men—inequalities in intelligence, talent, abilities of all kinds—were not extreme, and therefore did not justify a society of hereditary privilege (of "two races," as it were). This assumption we now know to be true, demonstrably true, as a matter of fact. Human talents and abilities, as measured, do distribute themselves along a bell-shaped curve, with most people clustered around the middle, and with much smaller percentages at the lower and higher ends. That men are "created equal" is not a myth or a mere ideology—unless, of course, one interprets that phrase literally, which would be patently absurd and was never the bourgeois intention. Moreover, it is a demonstrable fact that in all modern, bourgeois societies, the distribution of income is also along a bell-shaped curve, indicating that in such an "open" society the inequalities that do emerge are not inconsistent with the bourgeois notion of equality.

It is because of this "natural tyranny of the bell-shaped curve," that contemporary experiments in egalitarian community-building—the Israeli kibbutz, for instance—only work when they recruit a homogeneous slice of the citizenry, avoiding a cross-section of the entire population. It also explains why the aristocratic idea—of a "twin-peaked" distribution—is so incongruent with the modern world, so that modern versions of superior government by a tiny elite (which is what the Communist regimes are) are always fighting against the economic and social tendencies inherent in their own societies. Purely egalitarian communities are certainly feasible—but only if they are selective in their recruitment and are relatively indifferent to economic growth and change, which encourages differentiation. Aristocratic societies are feasible, too—most of human history consists of them—but only under conditions of relative economic lethargy, so that the distribution of power and wealth is insulated from change. But once you are committed to the vision of a predominantly commercial society in which flux and change are "normal," in which men and resources are expected to move to take advantage of new economic opportunities—then you find yourself tending toward the limited inequalities of a bourgeois kind.

This explains one of the most extraordinary (and little-noticed) features of 20th-century societies—how relatively invulnerable the distribution of income is to the efforts of politicians and ideologues to manipulate it. In all the Western nations—the United States, Sweden, the United Kingdom, France, Germany—despite the varieties of social and economic policies of their governments, the distribution of income is strikingly similar. Not identical; politics is not entirely impotent, and the particular shape of the "bell" can be modified—but only with immense effort, and only slightly, so that to the naked eye of the visitor the effect is barely visible.[3] Moreover, available statistics suggest that the distribution of income in the Communist regimes of Russia and Eastern Europe, despite both their egalitarian economic ideologies and aristocratic political structure, moves closer every year to the Western model, as these regimes seek the kind of economic growth that their "common men" unquestionably desire. And once the economic structure and social structure start assuming the shape of this bell-shaped curve, the political structure—the distribution of political power—follows along the same way, however slowly and reluctantly. The "Maoist" heresy within Communism can best be understood as a heroic—but surely futile—rebellion against the gradual submission of Communism to the constraints of the bell-shaped curve.

So bourgeois society—using this term in its larger sense, to include such "mixed economies" as prevail in Israel or Sweden or even Yugoslavia—is not nearly so fragile as its enemies think or its friends fear. Only a complete reversal of popular opinion toward the merits of material prosperity and economic growth would destroy it, and despite the fact that some of our citizens seem ready for such a reversal, that is unlikely to occur.

The concern and distress of our working- and lower-middle classes over the bureaucratization of modern life can, I think, be coped with. One can envisage reforms that would encourage their greater "participation" in the corporate structures that dominate our society; or one can envisage reforms that would whittle down the size and power of these structures, returning part way to a more traditional market economy; or one can envisage a peculiar—and, in pure principle, incoherent—combination of both. My own view is that this last alternative, an odd amalgam of the prevailing "Left" and "Right" viewpoints, is the most realistic and the most probable. And I see no reason why it should not work. It will not be the "best" of all possible societies—but the ordinary man, like Aristotle, is no utopian, and he will settle for a "merely satisfactory" set of social arrangements and is prepared to grant them a title of legitimacy.

But the real trouble is not sociological or economic at all. It is that the "middling" nature of a bourgeois society falls short of corresponding adequately to the full range of man's spiritual nature, which makes more than middling demands upon the universe, and demands more than middling answers. This weakness of bourgeois society has been highlighted by its intellectual critics from the very beginning. And it is this weakness that generates continual dissatisfaction, especially among those for whom material problems are no longer so urgent. They may speak about "equality"; they may even be obsessed with statistics and pseudo-statistics about equality; but it is a religious vacuum—a lack of meaning in their own lives, and the absence of a sense of larger purpose in their society—that terrifies them and provokes them to "alienation" and unappeasable indignation. It is not too much to say that it is the death of God, not the emergence of any new social or economic trends, that haunts bourgeois society. And *this* problem is far beyond the competence of politics to cope with.

NOTES

EDITOR'S INTRODUCTION

1. The term "the new egalitarianism" has been employed by Charles Frankel (see "The New Egalitarianism and the Old"), among others, to describe the movement represented by Jencks and Rawls.

2. See the comments by Elliott Abrams, Midge Decter, Carl Gershman, and Diane Ravitch in the symposium "What Is a Liberal—Who Is a Conservative?" *Commentary* 62, no. 3 (September, 1976).

3. *A Theory of Justice*, pp. 136–161, 206–7. Cf. David Lewis Schaefer, "A Critique of Rawls's 'Contract' Doctrine," *Review of Metaphysics* 28, no. 1 (September, 1974): 89–115.

4. *A Theory of Justice*, pp. 102, 532.

5. See Herbert Marcuse, *An Essay on Liberation* (Boston, 1969), pp. 20–22, 91; Friedrich Nietzsche, *Thus Spoke Zarathustra*, in *The Portable Nietzsche*, ed. Walter Kaufmann (New York, 1954), pp. 129–130; Rawls, *A Theory of Justice*, pp. 429–432; David L. Schaefer, "Ideology in Philosophy's Clothing: John Rawls's *A Theory of Justice*," *Georgia Political Science Association Journal* 4, no. 2 (Fall, 1976): 42–44.

6. James Madison to Thomas Jefferson, February 8, 1825, in *The Writings of James Madison*, ed. Gaillard Hunt (New York, 1900), vol. 9, pp. 218–19; see also Martin Diamond, "The Revolution of Sober Expectations" (American Enterprise Institute Bicentennial Lecture Series, Washington, D. C., 1974), p. 4.

7. See Plato, *Republic*, 488a–495c, 592a–b; Allan Bloom, *The Republic of Plato* (New York, 1968), p. 345; Aristotle, *Politics*, 1267a 5–13; idem, *Nicomachean Ethics*, X, 7–8.

8. See Leo Strauss, "Liberal Education and Mass Democracy," in Robert A. Goldwin (ed.), *Higher Education and Modern Democracy* (Chicago, 1967), pp. 73–96; Allan Bloom, "The Crisis of Liberal Education," ibid., pp. 121–140; Bloom, "The Democratization of the University," in Goldwin (ed.), *How Democratic Is America?* (Chicago, 1971), pp. 109–136.

Daniel Bell, "ON MERITOCRACY AND EQUALITY"

1.   A theoretician of the Technicians Party, Professor Eagle, had argued that
marriage partners, in the national interest, should consult the intelligence register,
for a high-I.Q. man who mates with a low-I.Q. woman is wasting his genes. The
activist women, on the other hand, took romance as their banner and beauty as their
flag, arguing that marriage should be based on attraction. Their favorite slogan was,
"Beauty is achievable by all."

2.   But there was usually some kind of sorting device. In the Midwestern systems,
anyone with a C average or better in high school could enter the state university,
but a ruthless examination system would weed out the poorer students by the end
of the first or second year. In the California system, any high school graduate could
go on to higher education, but a grade tracking system put the top 10 to 15 percent
directly into the universities (e.g., Berkeley, U.C.L.A.), the next 25 percent into the
state colleges, and the remainder into junior or community colleges.

3.   In full acknowledgement of this principle, the Union Theological Seminary
on June 1, 1972, voted that blacks and other minority groups would henceforth
make up one third and women one half of all students, faculty, staff, and directors.
(At the time, blacks made up 6 percent of the 566 students and 8 percent of the
38 faculty members; women 20 percent of the student body and 8 percent of the
faculty.) "It is unrealistic," said the Seminary, "to educate people in a pluralistic
society in an environment that is overwhelmingly white and male-oriented." The
figure of 50 percent women was chosen to reflect their representation in society;
the one third figure for minorities as a "critical mass" to give them presence. *New
York Times,* June 1, 1972.

4.   The first discussion of the report was in *The Public Interest,* No. 4 (Summer,
1966), where Coleman summarized his conclusions in an article entitled "Equal
Schools or Equal Students." As the debate widened, Coleman discussed the implications of the Report in *The Public Interest,* No. 9 (Fall, 1967), in the article
"Toward Open Schools." He argued for the utility of integration on the following
grounds:

The finding is that students do better when they are in schools where their fellow
students come from backgrounds strong in educational motivation and resources.
The results might be paraphrased by the statement that the educational resources
provided by a child's fellow students are more important for his achievement than
are the resources provided by the school board. This effect appears to be particularly
great for students who themselves come from educationally-deprived backgrounds.
For example, it is about twice as great for Negroes as for whites.

But since family background is so important, Coleman warned that "the task of
increasing achievement of lower-class children cannot be fully implemented by school
integration, even if integration were wholly achieved—and the magnitude of racial
and class concentrations in large cities indicates that it is not likely to be achieved
soon."

The most comprehensive discussion of the Coleman Report took place in a
three-year seminar at Harvard University initiated by Daniel P. Moynihan. The
various papers analyzing the report, and Coleman's reply to his critics, are in *On
Equality of Educational Opportunity,* edited by Frederick Mosteller and Daniel P.
Moynihan (New York, 1972).

5.   Jencks's key argument, to repeat, is that "economic success seems to depend
on varieties of luck and on-the-job competence that are only moderately related
to family background, schooling or scores on standardized tests." And, as he concludes, "Nobody seems able to say exactly what 'competence' in this sense entails,

including employers who pay huge sums for it, but it does not seem to be at all similar from one job to another. This makes it harder to imagine a strategy for equalizing such competence. A strategy for equalizing luck is even harder to conceive."

Since the factors which make for success are, for Jencks, simply wayward, there is no ethical justification for large disparities in income and status; and since one cannot equalize luck in order to create equal opportunity one should seek to equalize results.

While Jencks's findings are important against the vulgar Marxist notion that inheritance of social class background is all-important in determining the place of the child, and they disprove, once again, the stilted American myth that each person of ability finds a place commensurate with his merit, the inability to find a consistent set of relationships leads Jencks to emphasize "luck" as a major factor. But in his analysis, "luck" is really only a *residual factor* which is inserted because all other variables do not correlate highly. In and of itself, luck cannot be measured as a positive variable. While it may be true, as many studies show, that there is a low correlation between the career one thinks a man is educating himself for and the final outcomes, and there is a measure of "luck" about the job one finds in relation to one's talents to fulfill the job, the fact remains, nevertheless, that on the job, particularly at the professional level, there is a high degree of talent and hard work required to succeed. By emphasizing "luck" Jencks seeks to use the randomness of an occupational roulette wheel to minimize the *earned* quality of success and to justify policies which "equalize result." And it may be that there is much more luck to the occupational system than Marxists or Meritocrats would like to admit. Yet "common observation" (that other residual category of analysis) would indicate that—again, on the professional level at least—hard work is a necessary condition for success, and that if a rough equality of opportunity has allowed one man to go further than another, he has *earned* the unequal reward—income, status, authority—which goes with that success. The important question of justice—as I argue later—is really "how much" unequal reward, in what dimensions, and for what.

6.   Calhoun argued that agreement requires a consensus of all the major interests or factions, rather than a simple majority of people which cuts across such natural or social lines as regions, groups, or classes. This was a caricature, though a brilliant one, of the Madisonian model. It was a philosophical argument about representation in a heterogeneous rather than a homogeneous society, in order to sustain human inequality, white supremacy, states' rights, anti-majoritarianism, and minority power. It came, one should also note, at a time when American parties had begun to splinter.

7.   John Rawls, *A Theory of Justice.* Justice, for Rawls, does not encapsulate all the energies of the society; it is a principle of distributive standards, and is itself part of a larger social ideal to which a society commits itself. He writes:

A conception of social justice, then, is to be regarded as providing in the first instance a standard whereby the distributive aspects of the basic structure of society are to be assessed. This standard, however, is not to be confused with the principles defining the other virtues, for the basic structure, and social arrangements generally may be efficient or inefficient, liberal or illiberal, and many other things, as well as just or unjust. A complete conception defining principles for all the virtues of the basic structure, together with the respective weights when they conflict, is more than a conception of justice; it is a social ideal. The principles of justice are but a part of such a conception. A social ideal in turn is connected with a conception of society, a vision of the way in which the aims and purposes of social cooperation are to be understood . . . Fully to understand a conception of justice we must make explicit the conception of social cooperation from which it derives.

8.   As Rawls further notes, "The naturally advantaged are not to gain merely because they are more gifted, but only to cover the costs of training and education and for using their endowments in ways that help the less fortunate as well."

9. In an interesting comparison, Rawls (like Rousseau) takes the metaphor of the family as the model for this principle:

> The family in its ideal conception, and often in practice, is one place where the principle of maximizing the sum of advantages is rejected. Members of a family commonly do not wish to gain unless they can do so in ways that further the interests of the rest. Now wanting to act on the difference principle has precisely this consequence.

The difficulty with this argument—if one regards society as the family writ large—is that the family, as Freud has argued, holds together by love, which is specific. One loves one's wife and children—and tries to pass on one's advantages to them. Where love is generalized to the society, it becomes "aim-inhibited" (because one loves all) and is consequently weak and ineffective. For this reason, Freud argues in *Civilization and its Discontents* that communism is impossible in the larger society.

10. The claims of the poor are, of course, among the oldest traditions in Western thought and are central to the idea of Christian love. But Christian love—charity as *caritas*—accepted the poor as worthy in themselves and loved the poor as poor without endowing them with higher qualities than they possessed. In that sense, classic Protestant liberalism—with its sympathy and humanitarianism, rather than love—corroded the social conscience of the Catholic world. From a different source, the romanticizing of the poor, a tradition going back to Villon, also led to the erosion of *caritas* toward the poor. For a defense of Christian love as the basis of society, and a biting attack on English moral philosophy (i.e., Hutcheson, Adam Smith, Hume), see Max Scheler's *Ressentiment*.

11. It is striking that Rawls, like Jencks, does not discuss either "work" or "effort"—as if those who had succeeded, in the university, or in business or government, had done so largely by contingent circumstances of fortune or social background. There is a discussion of meritocracy, but not of merit. This itself is a measure of how far we have moved from nineteenth-century values. It is equally striking that, in the "issue-attention cycle," the policy concern a decade ago was with "excellence." The Stern Fund sponsored a major study on the identification of excellence; John Gardner wrote a book about excellence. At that time, meritocracy was a positive word—so much so that Merrill Peterson, in his magisterial biography of Thomas Jefferson, said that Jefferson would have used the word "meritocracy" to define his "natural aristocracy" if he had known the term. Today the concern is almost entirely with equality and the disadvantaged. Will the "issue-attention cycle" come full circle in the future?

12. What if the "least fortunate" are there by their own choice? Christopher Jencks points out that while "we have already eliminated virtually all economic and academic obstacles to earning a high school diploma ... one student in five still drops out." And while one may guarantee working-class families the same educational opportunities as middle-class families, what happens if they don't want to use this opportunity? Society may have an obligation to those who are kept down or cannot advance because it is not their fault. But if individuals—for cultural or psychological reasons—do not avail themselves of opportunities, is it the society's responsibility, as the prior obligation, to devote resources to them? But if not, how does one distinguish between the genuinely disadvantaged and those who are not? This is the inextricable difficulty of social policy.

13. Rawls avoids the difficulty of the Arrow impossibility theorem by rejecting the condition of majority rule. He writes:

> It is evident from the preceding remarks that the procedure of majority rule, however it is defined and circumscribed, has a subordinate place as a procedural device. The justification for it rests squarely on the political ends that the constitution is designed to achieve, and therefore on the two principles of justice ... A fundamental part of the majority principle is that the procedure should satisfy

the conditions of background justice... When this background is absent, the first principle of justice is not satisfied; yet even when it is present, there is no assurance that just legislation will be enacted.

There is nothing to the view, then, that what the majority wills is right... This question is one of political judgment and does not belong to the theory of justice. It suffices to note that while citizens normally submit their conduct to democratic authority, that is, recognize the outcome of a vote as establishing a binding rule, other things equal, they do not submit their judgment to it.

Rawls is right of course, as with most traditional conceptions of justice, that the action of a majority does not make any decision right. The tyranny of a majority has long been recognized as a source of injustice, as much as the tyranny of a despot. The procedural question, however, is whether, as a *consistent rule* there is a better method than majority vote, subject to the democratic check of a minority having the right and ability to change the decision and become a majority, in reaching consensus.

14.　Rawls writes: "One is not allowed to justify differences in income or organizational powers on the ground that the disadvantages of those in one position are outweighed by the greater advantages of those in another. Much less can infringements of liberty be counterbalanced in this way." His argument is puzzling. In any interdependent society one forgoes certain liberties—in traffic and zoning regulations —to enhance others. Nor is it clear why one has to redress inequalities in every sphere rather than allow individuals to choose which sphere represents the most nagging inequality to them. As a political principle, it is unlikely that any single rule can dominate a policy without disruption. In the *Politics,* Aristotle distinguished between two kinds of justice, numerical equality (equality of result) and equality based on merit. As he concluded: "To lay it down that equality shall be exclusively of one kind or another is a bad thing, as is shown by what happens in practice; no constitution lasts long that is constructed on such a basis."

15.　W. G. Runciman, "'Social' Equality," *Philosophical Quarterly* 17 (1967), reprinted in his *Sociology In Its Place* (London, 1970).

Richard W. Crosby, "EQUALITY IN AMERICA"

*Adapted from a paper originally presented at the 1973 meeting of the Northeastern Political Science Association.

1.　Christopher Jencks et al., *Inequality,* title of chap. 1.

2.　Thomas Hobbes, *De Cive,* chap. 1, sec. 3; also, *Leviathan,* chap. 13, beginning.

3.　"The question of who is the better man has no place in the condition of mere nature.... The inequality that now is has been introduced by the laws civil. I know that Aristotle in the First book of his *Politics,* for a foundation of his doctrine, makes men by nature some more worthy to command, meaning the wiser sort such as he thought himself to be for his philosophy, others to serve, meaning those that had strong bodies but were not philosophers as he; as if master and servant were not introduced by consent of men but by difference of wit, which is not only against reason but also against experience." (*Leviathan,* chapter 15: the ninth law of nature.)

4.　This discussion is greatly indebted to Harvey C. Mansfield, Jr., "Hobbes and the Science of Indirect Government," *American Political Science Review* 65, no. 1 (March, 1971): 98-100.

5.　*Leviathan,* chap. 13.

6.　Ibid., chap. 14, beginning.

7.　*De Cive,* chap. 10, sec. 4.

8.　Ibid.

9.　*Leviathan,* chap. 13.

10.　Robert Goldwin, "John Locke," in Leo Strauss and Joseph Cropsey (eds.), *History of Political Philosophy* (Second edition, Chicago, 1972), p. 460.

11. John Locke, *Two Treatises of Government*, vol. 2, sec. 4.
12. Ibid., sec. 7.
13. Ibid., sec. 123.
14. Ibid., sec. 131. It should be noted that equality is given up entirely, for the sake of the preservation of liberty and property.
15. For a discussion of this issue see Harry V. Jaffa, *Crisis of the House Divided: An Interpretation of the Issues in the Lincoln-Douglas Debates*, pp. 318-321.
16. Joseph Cropsey, "The Right of Foreign Aid," in Robert A. Goldwin (ed.), *Why Foreign Aid?* (Chicago: Rand McNally, 1962), p. 123.
17. When political equality achieves the status of an end in itself, equality of results in all spheres of life can be demanded in its name. See Robert Dahl, *After the Revolution* (New Haven, 1970), pp. 12-13, 108, 112-113.
18. Jaffa, *Crisis*, p. 379.
19. Hamilton, Madison, and Jay, *The Federalist*, #22, end.
20. See William B. Allen, "Federal Representation: The Design of the Thirty-Fifth *Federalist* Paper," *Publius* 6, no. 3 (Summer, 1976), pp. 61-72.
21. *Federalist* #10.
22. Harry V. Jaffa, *Equality and Liberty*, p. 19.
23. *People of Plenty* (Chicago, 1954), p. 92.
24. *Federalist* #10.
25. Alexis de Tocqueville, *Democracy in America*, transl. Phillips Bradley, 2 vols. (New York, 1945), vol. 2, p. 40.
26. Ibid., 2: 23.
27. Ibid., 2: 23 and 27.
28. Ibid., 2: 39.
29. Quoted in Marvin Zetterbaum, *Tocqueville and the Problem of Democracy*, p. 127.
30. Tocqueville, 2: 23.
31. Ibid., 2: 18.
32. Ibid., 2: 144-145.
33. Ibid., 1: 56.
34. Ibid., 1: 59 and 208; see also pp. 336-337.
35. Ibid., 2: 336-337.
36. Jencks et al., pp. 263-265.
37. See the analysis of McGovern's defeat by S. M. Lipset and Earl Raab in *Commentary* 55, no. 1 (January, 1973): 43-50.
38. "About Equality " [reprinted in this volume—ed.]

Irving Kristol, "OF POPULISM AND TAXES"

1. The present 50 percent maximum tax on earned income seems to me to strike just about the right balance.
2. One such plan was described by Charles M. Haar and Peter A. Lewis in "Where Shall the Money Come From?" *The Public Interest*, no. 18 (Winter, 1970), pp. 101-112.
3. I am not even thinking of those famous depletion allowances for firms that produce oil, gas, and minerals. If such allowances were completely eliminated, the Treasury would get an extra $1.5 billion in revenue. And no one is even advocating their *complete* elimination! Rarely can so much publicity have been generated by the prospect of so little tax revenue. In a way, the fuss over depletion allowances is a perfect illustration of how the populist vision distorts economic reality.
*(Editor's note): By the beginning of 1977 inflation had naturally pushed these figures up, but without altering the author's point. At this time the top 5 percent of families were reported to earn an annual income of $40,000 or more, while the

top 10 percent earned at least $30,000. Persons earning $30,000 or more in 1974 (the most recent year on which tax data were available in early 1977) paid an average of 31 percent of their income in income taxes. See Frederick Andrews, "The Top Ten Per Cent May Not Be Rich," *New York Times,* January 9, 1977, section 3, p. 26.

Bertrand de Jouvenel, "THE SOCIALIST IDEAL"

1. James Edward Meade, *Planning and the Price Mechanism* (London, 1948), p. 42.
2. Romans, 7: 6.
3. See my "Essai sur la Politique de Rousseau," in introduction to my critical edition of *Du Contrat Social* (Geneva, 1946).
4. James, 3: 18.
5. Christ's bidding to the rich is most imperative. It is necessary to stress that while he urged the rich young man to "distribute unto the poor," he did not tell the poor to take upon themselves to distribute by taxation the rich young man's wealth. While the moral value of the first process is evident, that of the second is not.
6. The socialist alluded to in this place is not the "utopian" socialist mainly preoccupied with the brotherhood of man, but the "organic" socialist who reasons in terms of the society as a whole.
7. Indeed there are some redistributionists who would be less satisfied by a lifting-up of the whole scale of incomes, preserving their present inequality, than by a flattening down of the inequalities.
8. Cf. Bernard Shaw: "I hate the poor."
9. "If therefore the choice were to be between Communism with all its chances and the present (1852) state of society with all its sufferings and injustices; if the institution of private property necessarily carried with it as a consequence that the produce of labour should be apportioned as we now see it, almost in an inverse ratio to the labour: the largest proportions to those who have never worked at all, the next largest to those whose work is purely nominal, and so in a descending scale, the remuneration dwindling as the work grows harder and more disagreeable, until the most fatiguing and exhausting bodily labour cannot count with certainty on being able to earn even the necessities of life; if this or Communism were the alternative, all the difficulties, great or small, of Communism would be as dust in the balance." (John Stuart Mill, *Principles of Political Economy,* vol. 2: i, par. 3.)
10. The idea, mentioned in our quotation of Mill, that the higher incomes are probably undeserved is also operative. It is of course related to the aforementioned principle of fair reward. But we do not have to take it into account here, since the policies of redistribution make little use of it. The difference in treatment between earned and unearned incomes is slight; nor is any made according to the means of earning incomes—no more is allowed to the creator than to the man whose activity is purely repetitive and even whose "earnings" are drawn from a monopoly situation.
11. It is well known that "the people" are less critical of high-living than the *petite bourgeoisie.* When this high-living has a spectacular value, as in the case of aristocracy, or today in the case of film actors and similar public figures, there is great tolerance of it among "the people."
12. A. C. Pigou, *The Economics of Welfare,* 4th ed. (London, 1948), p. 89.
13. A. P. Lerner, *The Economics of Control,* 3rd ed. (1947), chap. 2, p. 29.
14. Lionel Robbins, *An Essay on the Nature and Significance of Economic Science,* 2nd ed. (London, 1935), chap. 6.
15. Lerner, pp. 29–32.
16. A. C. Pigou, *A Study in Public Finance,* 3rd ed. (London, 1947), p. 90.
17. The remarkable consent of the British higher-income classes to a sharp fall

in economic status was got from their patriotism, during a war which threatened national existence. The "silent revolution" was really achieved by a war-waging national government. Whether so rapid a descent would have been accepted as willingly in peace, for an avowed purpose of social redistribution, is a matter for doubt. It might then have bred an upper-class resentment which tends to weaken a commonwealth.

18. In recent years, public opinion has been made increasingly aware of the part played by the accumulation of capital in economic progress. No attention has yet been paid to the relationship between the distribution of buying power and progress. Experience shows that progress is discouraged where inequality is excessive, hereditary, and where the scale of incomes is discontinuous. But also that it is discouraged where equality is enforced. There may be an optimal allocation of consuming power for the purposes of progress. This subject might be worth exploring.

19. It is permissible to retort that the rich Jameses put great parts of their incomes to less laudable uses, and to argue that the public powers, taking over the incomes of the Jameses, will do more for culture than the rich had done. There is a strong case here (compare what the princes did for the arts from the Renaissance to the eighteenth century, with the services rendered by the *bourgeois* rich in the eighteenth century); but it is to be noted that what comes into discussion now is redistribution of power from individuals to the State, and not redistribution from the rich to the poor. Whether or not the State is better qualified than the rich to support the arts (and that very much depends on the nature of the government and the nature of the wealthy class), if the State's warrant for taking over the incomes of the rich is its mandate to maximize satisfactions of the national consumers, it is not entitled by that warrant to apply its takings to another object, thus moving away from the position of maximum overall satisfaction.

Colin Welch, "INTELLECTUALS HAVE CONSEQUENCES"

*(Editor's note): Mr. Crosland died in February, 1977, after this article was written.

P. T. Bauer, "WESTERN GUILT AND THIRD WORLD POVERTY"

1. Several remarkable ones were cited by Daniel P. Moynihan in his celebrated article "The United States in Opposition," *Commentary* 59, no. 3 (March, 1975): 31-44.

2. On the other hand, of course, there was the Atlantic slave trade. But horrible and destructive as this trade was, it cannot legitimately be claimed as a cause of African backwardness. Indeed, the slave trade to what is now the Middle East began before the Atlantic slave trade and far outlasted it. (It was also even more brutal because the young males were usually castrated, often with fatal results.) And as it happens, the most backward parts of the continent, such as the interior of Central and Southern Africa and most of East Africa, were relatively unaffected by Western slavery, while the currently most advanced areas, notably West Africa, were much affected by it. (Asia was of course altogether untouched.)

3. Although these observations differ radically from the ideas reaching the public in the West, they should not come as a surprise. Some years ago, Sir Arthur Lewis noted in an important address that in the 1950s the terms of trade of primary producers were more favorable than at any time in the preceding eighty years (see "A Review of Economic Development," *American Economic Review,* May, 1965). Sir Arthur wrote before the subsequent upsurge in the prices of primary products and without reference to the favorable factors noted in the text. The exporters of primary products are far from the same as Third World exporters, but they are often identified in discussions of Third World poverty.

4. At an official level, a damaging international demonstration effect may indeed operate by encouraging the adoption of show projects and unsuitable technologies financed with public funds. But this is not usually what the exponents of the international demonstration effect have in mind. Nor is it appropriate to blame the West for the policies of Third World governments in adopting unsuitable external models.

5. See the *Washington Post,* May 6, 1975, for a report on this process.

Midge Decter, "THE LAST TRAIN TO NIHIL"

1. Shulamith Firestone, *The Dialectic of Sex* (New York, 1971), p. 193.
2. Louise Gross and Phyllis MacEwan, "On Day Care," in Leslie B. Tanner (ed.), *Voices from Women's Liberation* (New York, 1970), p. 201.
3. Firestone, p. 11.

Catherine H. Zuckert, "AMERICAN WOMEN AND DEMOCRATIC MORALS"

1. Henry James, *The American Scene* (Bloomington, Ind., 1968), p. 347. "The woman produced by a women-made society alone has obviously quite a new story.... What it came to, evidently, was that she had grown in an air in which a hundred of the 'European' complications and dangers didn't exist, and in which also she had had to take upon herself a certain training for freedom.... Thus she arrived, fullblown, on the general scene, the least criticized object, in proportion to her importance, that had ever adorned it. It would take long to say why her situation . . . may affect the inner fibre of the critic himself as one of the most touching on record.... For why need she originally.... have embraced so confidently, so gleefully, yet so unguardedly, the terms offered her to an end practically so perfidious. Why need she, unless in the interest of her eventual discipline, have turned away with so light a heart after watching the Man, the deep American man, retire into his tent . . . ? Would she not have said, 'No, this is too unnatural; there must be a trap in it somewhere—it's addressed really, in the long run, to making a fool of me.'"
2. Henry James, "The Speech of American Women," reprinted in *French Writers and American Women Essays* (Branford, Conn., 1960), p. 33.
3. F. O. Matthiessen and Kenneth B. Murdock, *The Notebooks of Henry James* (New York, 1961), p. 47.
4. Charles Thomas Samuels, *The Ambiguity of Henry James* (Urbana, Ill., 1973), p. 102; Alfred Habegger, "The Disunity of *The Bostonians,*" *Nineteenth Century Fiction* 24, no. 2 (September, 1969): 198; Irving Howe, *Politics and the Novel* (New York, 1957), pp. 188, 190.
5. S. Gorley Putt, *Henry James, A Reader's Guide* (Ithaca, N. Y., 1966), p. 184.
6. Henry James, "American Democracy and American Education," in *American Essays,* ed. Leon Edel (New York, 1956), p. 243. Consider also James's critical comment, in the same essay, on E. L. Godkins's *Unforeseen Tendencies of Democracy:* "One feels it to be a pity that, in such a survey, the reference to the social conditions as well should not somehow be interwoven: at so many points are they—whether for contradiction, confirmation, attenuation, or aggravation—but another aspect of the political" (ibid.).
7. Page citations refer to the Modern Library edition of *The Bostonians* (New York, 1956).
8. See P. R. Grover, "'The Princess Casimassima' and 'L'Education sentimentale,'" *Modern Language Review* 66, no. 4 (October, 1971): 760–71, on the superiority of James's analysis of political reality in terms of "types" to more factual literary accounts.
9. According to his notebook, p. 47, James initially contemplated the novel in

terms of the struggle that takes place in the mind of Verena Tarrant. Such a tack is truer to the technique of the later James but it is not true to the character. Verena's intelligence is not developed. The absence of a center of consciousness that some critics point out as a fault could lead to deeper insights into James's intention if readers were not so quick to think that they know the "real James." This "fault" in the novel in fact points to one of James's major conclusions: The American regime prevents the development of a fine consciousness. In his other novels, James's heroines or heroes have to go to Europe to develop, and they do so with varying degrees of success.

10. Henry James, "Emerson," in *American Essays*, p. 72.

11. Cf. Richard Chase, *The American Novel and Its Tradition* (Garden City, N. Y., 1957), pp. 121–30, for an Isabel Archer very like Olive.

12. There seems to be an ironic play in the old lady's name on the notion of a "birdseye view." On James's use of names see Joyce Taylor Horrell, "A 'Shade of a Special Sense'": Henry James and the Art of Naming," *American Literature* 42 (1970–71): 203–220; Lionel Trilling, "The Bostonians," *The Opposing Self* (New York, 1955). Some readers have been tempted to see historical figures such as Elizabeth Peabody in Miss Birdseye and Victoria Woodhull in Verena. James, however, emphatically denied that the characters had any source outside his "moral consciousness." See F. O. Matthiessen, *The James Family* (New York, 1947), p. 326.

13. See Louise Bogan, "The Portrait of New England," *Selected Criticism* (New York, 1955), pp. 297, 298, 300; Clinton Oliver, "Henry James as Social Critic," *Antioch Review* 7, no. 2 (June, 1947): 245; Philip Rahv, Introduction to *The Bostonians* (Dial Press edition, New York, 1945).

14. Basil wants to rule the minds of men. But it seems that the only place he will in fact rule, if at all, is his own hearth. James perhaps refers ironically to Basil's ambition in his first name, from the Greek for king, *Basileus*.

15. Peter Buitenhuis, *The Grasping Imagination* (Toronto, 1970), suggests that Basil "ransoms" Verena's sexuality. James may have used the poem he remembered Emerson delivering at the Music Hall in commemoration of the Emancipation Proclamation ironically, however:

> Pay ransom to the owner
> And fill the bag to the brim.
> Who is the owner? The slave is owner
> and ever was. Pay him!

16. Property is perhaps *the* bourgeois concern, and its extension into the human realm forms a major theme of James's writing, as in *The American, The Spoils of Poynton, The Wings of the Dove,* and *The Golden Bowl.* See Donald L. Mull, *Henry James' "Subtle Economy"* (Middletown, Conn., 1973).

17. "The Question of Our Speech," an address delivered to the graduating class at Bryn Mawr College, Pennsylvania, June 8, 1905, reprinted in Henry James, *French Writers and American Women Essays*, p. 20.

18. Alexis de Tocqueville, *Democracy in America,* transl. Phillips Bradley, (New York, 1945), vol. 2, p. 209.

19. Cf. James, *American Scene*, p. 347.

20. James took the outline of the plot of *The Bostonians* from Alphonse Daudet's *L'Evangeliste.* He considered Daudet the "best of all the novelists who have not the greater imagination, the imagination of the moralist" (*French Writers and American Women*, p. 3).

Robert F. Sasseen, "AFFIRMATIVE ACTION"

1. For a full and lucid exposition of the natural rights doctrine and the nature of the government it suggests, see Harry V. Jaffa, *Crisis of the House Divided: An Interpretation of the Issues in the Lincoln-Douglas Debates* (Garden City, N. Y., 1959), especially chaps. 9, 10, 14. For an analysis of the intentions of the founding fathers, see Martin Diamond, *"The Federalist,"* in Leo Strauss and Joseph Cropsey (eds.), *History of Political Philosophy* (Chicago, 1972). See, also, Morton J. Frisch and Richard G. Stevens (eds.), *American Political Thought: The Philosophic Dimensions of American Statesmanship* (New York, 1971).

2. Harvey Mansfield, Jr., "Impartial Representation," in Robert A. Goldwin (ed.), *Representation and Misrepresentation* (Chicago, 1968), pp. 91–113.

3. This is clear in James Madison's account of the Constitution's solution to the problem of faction in nos. 10 and 51 of the *Federalist*.

4. Section 202 (1) of Executive Order 11246 (September 24, 1965) as amended by Executive Order 11375 (October 13, 1967). Italics added. The quotation is taken from the Executive Order as found in U. S. Department of Health, Education and Welfare, *Higher Education Guidelines, Executive Order 11246*, 1972, p. A-2, hereafter referred to as *HEW Guidelines*.

5. *HEW Guidelines*, pp. 2–3. All italics added both here and below.

6. Ibid., pp. 8–9.

7. Ibid., p. 12.

8. Ibid., p. 14.

9. Ibid., p. 4.

10. Ibid., p. 10.

11. Ibid., p. 9.

12. Ibid., p. 8.

13. Ibid., pp. 4, 11.

14. See Michael J. Malbin, "Employment Report: Proposed Federal Guidelines on Hiring Could Have Far-reaching Impact," *National Journal Reports* 5, no. 38 (September 29, 1973): 1429–34.

15. *HEW Guidelines*, p. 3.

16. Ibid., pp. 3–4.

17. U. S. Department of Labor, Revised Order No. 4, Section 60-2, 10, *HEW Guidelines*, p. C-2.

18. *HEW Guidelines*, p. 3.

19. Ibid.

20. Ibid.

21. Edward C. Banfield, *The Unheavenly City* (Boston: Little, Brown, 1968), pp. 67–87.

22. Abraham Lincoln, "Address at Ottawa, Illinois, August 21, 1858," in Robert W. Johannsen (ed.), *The Lincoln-Douglas Debates of 1858* (New York, 1965), pp. 64–65. Also, "Address at Chicago, Illinois, December 10, 1856," in Philip Van Doren Stern (ed.), *The Life and Writings of Abraham Lincoln* (New York, 1940), p. 412.

23. Alexis de Tocqueville, *Democracy in America,* Transl. Phillips Bradley, 2 vols. (New York, 1956), vol. 2, pp. 102–3, 304–39.

Nathan Glazer, "IS BUSING NECESSARY?"

1. *Federal Civil Rights Enforcement Effort,* 1970, p. 14.

*(Editor's note): After this article was written, in *Keyes v. School District No. One, Denver, Colorado* (1973), the Supreme Court reversed that portion of the Court of Appeals' decision that had limited the Denver district judge's desegregation order.

Remanding the case to the district court, the Supreme Court "virtually instructed" the district judge "to order 'all-out desegregation.'" (Lino A. Graglia, *Disaster by Decree: The Supreme Court Decisions on Race and the Schools,* pp. 178–9).

**(Editor's note): The judgment of the district judge in the Richmond case ordering the reorganization of school districts for the purpose of racial integration was later reversed by the Court of Appeals for the Fourth Circuit. An appeal of the reversal to the Supreme Court ended in the Court's dividing 4–4, thus affirming the court of appeals' decision. By a 5–4 vote in *Milliken v. Bradley* (1974) dealing with the Detroit case, the Supreme Court once again refused to sanction the requirement that different school districts be consolidated in order to undo the effects of previous "segregation" in one of them. However, the Court let stand a questionable lower-court finding of "de jure" segregation in the Detroit schools, "although Detroit had never had explicit racial assignment and had early taken voluntary steps to further integration in spite of massive black population growth" (Graglia, p. 203). Graglia's book contains a thorough critical review of the Supreme Court's decisions in these and other busing cases.

2.   David R. Cohen, Thomas F. Pettigrew, and Robert S. Riley, "Race and the Outcomes of Schooling," in Frederick Mosteller and Daniel P. Moynihan (eds.), *On Equality of Educational Opportunity: Papers Deriving from the Harvard University Faculty Seminar on the Coleman Report.*

3.   *Equal Educational Opportunity: Hearings before the Select Committee on Equal Educational Opportunity of the United States Senate,* 92nd Congress, 1st Session, 1971, p. 4058ff.

Irving Kristol, "ABOUT EQUALITY"

1.   One of the reasons they are so incredulous is that they do not count as "income"—as they should—such benefits as tenure, long vacations, relatively short working hours, and all of their other prerogatives. When a prerogative is construed as a "right," it ceases to be seen as a privilege.

2.   As Professor Peter Bauer has pointed out, the very term "distribution of income" casts a pall of suspicion over existing inequalities, implying as it does that incomes are not personally *earned* but somehow *received* as the end-product of mysterious (and therefore possibly sinister) political-economic machinations.

3.   It must be kept in mind, of course, that retaining the shape of the curve is not inconsistent with *everyone* getting richer. The bell itself then moves toward a new axis.

SUGGESTIONS FOR FURTHER READING

CONTEMPORARY WORKS

Bauer, P. T., and Yamey, B. S. "Against the New Economic Order." *Commentary* 63, no. 4 (April, 1977): 25-31.

Browning, Edgar K. *Redistribution and the Welfare System.* Washington, D.C.: American Enterprise Institute, 1975.

Coleman, James, et al. *Equality of Educational Opportunity,* 2 vols. Washington, D. C.: U. S. Government Printing Office, 1966.

Decter, Midge. *The New Chastity and Other Arguments Against Women's Liberation.* New York: Coward, McCann, & Geoghegan, 1972.

De Jouvenel, Bertrand. *The Ethics of Redistribution.* Cambridge, England: Cambridge University Press, 1951.

Frankel, Charles. "The New Egalitarianism and the Old." *Commentary* 56, no. 3 (September, 1973): 54-61.

Gans, Herbert. *More Equality.* New York: Pantheon Books, 1973.

Glazer, Nathan. *Affirmative Discrimination: Ethnic Inequality and Public Policy.* New York: Basic Books, 1975.

Graglia, Lino A. *Disaster by Decree: The Supreme Court Decisions on Race and the Schools.* Ithaca, N. Y.: Cornell University Press, 1976.

Gross, Barry R. (ed.). *Reverse Discrimination.* Buffalo, N. Y.: Prometheus Books, 1977.

Jaffa, Harry V. *Crisis of the House Divided: An Interpretation of the Issues in the Lincoln-Douglas Debates.* Garden City, New York: Doubleday, 1959.

–––. *Equality and Liberty.* New York: Oxford University Press, 1965.

Jencks, Christopher, et al. *Inequality: A Reassessment of the Effect of Family and Schooling in America.* New York: Basic Books, 1972.

Koritansky, John. "Two Forms of the Love of Equality in Tocqueville's Practical Teaching for Democracy." *Polity* 6, no. 4 (Summer, 1974): 488-499.

Kristol, Irving. "Capitalism, Socialism, and Nihilism." *The Public Interest,* no. 31 (Spring, 1973), pp. 3-16.

–––. *On the Democratic Idea in America.* New York: Harper and Row, 1972.

Lipset, Seymour Martin. "Social Mobility and Equal Opportunity." *The Public Interest,* no. 29 (Fall, 1972), pp. 29-68.

Mosteller, Frederick, and Daniel P. Moynihan (eds.). *On Equality of Educational Opportunity: Papers Deriving from the Harvard University Faculty Seminar on the Coleman Report.* New York: Vintage Books, 1972.

Rainwater, Lee (ed.). *Inequality and Justice: A Survey of Inequalities of Class Status, Sex, and Power.* Chicago: Aldine, 1974.

Rawls, John. *A Theory of Justice.* Cambridge, Mass.: The Belknap Press of Harvard University Press, 1971.

Roche, George C., III. *The Balancing Act: Quota Hiring in Higher Education.* La Salle, Ill.: Open Court, 1974.

Schaar, John. "Some Ways of Thinking About Equality." *Journal of Politics* 36, no. 4 (November, 1964): 867–895.

Schaefer, David Lewis. *Justice or Tyranny? A Critique of John Rawls's "Theory of Justice."* Port Washington, N. Y.: Kennikat Press, 1979.

Simon, Yves R. *Philosophy of Democratic Government.* Chicago: University of Chicago Press, 1951, part 4.

Sowell, Thomas. *Affirmative Action Reconsidered: Was It Necessary in Academia?* Washington, D. C.: American Enterprise Institute, 1975.

Tawney, R. H. *Equality.* London: George Allen & Unwin, 1931.

Tucker, Robert W. *The Inequality of Nations.* New York: Basic Books, 1977.

Tyrrell, R. Emmett, Jr., (ed.). *The Future that Doesn't Work: Social Democracy's Failures in England.* New York: Doubleday, 1977.

Zetterbaum, Marvin. "Equality and Human Need." *American Political Science Review* 71, no. 3 (September, 1977): 983–998.

–––. *Tocqueville and the Problem of Democracy.* Stanford, Calif.: Stanford University Press, 1967.

CLASSIC PHILOSOPHIC WORKS

Aristotle, *Politics.* Transl. by Ernest Barker. New York: Oxford University Press, 1958.

Hobbes, Thomas. *Leviathan.* Edited by Michael Oakeshott. New York: Crowell, 1962.

Locke, John. *Second Treatise.* In Peter Laslett (ed.), *Two Treatises of Government.* New York: New American Library, 1960.

Nietzsche, Friedrich. *Beyond Good and Evil.* Translated by Walter Kaufmann. New York: Random House, 1966.

Plato. *Republic.* Translated by Allan Bloom. New York: Basic Books, 1968.

Rousseau, Jean-Jacques. *Discourse on the Origin and Foundations of Inequality Among Men.* In Roger Masters (trans.), *First and Second Discourses.* New York: St. Martin's Press, 1964.

Tocqueville, Alexis de. *Democracy in America.* Translated by George Lawrence. New York: Harper and Row, 1966.

ABOUT THE CONTRIBUTORS

P. T. Bauer is Professor of Economics (with special reference to the economic development of underdeveloped countries) at the London School of Economics. His books include *Economic Analysis and Policy in Underdeveloped Countries; Indian Economic Policy and Development;* and (with B. S. Yamey) *The Economics of Underdeveloped Countries* and *Markets, Market Control, and Marketing Reform.*

Daniel Bell is Professor of Sociology at Harvard University. Among his books are *The End of Ideology; The Cultural Contradictions of Capitalism;* and *The Coming of Post-Industrial Society.* He formerly served as co-editor of *The Public Interest.*

Richard W. Crosby is Assistant Professor of Political Science at Colgate University. His special fields of interest include political philosophy and American political thought. His forthcoming books include *Patriot v. Loyalist: The Hamilton-Seabury Controversy, 1774–1775;* and translations with commentary of Rousseau's *Social Contract* and Maurice Joly's *Dialogue in Hell between Machiavelli and Montesquieu.* He has been a Fulbright lecturer and has published a number of articles in scholarly journals.

Midge Decter is a senior editor with Basic Books and previously held editorial posts with *Harper's* and *Saturday Review-World* magazines. She is the author of *Liberal Parents, Radical Children; The Liberated Woman and Other Americans;* and *The New Chastity.*

Bertrand de Jouvenel, the distinguished French political theorist, econo-mist, and journalist, served for many years as director of the Société d'études et de documentation économique (SEDEIS), and edits its journal *Études futuribles,* which publishes research on "futurology." Baron de Jouvenel has taught at the University of Paris, Oxford, Cam-bridge, Yale, and Berkeley. Among the many books he has written are *Sovereignty; On Power;* and *The Pure Theory of Politics.*

Nathan Glazer is Professor of Education and Social Structure at Harvard University and co-editor of *The Public Interest.* His books include *American Judaism; Affirmative Discrimination; Remembering the Answers;* and (with Daniel P. Moynihan) *Beyond the Melting Pot.*

Irving Kristol is Henry R. Luce Professor of Urban Values at New York University and co-editor of *The Public Interest.* He is the author of *On the Democratic Idea in America* and has edited several books. His many articles have appeared in *Commentary, The Public Interest, The New York Times Magazine, The Wall Street Journal,* and other periodicals.

Harvey C. Mansfield, Jr., is Professor and former Chairman, Department of Government, Harvard University. His main field of interest is politi-cal philosophy. He is the author of *Statesmanship and Party Govern-ment: A Study of Burke and Bolingbroke;* of a forthcoming book on Machiavelli's *Discourses on the First Ten Books of Livy;* and of numerous articles, dealing especially with the philosophic foundations of modern representative government and of the modern political party system.

Robert F. Sasseen is Associate Academic Vice President, Dean of the Faculty, and Professor of Political Science at San Jose State University. He has contributed articles to several professional journals and has been awarded research grants by the National Endowment for the Humani-ties and the Center for the Study of Democratic Institutions.

David L. Schaefer is Associate Professor of Political Science at Holy Cross College. He is the author of *Justice or Tyranny? A Critique of John Rawls's "A Theory of Justice"* (1979). He edited *Americans and the Federal Principle: Some Reconsiderations* (published in 1976 as a special issue of *Publius*) and has contributed numerous articles to scholarly journals. He recently held a fellowship from the National

Endowment for the Humanities and was a resident at the Rockefeller Foundation Cultural Center in Bellagio, Italy. He is currently working on a book on the political philosophy of Michel de Montaigne.

Colin Welch is deputy editor of the London *Daily Telegraph* and has contributed to the *New Statesman, Encounter, The Spectator,* and other publications.

Catherine H. Zuckert is Assistant Professor of Political Science, Carleton College. Her special field of interest is political philosophy. She was the recipient of a fellowship from the National Endowment for the Humanities in 1974–75. She is the co-author (with Michael P. Zuckert) of "'And in Its Wake We Followed': The Political Wisdom of Mark Twain," published in *Interpretation,* and is co-editor of, and a contributor to, a forthcoming book on political thought in American literature.